Aiding and
Foreign aid failures and the 0.7% deception

Aiding and Abetting
Foreign aid failures and the 0.7% deception

Jonathan Foreman

Civitas: Institute for the Study of Civil Society
London

First Published December 2012

© Civitas 2012
55 Tufton Street
London SW1P 3QL

email: books@civitas.org.uk

ISBN 978-1-906837-44-0

Independence: Civitas: Institute for the Study of Civil Society is
a registered educational charity (No. 1085494) and a company
limited by guarantee (No. 04023541). Civitas is financed from a
variety of private sources to avoid over-reliance on any single
or small group of donors.

All publications are independently refereed. All the Institute's
publications seek to further its objective of promoting the
advancement of learning. The views expressed are those of
the authors, not of the Institute.

Typeset by Kevin Dodd
Printed in Great Britain by
Berforts Group Ltd
Stevenage SG1 2BH

Contents

Author

Jonathan Foreman is a writer, researcher and editor based in London and New Delhi. With an academic background in history and law, his primary areas of interest are urban policy, security and defence, South Asian affairs and film. He is currently co-editor of *The Indian Quarterly* and a Senior Research Fellow at Civitas.

Foreman was one of the founders for the British monthly magazine *Standpoint* and served as its deputy editor until 2009. In recent years he has reported from Beirut and Mumbai for *Standpoint*, from Pakistan for the *Daily Telegraph Magazine*, from Afghanistan for *National Review*, and from the Chad/Darfur border for *Men's Vogue*. In 2005 *Vanity Fair* sent him to Baghdad and Basra to report on Coalition efforts to train Iraqi security forces.

He was formerly based in New York, where he was at various times a war correspondent, leader writer and film critic for the *New York Post*, a contributing editor at the Manhattan Institute's *City Journal* and a contributing editor at the U.S. *National Law Journal*.

He has written for a variety of publications on both sides of the Atlantic including *The New Yorker, The Spectator, The Financial Times, The Sunday Times Magazine, the Daily and Sunday Telegraph, The Guardian, The Wall Street Journal,* and *The First Post.*

Acknowledgements

I should like to express my gratitude to my Civitas colleagues Justin Shaw, Director David Green and Editorial Director Robert Whelan for suggesting and shepherding this project; and to Elliot Bidgood for his assistance. I would also like to thank Justine Hardy, Maureen Lines and Baroness Cox – all of whom are outstanding examples of courage, integrity and the very best in aid work – for many inspiring and enlightening conversations about aid over the years. I also owe a debt to the anonymous referees who made many useful suggestions to improve the book.

Executive Summary

At a time of cuts in public expenditure, the UK government's commitment to increasing foreign aid to 0.7% of GDP seems perverse. Many recent non-altruistic justifications for the UK's lavish aid budget – such as the claims that more generous foreign aid will stop mass immigration, prevent wars such as that in Afghanistan and secure goodwill and economic benefits for the UK – have little or no basis in reality.

This paper argues for a radical rethinking of Britain's foreign aid policies and fundamental reform of the Department for International Development (DfID). Its position reflects not only the evident failure of six decades and more than three trillion dollars in official development aid (ODA) to foster economic growth in many poor parts of the world, but also the negative effects of much of that aid on the people and governments of some of the world's poorest and most unstable countries. Not only has there been no correlation between high levels of development aid and economic growth; there is evidence of an inverse relationship between the two, thanks to the corrupting effects of aid on fragile polities.

This paper also examines the complicated and often troubling realities that underlie emergency or humanitarian aid.

An understanding of what works and what does not work in the various forms of aid is hard to reach, partly because of the lack of genuine accountability and transparency in the aid industry and partly because dishonesty – for the best of motives – has so often been the industry's default setting.

Aid organisations behave as if good intentions matter more than outcomes. This is as true of Britain's DfID as it is of private non-governmental organisations (NGOs) and international organisations like UNHCR.

DfID compares well with other international donor bodies with regard to efficiency and transparency. It still stands accused of muddled thinking about priorities; self-deception about the feasibility of checking projects on the ground for waste and corruption; disingenuousness about the historical effectiveness of bilateral and multilateral development aid; and cultural inhibitions about using aid in ways that might benefit the United Kingdom and its people. In general, DfID's operations continue to be informed by an extreme absolutist view of aid, one that is suspicious of any benefits that may accrue to the UK. This is inappropriate for a government department.

Although this paper highlights the failings of development aid and the much less well-known problems intrinsic to humanitarian aid, it does not advocate the ending of all British foreign aid. Rather it urges that future UK aid be reality-based rather than faith-based, i.e. it should rest on realistic assumptions about the likely fate of donations to poor country governments, UN agencies, international bureaucracies, major global charities and local NGOs.

This paper does not take a position on the desirability of democratic and humanitarian conditions on aid, though it takes exception to the hypocrisy and inconsistency with which the UK government currently imposes such conditions. It makes little moral sense, for instance, to cut off aid to Malawi because of that country's treatment of homosexuals but to continue subsidising destructive regimes in countries like Ethiopia and Zimbabwe. Aid conditionality may well be desirable in general but it requires a pre-existing clarity about the primary goals of British aid.

Despite decades of lavish failure and negative outcomes including the enrichment of corrupt tyrants, the subsidising of warlords and the subversion of good government, aid work continues to enjoy uncritical support from sections of the media. This is not surprising given the existence of a nexus between Western media organisations and the aid agencies on which many of them depend for access and transport in conflict areas.

Recommendations

1) *Abandonment of the 0.7% target*
The 0.7% of GDP aid target should not be enshrined in law and should be abandoned. Britain's aid budget should be subject to at least the same austerity measures as those essential departments of state upon which the welfare and security of British citizens depend.

2) *A Royal Commission on Aid*
There needs to be an honest and public determination of the primary purposes of British aid, and the degree to which it should be designed to win influence for the UK or to serve other policy goals including the prevention of conflict and mass migration.

3) *Reabsorption of DfID into the FCO*
Given that DfID seems to be unwilling and unable to reform itself – and experience of other government departments indicates that even the most determined minister is unlikely to be able to reform it from above – the best hope for DfID would be reabsorption into the Foreign and Commonwealth Office.

4) *Budget Transfer to the MOD and Military Dual-Use Projects*
Up to one third of Britain's foreign aid budget should be diverted to the Ministry of Defence and the armed forces. The armed forces have the capacity to deliver certain key kinds of emergency aid more quickly and more effectively than any NGO or international aid agency.

While being able to transport emergency food and medical supplies over large distances and in the most difficult circumstances and terrain, they also have the capacity to maintain order in refugee camps, to defend themselves from predation by bandits, rebel groups and government forces, and to avoid the Goma syndrome in which refugee camps become guerrilla bases.

5) *DfID to pay for BBC World Service*
The BBC's World Service foreign language broadcasts, damaged by recent cuts, should be funded from the DfID's budget. These broadcasts are relied on by many millions of people around the world for their accuracy and have played a vital role in movements for liberty and better governance. The World Service genuinely wins influence for the UK.

6) *DfID to develop genuine counter-fraud and auditing capacity*
DfID should increase the budget and staff of its Counter-Fraud Unit and Internal Audit Department. Both units should recruit staff with appropriate financial forensic skills or borrow them from the Serious Fraud Office.

7) *DfID to shift focus from development to emergency/ humanitarian aid*
DfID should therefore shift the emphasis of its spending to emergency humanitarian aid. This is a form of aid that is unquestionably necessary, and that for all its pitfalls is less likely to do harm than many forms of overseas development aid.

8) *The UK to cut contributions to inefficient and wasteful multilateral agencies, in particular those of the EU*
DfID's recent commitment to focus more on multilateral aid is a recipe for greater waste.

9) *DfID to enshrine 'Do No Harm' as core principle of development and emergency aid*
Although the complexities of aid delivery make it impossible to achieve perfection, all DfID-funded projects need to be assessed for the likelihood that they will distort local economies, undermine existing state institutions, underwrite or prolong conflict or subsidise tyranny.

10) *In place of development aid, tax relief for immigrant remittances*
The UK government should offer tax relief for remittances by UK-resident migrants to their families in poor countries. These have proved to be an effective engine of economic growth in many Third World countries, providing capital whilst bypassing corrupt and inefficient bureaucracies.

11) *DfID to adopt pro-British policies*
DfID should abandon current practice and practise aid-delivery in ways that are mindful of the interests of the British citizens who pay for it. This should include an undertaking to publicise the British content of all British aid projects and to buy British where possible.

12) *No more UK subsidies for wealthy governments*
DfID, or any subsequent body formed after reunion with the FCO, should cut all development aid to countries with a space programme and/or a nuclear weapons programme, and also to all countries with their own foreign aid programmes. India qualifies for an aid cut-off on all three grounds, as do China and Russia.

Introduction

Aid and morality: The insufficiency of good intentions

> *'Something must be done; anything must be done, whether it works or not'*
> Bob Geldof, Live Aid (2005)

> *'Charity creates a multitude of sins'*
> Oscar Wilde, *The Soul of Man Under Socialism* (1891)

Few people in Western societies openly reject the idea that there is a moral obligation to help the poor and alleviate suffering in other countries. There is less consensus as to whether this charitable obligation should fall on states as well as on individual citizens, and regarding the forms that it should take.

Britain is among the most generous countries in the world in terms of the amount of money its citizens donate to private charities working around the globe. The generous response[1] in 2011 to the inaccurately labeled 'Horn of Africa Famine' showed that this generosity is undaunted by economic crisis. In that sense, the UK is already a 'development superpower' to use the phrase favoured by former Development Secretary Andrew Mitchell.*

To a considerable extent foreign aid is a concrete expression of the compassion we feel for those who suffer abroad. But however effective foreign aid may be as a public demonstration of compassion, its effectiveness as a

---

*The phrase was used in a speech of such self-congratulation and disingenuousness that it is worth quoting at length: 'My ambition is that over the next four years people will come to think across our country – in all parts of it – of Britain's fantastic development work around the poorest parts of the world with the same pride and satisfaction that they see in some of our great institutions like the armed forces and the monarchy. This is brilliant work that Britain is doing.' Groves, J., 'Backlash as Minister Boasts "Be as Proud of our £12bn Foreign Aid Bill as You are of the Army"' (2011) *The Daily Mail*, 6 June.

means of preventing and relieving suffering is more doubtful. This is important because it can be all too easy and seductive to confuse genuine generosity with what Rochefoucauld called 'the vanity of giving'.

In this regard, modern humanitarian and development aid are not so different from many previous expressions of compassion, solidarity and charity. It is easy to forget that the modern aid industry is descended not only from Henri Dunant's International Red Cross but also from the charitable explosion of the nineteenth century with its religious missionary and imperial components, and the anti-slavery movement that culminated in the Royal Navy's vigorous 'liberal interventions' of that era.

It is now commonplace to be sceptical of the motivations and the achievements of Christian missionaries of the colonial era, of the Raj officials who sought to bring justice and peace to their wards, and of all those imperialists who declared a belief in a European *mission civilizatrice'*. In their time however, their claims were taken more seriously, and their moral status was almost as high as today's aid workers and NGOs. In some places, their efforts, in Kipling's words, to 'Fill full the mouth of famine/and bid the sickness cease' had notable success. (One thinks of the French colonial doctor Eugene Jamot and his efforts to curb sleeping sickness, or Walter Reed and the American doctors who battled yellow fever in Panama.) Moreover, there is an argument that, unlike the better missionaries and Raj officials, the contemporary 'imperialists' of the overseas aid industry all too often really do immiserate their supposed beneficiaries while helping to deprive them of democratic freedoms.

There is even less consensus about the degree to which a moral obligation to help poor people abroad either justifies or requires reducing the autonomy of individuals and states that are the intended beneficiaries of foreign aid, even though many foreign aid programmes may have precisely that effect.

Understandably, the well-staffed marketing branches of the aid industry, in both its private and public incarnations, work hard to minimise public awareness of aid quandaries other than the need for more generous donations by government or individuals. However both humanitarian/ emergency aid, on the one hand, and development aid on the other, are activities that raise many complicated moral and practical questions.

This should not be surprising. Even the most basic individual acts of charity at home can raise difficult moral problems. Some people react to the importuning of a beggar on a city street by giving him or her money. Some try to guess by looking at the beggar if he is 'worth' giving money to. If he looks like a drunk or junkie, they may withhold their cash or extort a promise that their donation will not be used to buy alcohol or drugs. Others withhold their coins and instead donate to charities that work with the homeless or addicts or activist organisations that campaign for 'better' government policies. This they believe is 'really' helping the person on the street and others like him. All three responses are potentially problematic.

There is arguably something patronising and de-meaning about attempting to make sure that a beggar only uses your donation to buy food or for some other purpose that you believe is good for him or for society as a whole. Some would say that if he wants to 'misuse' your donation in a way that you find irresponsible but which he believes is a good idea, then any attempt to restrain that choice is treating him as a lesser being, or a child. True generosity, they might argue, is a matter of giving without worrying about the benefits to the recipient or the donor.

On the other hand, and this kind of argument certainly applies to many kinds of large-scale international aid, the giving of money to that same beggar could have many bad results both for him and for society as a whole, results that far outweigh the moral satisfaction of the donor or the apparent gratitude of the beggar.

After all, if the beggar goes off and buys crack cocaine or heroin with the money you have given him, you are then not only an enabler of an addiction that may further degrade him or even kill him; you have also sponsored a crime and contributed a subsidy to a criminal industry. You may have respected one individual's moral autonomy but at the cost of joining an international process that results in the assassination of judges, the torture of witnesses and the corruption of entire states.

Even if the beggar does not risk his health by buying drugs or booze, many critics would say you have fostered dependency, encouraged the socially undesirable practice of begging, undermined those groups who are trying to get the homeless off the street, and bought off your own conscience at a much lower price than working to improve the social problems that impoverished or degraded the beggar.

There are of course differences between the act of giving to a beggar and donations by wealthy countries, international aid agencies and non-government organisations to states, individuals and groups in poor countries. But it would be wrong and naïve to think that they are not often analogous or that the latter raises fewer moral and practical issues. (The tendency of the aid industry to treat Third World countries like children has long been a theme of complaint in Africa and elsewhere.)

Unfortunately, during the five or six decades of development aid and the simultaneous evolution and growth of the humanitarian aid sector, cries for 'action' have tended to obscure or silence some of these questions. For various reasons, some self-serving, both Western governments and those who hold power in the poorer parts of the planet have colluded in efforts to keep discussion of aid as simple and politically safe as possible. Much of the discourse on aid is dominated by the implicit or explicit notion that good intentions are a sufficient, perhaps even the only test of aid policy, and that questioning the effectiveness, still less the morality or utility, of various kinds of aid is inherently ungenerous.[2] A common position in the aid community is that such questioning is 'unconstructive' and only harms the poor. After all, it is indisputable that much aid helps the needy even if some fails because it is poorly conceived or executed, or is wasted or stolen, and even if some does actual harm.

It does not help that the discussion is often cabined by ideologically-determined 'political correctness' about the politics and economics of 'Third World' countries. For years it was considered 'unconstructive' for aid deliverers to dwell publicly on, or even to mention, problems of institutional corruption and incompetence, especially the former. (Rather than speak of either, the aid community prefers the euphemistic, 'non-judgmental' rubric of 'governance'.) This continues to be the case, especially in the humanitarian sector. Moreover, for many people in the aid community, it was and is an article of political faith that poverty and economic failure in 'developing' countries are almost entirely the result of malign behaviour by foreign countries and companies. According to this pervasive attitude, it is white foreigners, good or evil, who determine the fates of developing countries and their peoples. No matter how much breast beating it involves about past imperial crimes or the poverty supposedly caused by western indifference or exploitation, this is an attitude that reveals both a deluded sense of Western omnipotence and a 'bigotry of low expectations' that are all too common in the aid community.

Clear and honest discussion about the effectiveness, morality and utilty of aid is also hindered by two other phenomena. First there is the dominance of social scientists and a social science mindset in academic and policy discussions on the subject of development aid. This has led to a remarkably ahistorical approach to the key questions of how and why some societies develop faster than others at different times and in different places, and also a tendency to amnesia about previous efforts to make aid more effective.

Secondly there is an unhealthy, some might say corrupt nexus between Western media organisations and international aid agencies. In many parts of the world, the former depend on the latter not just as a vital source of information and stories but also for transportation, accommodation and other key services in remote areas. In an age of diminishing media organisation budgets, foreign journalists visiting many parts of Africa and Asia are entirely dependent on UN flights and NGO infrastructure. In return, the latter get stories shaped around their fundraising or policy needs. The aid agency 'line' on a particular crisis or the response to it is promoted by the journalist, and inconvenient information goes unmentioned.

Finally it is worth considering the argument made by aid critic David Rieff that foreign aid has become a means of avoiding responsibility, and that 'the whole discussion of aid avoids, or makes a kind of moral and historical end run around the problem of politics'. As Rieff put it in a debate on foreign aid in New York: 'There are these suffering people... We do or we don't have the modalities to efficiently succour them. That is the aid narrative and it is a narrative that largely speaking deprives the recipients of aid of their agency, infantilises them, and also makes aid a super-political, extra-political, moral question. Because it becomes a moral imperative we can't talk about the politics...'[3]

Foreign aid as sacred cow

The history of foreign aid is, among many other things both good and bad, a history of fads and fashionable jargon. At one point 'sustainable development' was all the rage, with its slightly disturbing implication that previous efforts were not designed to be sustainable. In recent years, alongside a new public concern for 'aid-effectiveness', one of the new buzzwords has been 'evidence-based aid'. Specifically this refers to aid programmes based on quasi-scientific experiments whereby analysts use randomised controlled trials, like those for new medicines, to assess aid projects in Third World countries. It is a good idea in many ways and researchers trying it out have had some interesting and useful results. But 'evidence-based aid' may be most significant because it implicitly reveals a troubling truth about other, previous forms of development aid that have cost the developed world more than two trillion[4] dollars over the past 60 years: That is that much foreign aid is not based on evidence that it works, or is useful, or does more good than harm.

It is based, instead, on other things, things like tradition, guesswork, momentum, inspiration, intuition, hope, and also greed, careerism, self-interest and cynicism. All too often, foreign aid is merely faith-based; not in the sense that it derives from religious belief, (though of course much modern altruism does indeed have its roots in Christian and other religious thought, and much of it is carried out by religiously inspired groups and individuals), but in the sense that foreign aid itself can be a kind of religion, believed in and supported by peoples and governments for reasons that have little or no connection with ascertainable facts.

Like any other organised religion, foreign aid fulfils deep psychological and emotional needs, while having both good and bad effects on the real world. It has its priests and followers. It employs large numbers of people.

It has state and private elements and is exploited by powerful political and economic interests. And like many religions, it requires that its adherents make leaps of faith when reality fails to match up with doctrine.

None of this necessarily makes foreign aid any less important or desirable. Nor does it make its practitioners any less courageous, selfless or competent. But it does make aid as an activity harder to analyse and discuss. As David Rieff has pointed out, an 'aura of sanctity'[5] surrounds foreign aid. Anyone who questions the amounts spent on it, let alone its justifications, is almost inevitably accused by its adherents of a monstrous lack of compassion.[6] Moreover, any open-minded outsider dealing with the 'aid industry' or, as insiders prefer, the 'aid community', cannot help but be struck by the self-righteousness and sanctimony that so often characterise responses to even the mildest outside questioning of aid methodology, let alone aid utility and morality.*

Furthermore, while 'transparency' and 'accountability' have recently become the watchwords of better aid organisations like Britain's Department for International Development (DfID), this was not the case for the first five decades of international development aid and for most of the history of humanitarian aid.[7] Indeed, secretiveness and the ruthless manipulation of information for public relations purposes have been and generally still are the default settings for the aid industry.

Aid workers confronted simultaneously by vast human distress and the apparent indifference of the rich world have

---

* The aid community would rather be analysed by insiders, though as Alex de Waal wrote in his seminal book *Famine Crimes – Politics and the Disaster Relief Industry*, this is 'as though the sociological study of the church were undertaken by committed Christians only: criticism would be solely within the context of advancing the faith itself'. de Waal, A., *Famine Crimes – Politics and the Disaster Relief Industry*, p.65.

often, perhaps understandably, resorted to distortion, hyperbole and outright lies to help those in their care. It is partly as a result of such pressures that there seems to be such a low bar for dishonesty in the aid community, especially in the gathering and dissemination of statistics. With so much at stake, and so many people to 'help', deliberately exaggerating the size of a famine or the number of people helped by a project can seem like a very venial sin.

This cultural characteristic of the aid industry, compounded by the practical obstacles inherent in its work in underdeveloped and often chaotic, corrupt and conflict-ridden states, and the paucity of truly reliable data, means that assessing the true impact of foreign aid is a complicated business.

Arguably, the really difficult part of aid is not raising money; it is delivering aid to those who need it. Unfortunately the aid community has historically avoided public and even private discussion of the enormous difficulty of delivering aid where it is supposed to go, lest governments and charitable individuals shrink their contributions.

For instance, right now in the UK, DfID is having to deal with the problem of a growing budget with a smaller staff. Rather than admit that it cannot handle the amount of money the Treasury is giving it, DfID is going to devote more of its 'spend' to direct budget support of poor country governments, the least accountable, least transparent and arguably least effective kind of foreign aid.

According to Margaret Hodge MP, chair of the Committee of Public Accounts of the House of Commons, in the Committee's report on DfID's finances, the increased spend in 'fragile and conflict-affected countries [presents a] danger to the taxpayer [because] there could be an increase in fraud and corruption. However, the Department could not even give us information as to the expected levels of fraud and corruption and the action they were taking to mitigate it.[8]

The reluctance to deal publicly with past failures and any current difficulties (other than lack of generosity from donor governments) pales as a disabling dereliction compared to the aid industry's general refusal to deal with the question of *actual harm* done by various kinds of aid. This can include the distortion of a local economy when aid agencies descend on an African town to set up nearby refugee camps. Not only do prices go up for everything from water to fuel, but skilled professionals give up their positions to work as interpreters and drivers for a hundred dollars a day (a standard international aid agency/media organisation rate even in countries where that is more than a doctor is paid in a month).

Some observers like Michela Wrong, the corruption expert and author of *It's Our Turn to Eat*, have become more concerned with the malign effect of aid on a country's politics and morale than with questions of aid 'effectiveness'. Wrong has reported on the way that civil society organisations, political dissidents and anti-corruption campaigners in countries like Kenya – a major recipient of UK aid – get discouraged when the continuation of that aid implies British approval of corrupt governments.

Then there is the question of autonomy that is raised by aid critics on both Right and Left. As Wrong says, countries which have up to 40 per cent of their operating budgets paid for by foreign donors, like, say, Kenya and Uganda, are not really independent.

Moreover, there is strong evidence that heavily-aided governments become less likely to spend their budgets in sectors like health and education, become more rather than less predatory on their citizens, and feel less need to be accountable to those citizens. If that were not bad enough, such aid-dependent states have rarely if ever enjoyed developmental success, in contrast to South East Asian and other countries that achieved development and prosperity having received much smaller amounts of aid.

Indeed there is a growing body of evidence and academic argument that there is an *inverse* relationship between the likelihood of economic success and the amount of development aid a country receives over time.[9] One of the factors explaining why a country like Ghana which in 1957 enjoyed a higher per capita GDP than South Korea,[10] had one that was lower by a factor of ten only thirty years later, seems to be the toxic effect of offical development aid (ODA) on the country's politics and economics.[11]

However, this evidence and these arguments have had little or no effect on aid policy especially in the UK.*

---

*As Moyo puts it, 'there is no other sector, whether it be business or politics, where such proven failures are allowed to persist in the face of such stark and unassailable evidence' (p .47). Dambisa Moyo, *Dead Aid*.

PART 1
British Aid Basics

1. The Basics of British Foreign Aid

'Just as the Americans are a military superpower, we are a development superpower – we are in the lead.'
Andrew Mitchell, Secretary of State for International
Development 2010–2012

The United Kingdom currently spends approximately £8 billion a year on foreign aid, a number that will rise to £11 billion over the next three years. Most of this sum is spent by the Department of International Development (DfID), though some is spent by the Ministry of Defence (MoD) and the Foreign and Commonwealth Office (FCO). DfID is essentially Britain's 'ministry of foreign aid'. Formerly known as the Overseas Development Administration, DfID was part of the Foreign Office until 1997, though it had an independent existence under previous Labour governments.

Not only is DfID now independent of the Foreign Office, it also has a much larger budget and a larger presence in many parts of the world.[1] Arguably it operates a parallel UK foreign policy that is neither initiated or controlled by the Foreign Secretary nor overseen by foreign policy committees in Parliament. Sometimes this parallel foreign policy conflicts with or undermines those of the Foreign Office and the Ministry of Defence. Yet despite the size of its budget and staff, it has a relatively low public profile in the UK, which enables it to formulate policy with minimal democratic scrutiny.

Bilateral aid

Currently more than one quarter of UK foreign aid takes the form of 'bilateral' aid that goes directly to developing country governments 'to spend on the priorities they set for themselves for helping their citizens out of poverty'.

3

This type of aid, which generally takes the form of 'budget support', is controversial because of the ease with which it can be stolen or wasted by the corrupt and incompetent government officials all too common in many poorer countries. There is convincing evidence that such corruption and incompetence – euphemistically labelled 'problems of governance' in aid jargon – is a major cause (rather than a symptom) of poverty and underdevelopment.

Multilateral aid

Another third of British foreign aid is 'multilateral' in that it goes to international institutions like the World Bank, the European Union's Aid Programme, various agencies of the United Nations and organisations like the Global Fund To Fight AIDS, Tuberculosis and Malaria (GFATM). Some of these institutions are known to be much more efficient and professional than others. The EU's aid programme for instance was memorably described by then International Development Secretary Clare Short MP as a 'an outrage and a disgrace',[2] and 'the worst development agency in the world' for its corruption, and inefficiency, and its propensity to divert aid to already wealthy Mediterranean countries. Currently almost one fifth of Britain's aid budget goes to the EU for distribution.

Humanitarian aid

Emergency or 'humanitarian' aid amounts to less than half-a-billion pounds per year of the UK's 10 billion plus aid 'spend', though it is the kind of aid most often depicted in aid industry marketing and is often cited by aid advocates to justify the entire aid budget, as when Prime Minister David Cameron told the House of Commons in July 2011 that the famine in the Horn of Africa 'once again' made the case for an increased foreign aid budget.[3] Under current policy, the UK government is increasing the amount given to DfID's Office of Coordination for Humanitarian Affairs from £10 million to £17 million even though, according to insiders and consultants who work for the department, 'it cannot even spend what it has'.[4]

Increasing and 'ring-fencing' the foreign aid budget

Although the Conservative-led Coalition government has in several areas changed policy direction or made U-turns in response to economic pressures that were not present or apparent during the general election campaign, it has held fast to David Cameron's commitment to 'ring-fence' Britain's foreign aid from cuts, and indeed to increase aid spending as a proportion of GDP from 0.56 per cent to 0.7 per cent. (The significance of this number is symbolic rather than empirically related to any particular aid goal as a later chapter will explain.)

Although the actual sum may change as British GDP drops, this meant as announced in 2010 that Britain's aid budget would rise by more than 34 per cent over four years and amount to £11.5 billion in 2014. That is more than the UK spends on the Royal Air Force or the Royal Navy and five times what the country is spending on the war in Afghanistan. It will cost every household in the country some £300-500 per year. To put it into another perspective, one billion pounds would pay for the salaries of 25,000 police constables or nurses.

The powerful momentum behind current aid policy seems to have much to do with the Conservative Party leadership's ongoing drive to 'detoxify' its 'brand' and market itself as 'compassionate'. To the extent that an increase in foreign development aid serves this public relations purpose, its effectiveness or lack thereof at delivering a better life and future for various poor peoples around the world is presumably beside the point, although at £11 billion per annum it amounts to one of the most expensive marketing campaigns in history.

In the late spring of 2011, criticism of this commitment within the Conservative party reached such a pitch after a leaked letter from then Secretary of Defence Liam Fox, that the Prime Minister felt obliged to make a spirited public defence of Britain's foreign aid expenditure and the fact that it had become proportionally the largest of any G8 country[5] despite this being a time of austerity and mounting international threats.

Among other justifications for the increase in expenditure, the Prime Minister and his then Secretary for International Development, Andrew Mitchell made much of a new direction in British aid policy, including the elimination of aid to some countries, increases to others, and new measures designed to ensure that less British aid might be wasted, misdirected or stolen than in the past.

The Prime Minister also claimed that foreign aid was vital to national security. This is an argument that has since been echoed with some frequency and even more forcefully by the Development Secretary,[6] along with the almost equally tendentious claim that foreign aid wins Britain significant goodwill abroad.

At one point the Prime Minister made the claim[7] that sending development aid to failing states now would prevent wars and save military expenditure in the future. In a distinctly unusual interpretation of recent history he wrote that: 'If we had put a fraction of our current military spending on Afghanistan into helping Afghanistan develop 20 years ago, just think what we might have been able to avoid over the past decade.'

Since then, the government has been obliged by a worsening financial situation to make many painful, previously unplanned economies including the raising of pension ages, the cutting of help to the disabled and other vulnerable citizens, cuts in police numbers, and more compulsory redundancies in the armed forces despite the ongoing war in Afghanistan and growing threats to national security. Again and again, the public is told – and largely accepts – that there simply isn't the money to pay for the services to be cut. Nevertheless the foreign aid commitment remains sacrosanct. And when it comes to funding the people and institutions involved in operations of dubious effectiveness for a goal that itself may be problematic, there turns out to be enough money in the exchequer.

The untouchability of the foreign aid budget and its planned increase seems all the more extraordinary given a report in October 2011 by Parliament's Public Accounts Committee[8] that cast doubt on DfID's ability to manage its budgets, its commitment to accountability and its ability to make efficient use of its resources. According to the report, DfID under its new secretary had actually stopped monitoring its own finance plan in 2010. The committee's chairperson Margaret Hodge MP stated that 'this must not happen again and DfID should report publicly on its financial management'. The report strongly disputed Andrew Mitchell's claims concerning the department's commitment and ability to monitor fraud and corruption abroad, and felt that its bigger budget would only make its weaknesses worse.

This paper argues that, even if the UK were still enjoying a boom rather than the worst economic crisis for many decades, there would still be a strong case for re-evaluating and changing the priorities, mechanisms and amounts of British foreign aid.

Not only is much of Britain's foreign aid budget destined to be wasted or stolen by recipient officials and institutions, much of that which does arrive in the right place fails to promote economic growth and often does

7

more harm than good to underdeveloped societies. Moreover the goodwill and security arguments for an increased aid budget are, as we shall see later, unsupported by evidence.

2. UK Aid and Unasked Questions

Arguably one of the biggest disappointments of the Cameron-Clegg Coalition government has been its failure to evaluate British foreign aid programmes from first principles and to ask the big and important questions about foreign aid. These include:

- Why should UK citizens – who give more to charity than the citizens of any other G8 country except the United States – also pay heavily for aid through their taxes?

- Does aid help poor people in the poorest and worst run societies or does it harm them?

- To the extent that aid can help people in poor countries, which kind of aid is least harmful and most effective?

- Should UK taxpayers subsidise a branch of government whose real function is arguably to subsidise a parasitic and often destructive industry whose employees come from the most privileged sections of British society and their equivalents abroad?

- Should UK taxpayers be subsidising an industry that replicates much that was bad about 19th century missionary activity and colonialism, that assumes moral superiority, and even with best intentions patronises and undermines those whom it is supposed to benefit?

Unfortunately, Britain's aid establishment under the supposedly reformist leadership of Development Secretary Andrew Mitchell preferred to avoid consideration of the bigger questions that surround the enterprise of foreign aid. Nor is there much discussion of them in Westminster or the media, despite the advent of the most severe economic crisis in three quarters of a century, a crisis that has prompted other Western nations to reconsider and decrease their foreign aid expenditure.[1]

Much of the discussion about British foreign aid that does take place is distorted by two things: the foreign aid 'Halo Effect' and popular confusion as to what aid actually is and how it works.

By the foreign aid Halo Effect, I mean the way an otherwise cynical society, that often chooses to think the worst of elected politicians, does the exact opposite when it comes to people and institutions involved in the activity of 'helping' the less fortunate abroad. As David Rieff has written of American public perceptions of aid workers: 'Here are people engaged in an activtity that is wholly admirable, and that one need not view sceptically.'[2] (It helps that their image has been burnished by what Rieff memorably called 'Niagaras of adulatory media attention'.[3])

The Halo Effect seems to be particularly strong in the UK where mega-charities like Save the Children are generally free from sceptical scrutiny.* In the UK, even UN agencies are presumed to be efficient organisations staffed by able, honest and altruistic individuals. (Exceptions to this general prejudice in favour of aid agencies and other international organisations include perceptions of the World Bank and the International Monetary Fund which are identified with the United States and 'heartless' capitalism.) Such is the presumption of benignity that print and televisions advertisements by organisations like Oxfam and Save the Children are not subjected to the level of scrutiny by the Advertising Standards Authority that is the norm for

---

*The discrediting of journalists and politicians may have made aid workers and the aid enterprise all the more attractive as notional icons of virtue and, perhaps, fed the fierce determination of the Cameron government to associate itself with both.

commercial organisations or even political parties.[4] (The latitude for exaggeration and even dishonesty that this allows NGOs was revealed by the ASA's lax approach to a 2010 Oxfam poster claiming that people '5,000 miles' away are being killed by climate change.[5])

Indeed, until the recent success of books like Dambisa Moyo's *Dead Aid* (2009), William Easterly's *The White Man's Burden* (2006) and Linda Polman's *War Games* (2010), the British public was largely unaware that there are searching questions to be asked about the effectiveness and morality of foreign aid in its various forms.

In the last decade or so, official 'development aid' (ODA) – the main form of aid given by Western governments and the largest form of aid worldwide, has fortunately come under increasingly sceptical scrutiny by academics and policy analysts. However, mainstream political discourse on the subject has generally taken little note of these fundamental debates about the overall effectiveness of foreign aid. The wider public has in the past been supportive of the general idea of foreign aid but ignorant of how and where it is delivered. Even the distinction between development aid and emergency aid, and the fact that the former is much larger than the latter, is little known.

This may well reflect the way that the whole enterprise of foreign aid is marketed by private aid agencies and non-government organisations (NGOs) on the one hand and the Department for International Development (DfID) on the other. Emergency aid is popular with the public; development aid is less so. Imagery of aid workers helping the victims of disaster is so predominant in aid agency PR that the public tends to assume that aid means humanitarian aid. Eliding this difference therefore serves a useful political purpose.

This confusion and this ignorance seems to have been

11

actively fostered by 'the aid community' – or as others call it, 'the aid industry' – the many thousands of mostly middle-class or upper class people who are profitably employed here and abroad by public and private aid agencies. (Both characterisations seem fair enough: these people represent both an industry and a community, and, equally important, an economic interest group with considerable political clout.)

Although analysts distinguish between government or public aid on the one hand and private or NGO aid on the other hand (usually assuming that the latter is principally engaged in emergency aid), in the UK that distinction can sometimes obscure certain larger realities. The big private aid agencies like Oxfam and Save the Children are prime overseas contractors for DfID and draw significant income from it.

This is not to say that the NGOs' agendas are therefore set by the government. If anything, the opposite is true.[6] DfID's agenda is heavily influenced by the big private aid agencies. It is not just that Oxfam and others publicly lobby DfID and use their influence to shape its agenda; many DfID officials are former activists from the NGO sector. The hegemonic ideologies of that sector have therefore predominated within DfID ever since it was split off from the Foreign and Commonwealth Office (FCO).

The aid sector is peculiarly under-scrutinised compared to other heavily subsidised parts of the British economy. This lack of scrutiny, compounded by an absence of honest self-interrogation, has ensured that official UK aid (and, less importantly, private aid) offers less value for money to the taxpayer, and is more vulnerable to waste, corruption and poor policymaking than even sectors like defence and trade.

Although DfID itself has a deserved reputation as one of the most professional, least inefficient and most transparent of the world's national and international aid agencies – a reputation akin to that of the British Army in military circles – the bar is unfortunately not a high one.* Moreover, while DfID's much vaunted 'new direction' under the Cameron-Clegg Coalition arguably represents mostly symbolic improvement, there is one major exception. There does seem to be at the top of the organisation a new, genuine concentration on 'aid-effectiveness' – the aid buzzword of our era – and therefore increased concern that the UK aid offers value for money both for the British taxpayer and aid beneficiaries. This seriousness is symbolised by the establishment of the Independent Commission on Aid Impact (ICAI), the first such institution of its kind.

However, it is not clear if Andrew Mitchell's enthusiasm for accountability and 'evidence-based' value for money won over long-term DfID staff and those within the permanent organisation who would prefer less scrutiny and a continuation of the free spending spirit fostered by Clare Short.

But other aspects of the new direction are troublingly incoherent, not least the department's new selectivity about which countries are to get bilateral UK aid. There is supposed to be a shift to very poor and conflict-ridden areas, despite the greater difficulty of ensuring accountability and guarding against corruption in such areas. There is also a shift to the Commonwealth countries, an

---

*As with other donor agencies, DfID is a sucker for well-written but misleading proposals. Linda Polman recalls coming upon a DfID-funded project in Sierra Leone that had been presented as 'supporting resettlement and reintegration of ex-combatants' and 'establishing resettled and reintegrated communities contributing in the long term to the estabishment of sustainable peace and security'. In reality, it amounted to a foreign aid worker standing over 25 teenagers who may or may not have once been child soldiers, whom he was paying 50¢ a day to dig holes by the side of the road, which they would fill in and re-dig the next day. Linda Polman, *War Games: The Story of Aid and War in Modern Times*, p.188.

unexceptional decision[7] except to the extent that it conflicts with the previous one, and the fact that it will entail giving British aid to some nasty and corrupt tyrannies. The supposed new focus on 'value for money' could undermine projects that are useful but offer little in the way of usable metrics. Moreover, this new emphasis, as sensible and admirable as it sounds, may represent a pipe dream given the unreliabity of aid statistics in general and the untrackability of moneys given in the form of budget support or to multilateral agencies.

More significant, however, is the fact that DfID has largely failed to assimilate a whole series of powerful critiques of development aid by independent economists and former aid agency officials including Paul Collier, William Easterly and Robert Calderisi.[8] Because of these critiques, overseas development aid is no longer an activity whose justification can simply be taken for granted by any principled person with responsibilty to the British public.

This is, after all, an enterprise whose core assumptions may be fundamentally flawed and hubristic, whose history the evidence shows to have one of overwhelming failure (at least with regards to the promotion of economic growth), whose implementation has historically been marred in practice by inefficiency, corruption and unacceptable moral and political compromise, and finally one which has had dreadful unintended consequences including: fostering corruption and enriching kleptocrats; the preservation in power of tyrannical and exploitative regimes; the subsidising of war and ethnic cleansing; the fostering of aid dependency rather than economic activity; and finally the undermining of local economies (food aid in particular has caused agricultural sectors to shrink and made famine more rather than less likely).[9]

The very fact that the Department continues to adhere to the 0.7 per cent of GDP target and the Millennium

Development Goals – both of which have origins not in empirical research but in rich-country political grandstanding and activist marketing – is telling.

Arguably DfID's continuing failure to confront some of the more awkward aspects of the history of development aid or the complex intellectual, practical and philosophical issues inherent in aid policy does not indicate a leadership – or a staff – that is fit for purpose, especially given the department's duty to the British public to ensure that British generosity is not wasted.

This failure also represents a dereliction of DfID's secondary duty to the purported beneficiaries of aid abroad. If, as seems to be the case, per-capita income is higher in virtually unaided, failed-state Mogadishu than in heavily-aided Nairobi,[10] a responsible and well-informed aid minister would be asking his or her advisers some difficult fundamental questions.[11] However Mr. Mitchell was either unaware of such facts or unwilling to admit them.

At a time of extreme economic distress in the UK, it is unconscionable for a government department and its head to take so little note of its responsibility to both the British public and the notional beneficiaries of British aid abroad.

Being seen to 'care' and to 'give', expensively, may make for good marketing and moral pride on departmental and even a national level. It certainly serves the perceived party-political needs of the Conservative-Liberal Coalition and the Tory Party leadership's overriding concern with 'rebranding'. However, this is not the same as actually helping the world's poorer peoples. Too often it amounts to an expensive version of what might be called 'aid theatre'[12] – charitable activity or expenditure whose primary function is not 'saving lives' or improving the lives of people in poor countries but rather the provision of political, moral, emotional and psychological benefits to powerful individuals and groups in donor countries.

15

Class and the Coalition's aid agenda

It is hard to see any principled argument behind the steadfast refusal of the current government to include the foreign aid budget in the cuts that will have a negative impact on almost every public service in Britain, from libraries destined to close to the police and military lay-offs that may imperil the safety of British citizens and businesses at home and abroad. It is a refusal that is accompanied by the throwing of accusations of 'hardheartedness' at those who question it. Yet this is a country and a government which has not yet budgeted for the long-term treatment and care of the 2,500 to 3,500 severely wounded veterans of the Iraq and Afghanistan wars who will never be able to work again. The costs of looking after these men, many of them multiple amputees with other debilitating injuries, and most from relatively poor families, are estimated by defence experts to cost between £2.5 and £4 billion, assuming a life expectancy of only 15 years.[13] Taxpayer money that could be devoted to these men who have sacrificed so much for their country is instead going to an aid enterprise that is largely as quixotic and self-indulgent as Andrew Mitchell's dream of Britain as a 'foreign aid superpower'.

It would seem that for the Cameron-Clegg government, notionally helping poor people in Africa and South Asia (or sending money in their general direction) simply ranks as a higher moral or political priority than the suffering of vulnerable people at home.* This is perhaps explicable as an aspect of the well-heeled, expensively educated culture from which many of the Coalition's leaders come. Among the wealthy 'Notting Hill set' and its neighbours in that

---

*This is an attitude sometimes called Jellybyism after the Charles Dickens's character Mrs Jellyby in *Bleak House* who gave all her money and attention to African charitable causes while neglecting her own family.

fashionable quarter, foreign charity is a common enthusiasm. Such people are perhaps more likely to engage with poor Africans and South Asians on their holidays than they are to encounter needy or vulnerable people in their own country. And it is hard to escape the impression that it is for this reason (rather than pure snobbery) that the PM and his circle apparently find it harder to empathise with a 'chav' in a wheelchair – even if he lost his legs in Afghanistan – than they do with disadvantaged people in the Third World.

3. Aid Myth and Aid Reality

'To call official wealth transfers 'aid' promotes an unquestioning attitude. It disarms criticism, obscures realities and prejudges results. Who can be against aid to the less fortunate? The term has enabled aid supporters to claim a monopoly of compassion and to dismiss critics as lacking in understanding and compassion.'   Peter Bauer[1]

In vibrant village markets all over Africa and in parts of South and Central Asia, the traveller often comes across sacks of grain that have marked on them 'not for sale – this is a gift of the American people' or the logo of the World Food Programme. Similarly, dusty local pharmacies often contain medicines bearing stickers that read 'donated by' and 'not for sale'. They are visible reminders of realities of foreign aid that contradict the world evoked by aid statistics and aid marketing. The claims of people fed, children schooled, buildings raised, institutions built, and consciousnesses raised often have little basis in objective reality. Aid projects are like the French Resistance – if all the people in post-war France who claimed to have been members of the Resistance had actually been in it, the Germans would not have been able to occupy France for more than a couple of days. Similarly if all the roads/schools/clinics and orphanages that that aid agencies claimed to have created in the Third World really existed and functioned as they were supposed to do, then much of today's poverty and misery would have been eliminated.

When an aid agency like DfID claims in its publicity materials that one of its programmes 'is educating' or has educated 'x million' children, it is practicing what is at best a form of ellipsis. The only certain truth of the claim is that a particular programme was created to perform that function and that funds were allocated to it. Whether or not the schools were completed, whether the country in question supplied teachers, whether the DfID funded schools had sufficient furniture, books or electricity to actually function might be a very different matter.[2]

One of the causes of poverty and underdevelopment that is least appreciated by the general public is the existence of Potemkin Projects or 'ghost' institutions in developing countries. 'Ghost schools' in particular, i.e. schools that exist only on paper, along with 'ghost clinics' are extremely common on the books of heavily aided Third World countries.

For instance, when General Musharraf first took power in Pakistan he sent military auditors to every community in the country. (In many villages it was the first time since independence that they had been visited by an official of the central government.) They found that Pakistan had at least 5,300[3] 'ghost schools.'

In the early 1990s, the head of a small American NGO planning to build a school in a village in the Baltistan region of Pakistan's Northern Areas was told by the Ministry of Education in Islamabad that the village already had a government school. The American had just been in the village and there was no school there. He asked a provincial official what had happened to the school. The official replied: 'it is a probably a Mitsubishi Pajero driving around Islamabad'.[4] [5]

Unfortunately it is not only government schools and clinics in South Asia and Africa that have a mere paper existence, as DfID discovered in Kenya when its £1 million budget for education went missing in 2009.[6] Although it is harder for local officials to steal whole projects funded by foreign aid agencies than it is to steal from their own government budgets, it does happen.[7]

Also, as with the schools, clinics and roads built by local governments, it is vital to ask of any notionally successful project whether or not the school or clinic is actually staffed and whether or not a completed road is subsequently maintained. Sub-Saharan Africa is littered with the shells of empty schools and roads and bridges that have fallen into disuse because they were not maintained in safe condition. South Asia has thousands of schools and clinics where the teacher or doctor rarely if ever turns up but collects a salary all the same (the official in charge of attendance being suitably bribed).[8]

Indeed it is fury at such dereliction that has inspired Maoist revolutionary movements in Nepal and India and won public support for Islamist militant groups in Pakistan – all three of which countries are major recipients of British aid.

Claims of aid project success need to be subjected to questions such as: Was the design suitable for the climate/ the culture/the local practices? Was it built with the specified or correct materials? Was it built in the right place? Was it really needed? Were funds included for maintenance or has some local institution agreed to maintain it? Is the recipient government able or willing to staff the school or clinic or orphanage?

All too often, even if a school/clinic/orphanage were built in the wrong materials in the wrong place in the wrong dimensions and is already falling apart, it may be counted as a success. After all, the workers in the field have a strong personal and institutional incentive to give good news to their bosses at home, who in turn need to supply good news to donors. Moreover, it may well be claimed as a success by more than one aid agency. Competition among aid agencies and NGOs is so fierce that it is common for groups to send photos home to donors of other agencies' projects.[9]

Then there is the question of numbers and statistics (dealt with in more detail below). Most statistics from very poor and/or disorderly countries are in fact little more than guesses; some are outright inventions. This is true of estimates of everything from GDP to the numbers of people sick with malaria, to the numbers of people who are allegedly benefiting from UK aid.

When DfID's website asserts, for instance, that EU aid, part paid for by Britain, has 'help[ed] 24 million of the world's poorest people get food', 'enabl[ed] nine million people to enrol in primary school' and 'help[ed] 31 million households gain access to better drinking water', all it really means that those vast numbers were targeted by a plethora of programmes, some of which may possibly have succeeded in those goals. Every aspect of those claims ranging from the superiority of 'better drinking water' to the functionality of the primary schools to numbers like '24 million' would be unlikely to stand up to close empirical scrutiny – and almost certainly has never been subjected to such scrutiny.

One aid critic points out that in 2003 'estimates of the number of Liberians who were in acute need because of the war varied from 'hundreds of thousands' (UN) and 'one million' (AP) to 'practically the entire population of 3.2 million souls' (American Black Caucus). The only certain fact about the condition of the Liberian people is that nobody knew what it was. AP alone gave a source, after a fashion, for its guesstimate: international aid organisations attempting to raise funds for Liberia.[10]

Moreover, as Alex de Waal, the co-director of Justice Africa and author of *Famine Crimes* has written, in Africa people 'never, never die in the numbers predicted by aid agencies[11]'.

The other problem with the core arguments of aid enthusiasts is one of basic credibility. The history of foreign aid is to an astonishing and depressing degree a history of untruths – of lies told for the greater good, of false or unverifiable claims of success,[12] of exaggerated natural catastrophes and of dishonestly hidden deals with dictators and rebel forces.

These and other grubby realities are no secret within the aid community. Indeed, spend time in a bar with expatriate aid workers in any Third World country and you will soon hear stories that will make you hesitate ever again to put coins in a charity box. However, nothing of mistakes, errors, waste, corruption or anything else likely to inspire diminished enthusiasm and generosity ever makes it into official agency reports or NGO marketing materials. This is equally true of both development and emergency aid.

Within the aid community, people know perfectly well that even their least inaccurate data are only guesstimates, because the societies they work to improve are, inevitably, those in which gathering accurate statistics is extremely difficult, and becomes even harder the further you get from the relative order and sophistication of the capital city.

Within the aid community you can even find aid workers and officials who will dissent from the standard line[13] that the transfer of aid wealth to plundering dictators like Zaire's Mobutu, Haiti's Baby Doc Duvalier and Jean-Bedel Bokassa of the Central African Republic was a specific mistake made by a paranoid anti-communist West during the Cold War phenomenon and that since then aid has stopped being an endless slush-fund for what Africans call the *WaBenzi*[14] – the big bosses whose Mercedes cars are a symbol of power and wealth. Similarly there are those within the aid community who, at least in private, will break from the Orwellian aid tradition of claiming one unsullied development victory after another.[15]

However, for the most part, dishonesty and disingenuousness about the way aid really works or does not work in the field is a default setting for aid advocates and practitioners. It is as if the small lies that aid workers 'have' to tell their bosses or donors at home become so habitual that larger lies in the service of aid's good intentions become easy to tell.

Fortunately, the truth that all too often lies behind the bland language or impenetrable jargon[16] of aid agency reports – 'empowerment', 'capacity-building', 'stakeholder', 'facilitator' and so on – sometimes emerges in blogs and websites run by current and former aid workers. They know from personal experience* that 'civil society involvement' often really means 'consulting a few middle-class local employees of foreign NGOs', that 'capacity building' can simply mean 'a highly salaried staff member flying in for three days of lectures',[17] and that 'beneficiaries' translates to 'the people who make it possible for us to be paid'.[18]

This is as true for expats working for small charities out in the bush as it is for those who work in the NGO equivalent of multinational corporations and for those who work for the UK's DfID. After all, to get money from governments like that of the UK, private aid agencies have to parrot the latest, trendiest developments in aid theory, filling both their proposals and their progress reports with the appropriate jargon whether it concerns 'participatory development' (1980s) 'sustainable development' (1990s) or 'evidence-based aid' (2010s). Invariably, new slogans accompany the 'new' theories and practices. When 'women in development' became fashionable in the mid 1980s, the slogan went: 'teach a man and you teach an individual; teach a woman and you teach a family'. The great advantage of a phrase like 'sustainable development' is that it can be

---

*A friend of mine witnessed a classic example of 'awareness building' in Afghan village where he was negotiating to build a school. A fleet of landcruisers arrived one afternoon. The World Bank staffers they brought put out tables with the tea and biscuits required to get a crowd. The aid workers handed out leaflets to everyone explaining the benefits and methodology of microfinance. Satisfied with having reached another community and brought to them the benefit of microcredit, the aid workers jumped back into their landcruisers and raced back to Kabul. What they did not know was that no one in the village was literate enough to read their leaflets and their efforts had achieved absolutely nothing except the ticking of a box on a form.

applied to almost anything from literacy to women's rights. In the realm of project proposals, many of these phrases can be used interchangeably and still fulfil their real purpose of box-ticking. For instance, as Linda Polman points out, a typical aid project proposal might equally assert that 'women's rights are the key to democratisation' or 'democratisation is the key to women's rights'.[19]

PART 2

What Aid Does and Does Not Achieve

'International responsibility for the alleviation of suffering is one of the most noble of all human goals. Nobility of aim does not confer immunity from sociological analysis or ethical critique, however.'

Alex de Waal, *Famine Crimes*

'Aid has been, and continues to be, an unmitigated political, economic and humanitarian disaster for most parts of the developing world.'

Dambisa Moyo, *Dead Aid*

'The real debate is not about whether aid works or not, but about (a) under what circumstances it actually works; (b) how it can be reformed, in principle, to become more effective; and (c) how likely is it that the requisite reforms can in fact be undertaken.'

Dani Rodrik[1]

Introduction

Overseas development aid in its various iterations since the 1950s seems to have failed to achieve its core economic task. Buttressed by convincing data, this finding is accepted by aid critics on the left as well as on the right, with left critics arguing that aid has failed mainly because there has not been nearly enough of it, or because it has been too often 'tied' to donor country interests, or that it has been based on incorrect 'neo-liberal' or 'Washington Consensus' ideology.

Aid critics on all sides say that, despite claims made by the aid industry, the real beneficiaries of overseas aid have not been the world's poorest people but Third World tyrants and ruling élites, Swiss bankers, European and American agribusiness, Paris couturiers, and the aid industry itself.

However, those who make British aid policy have generally been unwilling to address the economic critiques of development aid *per se*. In particular, the presumption underlying budget support that developing country governments genuinely care about the welfare of their citizens is never questioned. This refusal is so complete and so adamant that it is hard not to see in it a significant degree of self-interest.

If that were not bad enough, aid critics in the West and increasingly in the developing world have made a powerful case that aid has actually done a great deal of harm. Dambisa Moyo, for instance, the Zambian economist and banker, has written that: 'Aid has been, and continues to be, an unmitigated political, economic and humanitarian disaster for most parts of the developing world.'[1] Such critics argue that, even with the best intentions, and even when administered using best practices, aid frequently fosters corruption, underwrites the cruelties of tyrannical regimes, demeans and infantilises its beneficiaries,

27

subsidises armed conflict, subverts government account-ability, undermines enterprise, demoralises democratic reformers, distorts local economies, and makes sustainable development less rather than more likely.

4. The Claims of Development Aid

Aid and economic growth

'Growth is not a cure-all, but lack of growth is a kill-all.'

Paul Collier, *The Bottom Billion*

Growth has long been the primary goal of most official development aid. There are strong arguments that the bilateral or government-to-government aid historically provided by the UK to poorer nations has not only failed to fuel or ignite economic growth but has often actually hindered it while undermining other other aspects of 'development' and 'governance'. Critics say that this form of development aid has all too often fostered and funded government corruption, encouraged dependence, subsidised political repression and violent conflict, demoralised and disempowered responsible political and civil forces, and made Third World governments less accountable to their subjects[1].

Multilateral aid, i.e. aid given to international bodies like the World Bank and then provided to Third World governments, international agencies or NGOs, has often had the same – and other – negative effects though usually entailing much larger bureaucratic costs.

It is telling that the great developmental and economic success stories of the last two decades, in particular in East Asia, but more recently in parts of Latin America and even in Africa, seem not only to be causally unconnected to foreign aid but to have an inverse correlation with the amount of aid those countries received. Somaliland's growth is probably the most extreme example of this today[2][3]. (In the late twentieth century, Hong Kong and Singapore became wealthy without benefit of aid. Taiwan and South Korea began their impressive economic rises *after* large-scale aid from the US came to a halt.[4])

However there is little in current British aid policy to indicate that much account has been taken of *what actually worked* to bring about growth and prosperity in countries like Japan, South Korea, Taiwan, and more recently in Brazil, India and China.*

This partly represents the more general failure within the aid industry (and also among academic analysts of aid) to deconstruct the notions of 'development' and 'underdevelopment'. ('Underdeveloped' is arguably a euphemism, as were previously fashionable, politically-correct terms for poor non-Western countries such as 'Third World', 'the South' and most recently 'less developed countries' or 'LDCs').

The very term 'development' takes for granted the idea that there exists a teleological process by which nations eventually achieve the wealth, technological sophistication, and political institutions of the wealthy West. However, few of those who believe that foreign aid can promote development take much note of the real-life history of development in countries like Britain, France and the United States, preferring instead models offered by the social sciences. This has become more problematic, as thorough academic analyses such as those by Raghuram G. Rajan and Arvind Subramanian[5] indicate that foreign aid, while it may achieve other goods, seems to have little if any benign effect on economic growth.

Some aid critics on the left also point out that even in the few countries where large aid receipts have coincided with economic growth, that growth has not necessarily led to a decrease in poverty[6] and can often lead to greater inequality.

---

*Many critics of aid coming from a free market perspective also take too little note of the protectionism and state subsidy of key industries that seem to have played an important role in the rise of some of their own countries.

William Easterly, arguably the most important mainstream critic of development aid in its current form, believes that aid can achieve less ambitious goals than it has previously been set. Other critics like Robert Calderisi – a long time practitioner of foreign aid – believe that development aid should only go to countries where the metaphorical soil is suitable for planting, in other words where there is a modicum of peace and order, where the rule of law exists and the ruling élite shows some signs of public spirit and civic sense.[7]

The problem, of course, with the argument that development aid should mainly go to states that are reasonably uncorrupt, competent, orderly and consensual is that they may have the least need of aid: their citizens are less likely to suffer from famine and other ills. They are also, as Lord Bauer explained, likely to be more prosperous and to receive more foreign and domestic investment:

> Poverty or riches, personal and social satisfaction, depend on people, on their culture, and on their political arrangements. Understand this sequence, and you understand the most important cause of wealth or deprivation… Development aid is thus clearly not necessary to rescue poor societies from a vicious circle of poverty. Indeed, it is far more likely to keep them in that state. It promotes dependence on others. It encourages the idea that emergence from poverty depends on external donations rather than on people's own efforts, motivation, arrangements, and institutions… By maintaining a minimum level of consumption, the subsidies avert total collapse and conceal from the population, at least temporarily, the worst effects of destructive policies. These subsidies also suggest external endorsement of damaging policies. These results in turn help the governments to remain in power and to persist in these policies without provoking popular revolt.[8]

Other claims for development aid

Tellingly, defenders of overseas aid when challenged in debate[9] almost invariably resort to boasts about the eradication or near eradication of diseases like river blindness, guineaworm and smallpox in Africa or elsewhere. These are genuine accomplishments.[10] (And, as William Easterly points out, many children still die in poor countries who could be saved by medicines that cost less than ten pence per dose.) However there have been less than a handful of such victories. Moreover, the core goals of overseas development aid have always been fundamentally economic. While it is of some economic benefit as well as an all-round good thing to eradicate crippling diseases, these rare public health triumphs scarcely justify the more than *two trillion* dollars that the West has provided in development aid in the past five decades.

In this context, it is worth remembering that the UK's International Development Act of 2002 (which replaced the Overseas Development and Cooperation Act of 1980) explicitly states that the purpose of DfID is 'poverty reduction' – *not* the eradication of diseases, the promotion of human rights or fostering improvements in what the aid industry euphemistically calls 'governance'. (This latter is a catch-all term for the various political phenomena including tyranny, endemic corruption, patrimonial politics, weak state institutions and so forth that have fostered poverty and undermined growth in 'under-developed' countries.)

It is, unfortunately, significant that the Labour authors of the 2002 act and creators of DfID led by Clare Short chose the term 'poverty reduction'. This was not only because a growing academic consensus was casting doubt on the ability of traditional foreign aid to bring about economic development and growth. Among the general public and in mainstream politics, economic growth is generally seen as the key to making people wealthier. However, growth is not seen as unalloyed good either by 'hard' environmentalists or by anti-capitalists within the aid community who fear that growth may foster inequality and injustice. 'Poverty reduction' by contrast allows for a welfare model of aid, according to which benign foreigners play a permanent role as benefactors to the helpless.

Arguably a welfare model according to which foreign agencies and charities distribute money or other goods to the needy runs counter to the modern notion of 'sustainable development'. But it has the triple advantage for those on the left of the aid establishment of (i) convenient metrics (it is easier to measure cash or goods distributed than evidence of growth that has been fostered); (ii) avoidance of ideologically uncomfortable questions about the comparative efficacy of free-market capitalism in promoting growth; and (iii) heightened emotional and moral rewards for donors and officials and workers who get to play the role of benefactor.*

Geostrategic considerations and UK aid

Two factors have made the debate about ongoing or increased British aid to Africa and Asia more complicated. One is the growing influence of China, and its use of aid, investment and bribery to obtain mineral resources, agricultural land and votes at the UN and in other international bodies. (The latter is a form of influence rarely considered in the UK, but if you spend time in the poor countries in Africa, the Caribbean and Asia you soon

---

*The welfare model also suits those who cultivate a sense of colonial or 'neo-colonial' guilt and its resulting obligations. In general, and this reflects the fact that aid careers (outside the World Bank) tend to attract left-wing young people, aid workers operate on the assumption that poverty and underdevelopment in Africa and South Asia are the result of malefaction by the West and the developed world in the form of colonial exploitation and its contemporary analogues. This idea that vastly powerful and malevolent outside forces controlled by white Westerners are responsible for the misery of the bottom billion is also popular among ruling elites in Africa and South Asia, and underlies some of their rhetoric justifying welfare-like foreign aid expenditure.

notice that the presence of Chinese or Taiwanese aid projects has a correlation with whether or not the country in question recognises Beijing or its Formosan rival.) The other is the spread of Islamist extremism, especially in East Africa.

In Africa, as in Pakistan and elsewhere, extreme Islamist sects have successfully won influence by providing education, medical help and other services that incompetent and corrupt states fail to deliver. Mosques, some of them funded by Saudi Wahabist charities, have appeared in hundreds of traditionally animist or Christian villages in many countries between the Horn and the Cape. This is of obvious concern to the UK and other Western governments. If it were possible for DfID and its partners to administer competing education and medical programmes with the same degree of effectiveness as these militant charities, it might serve an important British interest.

The other region where there are genuine, urgent geostrategic implications for British aid is Afghanistan and Pakistan. Unfortunately DfID's activities in both countries have often illustrated the foolishness of assuming that spending money in a conflict zone automatically translates into political benefits for the donor country.

DfID's notoriously inept performance in Afghanistan, where its cultural antipathy to the military and absurd health and safety rules have all but ensured failure on many levels,[11] has not helped it to win hearts and minds for Britain. Only last October it was found that DfID had paid more than £3.2 million to a German NGO in Afghanistan which was supposed to be resettling failed asylum seekers but which made little real effort to do so and is now being investigated for fraud by the German government.[12] In March 2012, a report[13] by the UK's Independent Commission for Aid Impact (ICAI) raised multiple concerns about DfID's management of its projects in Afghanistan and found that DfID was 'not proactive enough in detecting fraud and corruption'.[14]

Unfortunately DfID's poor record of effectiveness in Afghanistan is not untypical of aid agency efforts in that country.[15] As one British former security adviser in Afghanistan puts it: 'The only Afghan lives I've seen transformed by Western aid agencies are warlords who've used siphoned funds to build mansions, amass huge overseas property portfolios and arm private militias.'[16]

There is a powerful argument that foreign aid, including British aid, has actually tended to foster extremism in Pakistan rather than cure it. Certainly, convincing studies show, and my own experience of the country confirms, that Islamist and anti-Western extremism in Pakistan tends to be strongest among the educated and semi-educated middle classes.

The failure of aid to secure goodwill or neutralise extremism in both countries partly reflects DfID's insistence on not publicising or marketing British aid in those countries, a failure that renders aid useless as a tool for winning influence even if schools and clinics may help decrease the population's vulnerability to extremism.

While it is true, as DfID officials often point out, that in both Pakistan or Afghanistan the marking of a project with an Union Jack might make it a target for attack by militants, the truth is that (a) girls' schools and women's clinics are bombed regardless of who funds them, and (b) everyone knows that charity projects are funded by Western foreigners and it makes no negative difference to aid worker security if a project is labeled as British or not labeled at all.

Though it has become customary in the UK aid community to blame security concerns for all aid failures in countries like Afghanistan and Iraq, it is likely that aid failures by DfID and its subcontractor NGOs have actually worsened the security situation. This is partly because the gap between aid agency promises and delivery alienates those whose hearts and minds are up for grabs, especially where the 'other side' is believed to keep its promises. The infamous case of the Helmand washing machine, discussed below, is an example of this.

That failure and others make DfID's stated objective of shifting British aid to the most conflict-torn and poorest countries seem all the more quixotic or disingenuous. Indeed the evident inadequacy of DfID's efforts in Afghanistan is a strong argument for transferring the delivery of conflict-area aid to a suitable branch of the armed forces. Military civil affairs units can reach the most remote areas, can defend themselves and have the additional advantage of significant civil engineering capacity. Unlike DfID, which has assimilated an inappropriate ideology of neutrality from organisations like the ICRC, military civil affairs aid workers would not be troubled to the point of paralysis by the idea of assisting NATO or the Afghan government.

Aid effectiveness and the UK national interest: the claims of security/immigration/influence

To estimate the effectiveness of aid, you have to know what you want aid to achieve. Despite the desires of aid purists and altruistic absolutists, British official aid has never been justified to the public as an entirely altruistic exercise.

Recently, the Cameron government has defended its commitment to 'ring-fencing' foreign aid from cuts, and indeed to increasing UK aid, by claiming that such aid will benefit Britain by (a) making future military interventions less necessary and (b) making it less necessary for the poor and desperate of the Third World to migrate to the UK.

Put gently, neither of the Prime Minister's claims can be said to be based on evidence, because there is little or no evidence of foreign aid having such effects. Indeed, until the Cameron government employed these justifications for ring-fencing the aid budget from otherwise universal austerity measures, they were not even part of the marketing arsenal of aid enthusiasts.

If it could at least be plausibly argued that foreign aid has at some point in its history brought peace to a troubled region, or that foreign aid generally brings about prosperity, then Mr Cameron's claims could have some intellectual integrity – assuming that British foreign aid programmes were known to be effective ones.

However most modern literature on the subject indicates that peace is a *precondition* to the effective functioning of foreign aid of all kinds, not the other way round.

Arguably, no British foreign aid effort in the last thirty years has saved as many lives or done more for economic growth in a Third World country than the successful UK military intervention in Sierra Leone in 2000, which ended that country's civil war and enabled the restoration of economic life and effective humanitarian aid.

However, the Sierra Leone example is an awkward one for DfID and the aid industry in general. It suggests that dealing with the violence and disorder that cause or exacerbate poverty and underdevelopment may be more effective and offer more value for money than more conventional aid efforts. It is doubly awkward given that the UK military, despite evidence that its effectiveness genuinely secures influence and commercial advantage for Britain, is being subjected to savage, even crippling cuts.

Moreover given that so many of the things that undermine aid and that make it necessary in the first place are a result of failed states or ineffective, corrupt, predatory state institutions, there is an argument that if the wealthy world genuinely cared about the world's poor it would intervene militarily and impose quasi-colonial government as advocated by the Indian development expert and thinker Deepak Lal.[17]

5. Assessing the Impact of Aid

Direct and indirect impacts

Assessing the impacts of aid, good and bad, is a complicated and difficult business. It is relatively easy for donors and aid agencies to supply statistics for direct impacts such as the number of new schools that have allegedly been built or the number of children who have been vaccinated by a particular programme. The same goes for negative direct impacts such as the number of people displaced by a dam project, though such inevitable side-effects of development tend to get much less space in official aid agency materials.

Other, more indirect impacts, both good and bad, are hard to measure. Aid agencies can and do assert triumphs in fields like women's empowerment, but claims to have brought enlightenment to thousands of members of this or that group may well amount to little more than aid workers turning up in a fleet of white landcruisers in flyblown villages to hand out leaflets. Negative indirect impacts of aid, like the undermining of links between the state and the citizen, are even less amenable to capture within statistics.

DfID's new approach, with its concentration on 'evidence-based aid' and 'accountability', may sound like a guarantee of greater effectiveness, but it is possible that a greater emphasis on easily measurable and reportable 'metrics' will actually undermine or disincentivise some of the better British aid programmes. It is in that sense similar to the 'target' culture adopted under New Labour that has arguably had disastrous effects on policing, healthcare and other public services in the UK. Moreover, the new emphasis on direct, measurable impacts will impose heavy burdens and increase paperwork requirements not just from DfID workers and subsidiary NGOs but also on Third World governments already filling out reports for hundreds of foreign aid agencies.

Pushing for direct impacts is believed by experts like Clare Lockhart to be problematic because it can 'obscure the need to make more systematic changes'[1] and have unintended negative consequences. She believes that it is better to use British aid as a catalyst or as leverage to prompt governments like that of Afghanistan to do good things like inoculate more children.

Lack of reliable data

It is much more difficult to get accurate statistics about aid effectiveness than people in the aid industry like to admit.

Peter Bauer long ago pointed out that one of the problems with development aid policy was reliance on dubious assessments of per capita income in what were then called Less-Developed Countries: 'It was in 1963 that Professor Usher first showed that these biases (which, moreover, do not remain constant over time) amount to **several hundred percent**, and it was in 1968 that he explained his findings in great detail. They have been authoritatively endorsed. It has also become evident that the population statistics of some large Third World countries are quite unreliable. Yet advocacy of aid for redistribution still relies on conventional national income statistics which claim to estimate Third World incomes to a few percentage points'[2] (emphasis added).

This unreliability is partly because of inadequate statistical collection by Third World governments, and partly because of the difficulties and dangers of travel in many African states and in other poor and chaotic countries that receive UK aid.

The sad fact is that if a school or clinic or other project is more than a day's drive from a major city, it is unlikely to be checked on by DfID expatriate staff, whatever they or their bosses in London may claim. Very few of the DfID staff living in Third World capitals spend much time in the bush; often not more than a day per year.[3]

The local staff who may be sent (in their stead) out to the project in the sticks sometimes genuinely make the trip instead of retiring to a shebeen for a couple of days, and sometimes report accurately on whether or not the school or clinic has been completed, whether the teacher or doctor actually turns up, whether there are sufficient books or medicines. Some report good news because they know that is what their foreign employer wants to hear; others are paid off by the contractor who has failed to finish the school or by the absentee teacher or doctor.

The radical unreliability of the statistics relied upon by the aid community – and by those who analyse aid impact – does not in the least restrain the former from making grand claims. An all-too-typical example was an Oxfam announcement that: 'The G8's aid increase could save the lives of five million children by 2010 – but 50 million children's lives will still be lost because the G8 didn't go as far as they should have done. If the $50 billion increase had kicked in immediately, it could have lifted 300 million people of poverty in the next five years.' To call such a statement tendentious would be understatement. It shows almost as much contempt for statistics as it does for the intelligence of the public. Even so it is not as intellectually bankrupt as former Prime Minister Gordon Brown's exhortation: 'Let us double aid to halve poverty'.

Because a school has been paid for, or new clinic has been paid for, does not mean that they exist or will ever come to exist, except on paper. When genuine checks take place, the results can be shocking, as with the well known Reiikka and Svenssson study in Uganda in 1996. It looked at the government's system of giving per student grants to rural schools to maintain buildings and buy textbooks, and found that only 13 per cent of the funds ever reached the schools.[4] The rest of the funds were embezzled by district officials.*

Dubious statistics in a noble cause

You frequently read that four to six million have been killed in the endless fighting in the Democratic Republic of Congo (DRC) the mineral rich country formerly known as Zaire. Just where that terrible number comes from is something of a mystery. It is a statistic that is never properly questioned or examined because a great many people have certainly died, and because that enormous number with its deliberate historical echo is a useful stick for those agencies and activists who want to get the world's attention or raise money for aid to DRC.

However, the real number, though dreadful, is likely to be much smaller than four million. As experienced experts in African warfare know, large scale conflict in places like Congo invariably and inevitably leads to mass migration away from the fighting, just as they do from famine areas or places of disease. No such mass flight to safer zones and countries has yet taken place from the areas of DRC where the four to six million are said to have been killed.[5]

The vast numbers who have perished – for there is unquestionably an enormous human catastrophe taking place in the Congo, where various predatory militias, guerrilla bands, bandit gangs and armies from neighbouring countries fight over minerals and the ordinary spoils of combat, and commit vast amounts of

---

*Interestingly, after the results of the study were released and publicised in Uganda, the situation improved – which would imply that openness about such matters does far more good than the habitual secretiveness and disingenuousness of the fundraising-obsessed aid community.

sexual violence – mostly died not in fighting but from disease and malnutrition caused by the violent chaos.

This is *not* an argument for paying less attention, sending less aid, pulling out the all-too-ineffective UN 'peacekeeping' force. (Indeed the genuine horrors of DRC would justify a more vigorous or militarily serious foreign intervention.) But it is an all-too-representative example of the statistical carelessness and dishonesty – all in a good cause – so common in responses to Third World humanitarian crises.

Circumstantial evidence: the sad fates of the world's most aided countries

Those countries that received the most aid[6] during the last six decades seem to have a disproportionate tendency to collapse into anarchy. These include Somalia, Liberia, Zaire and Haiti. Although it would be argued by development aid adherents that there is no causal connection and that these countries received so much aid because they were already deeply troubled basket-cases, all suffered a major decline in state effectiveness after they became aid-dependent. Some examples follow.

a) Haiti

Even before the disastrous 2010 Earthquake, Haiti was one of the world's biggest recipients of development aid. Over half a century, it was given more than $6 billion, mostly by the United States. Per person, that works out as *four times* the amount that shattered post-war Europe received as Marshall Aid. Despite this – or arguably because of it – Haiti was one of the world's poorest countries by 2010 (though its kleptocratic light-skinned élite had grown wealthy) with a per capita income less than two thirds as high as it had been in 1960.[7] (Among other disasters, US food aid during the Clinton administration bankrupted hundreds of thousands of farming families, who then moved to shanty towns in the capital and found themselves without work.)

Haiti's extreme poverty on the eve of the earthquake was in contrast to the relative prosperity of the Dominican Republic which occupies the other half of the island of Hispaniola and which has an identical climate and similar history of colonisation, slavery and dictatorship.

Haiti's post-earthquake history is even more of an indictment of the aid industry. After initial relief successes, disorganisation, duplication, waste and a radical underestimation of the corruption that afflicts Haitian civil society and political culture crippled reconstruction efforts despite the expenditure of billions and the efforts of thousands of relief workers. (As so often most NGOs concentrated their efforts in the capital – with all its opportunities for expat social life and beach access – and neglected the provinces.) Significantly, the most successful single piece of reconstruction in post-earthquake Haiti was the rebuilding of the Iron Market area of the capital by a private company, Digicel, owned by the Irish billionaire Denis O'Brien.[8]

If all that were not bad enough, in 2011 UN staff prompted a deadly cholera outbreak[9] by dumping raw sewage into the river that waters Port au Prince. More than 7,000 died and half a million more people were affected, despite the presence of more than 12,000 NGOs[10] and the fashionable, much vaunted, 'cluster' system of organisation by the UN's Office of Coordination of Humanitarian Affairs.

b) Nepal

Nepal has long been one of the most aided countries in the world, and one with one of the largest populations of expatriate aid workers. (Aid organisations and workers understandably love working in Nepal.) Like so many

43

heavily aided countries, its state became thoroughly corrupted and decreasingly competent and responsible as the years went by. Parallel educational and health institutions funded by foreigners took quality personnel and money that might otherwise have worked for official ones. The NGO sector became the most important economic force in the country by the 1990s, bigger even than tourism, or the money the state made by supplying troops to UN peacekeeping operations. Eventually the state collapsed under the weight of its aid-funded corruption and a long running Maoist rebellion was able to overthrow the monarchy in 2008.

c) Somalia

For a decade before the 1992 famine, Somalia was the largest recipient of aid in sub-Saharan Africa, though its population (some six million) saw little benefit from it. (The country, like many other parts of Africa, has always been famine prone. But pre-civil war Somalia had a 'well-established system for dealing with regular cycles of drought'.[11] Moreover, it was self-sufficient in grain through the 1970s.) Its longtime ruler Mohammed Siad Barre had successfully played off the USA and the USSR so that both sides in the Cold War competed to give Somalia money in return for Somalia's ever switching allegiance. By the time the state disintegrated in the midst of clan fighting in 1990, the country had become completely dependent on foreign aid.

6. Assessing the Impact of Aid on Africa

'If aid were the solution to Africa's problems, it would be a rich continent by now.'
Richard Dowden, chairman of the Royal African Society[1]

One of the interesting and telling aspects of recent debates about aid is the way that both advocates and critics talk about sub-Saharan Africa – the continent that is almost literally the 'poster-child' for Third World distress. Africa is the most aided continent and is often said to be a basket-case by both advocates and critics of aid.

Yet some little-known statistics that tend to be obscured by the mutually beneficial *de facto* alliance of Western aid agencies and African kleptocrats with their heart-rending calls for more aid, include the fact that thrusting India may well have worse malnutrition rates than sub-Saharan Africa[2], and that many indicators of underdevelopment including illiteracy are worse in the oil-rich Arab states of the Gulf than in sub-Saharan Africa.

Statistical disingenuousness, earnestly and ardently expressed, is unfortunately a default setting in the marketing of both development and humanitarian aid. For instance, as the Nobel-Prize-winning economist Amartya Sen[3] and other calm heads have pointed out, it is not necessarily a monstrous thing that a billion people live on less than a dollar day. There are many places in the world where a dollar can easily feed an entire extended family for a day with considerable change left over. Though used to evoke horror, this is a datum that takes no account of lower costs of living in most poor countries. (In Kenya where the IMF says that half the population lives on an income of less than a dollar a day, 75 per cent of the adult population has a mobile phone.[4]) What is a real horror is that there are so many people who lack sufficient food, access to education, basic healthcare and personal freedom.

When aid advocates appeal for more money from governments and individuals for Africa, they cite statistics of poverty, illiteracy and disease on the continent that seem terrible. Aid critics cite the very same data as evidence of the failure of aid. When aid critics ask the adherents why these grim statistics have worsened despite the trillion dollars Africa has received in the last 50 or 60 years (more than seven times the amount given to Europe in Marshall Aid in today's dollars) the aid advocates not only say that more money is needed, but also point to other statistics that highlight progress in Africa and therefore 'prove' the utility of aid. The question becomes one not of numbers but of correlation and causation.

But African statistics can be extremely misleading. As Africa expert and author Michela Wrong points out,[5] 'if you go to Nairobi you don't see people sleeping on the streets despite all the unemployment and underemployment and the lack of formal jobs.'

Moreover many businesspeople have a different view of Africa, based on a combination of impressive growth data and investment profits. Ethiopia, for instance, one of the largest recipients of British aid, has apparently enjoyed higher growth than China, India or Vietnam over the past seven years.[6] Rwanda too has enjoyed growth rates similar to those of the Asian Tigers, without the benefit of either mineral resources, oil or even abundant high-value commodities like coffee or cocoa. There has been occasional media coverage of Africa's recent economic success stories,[7] but the overwhelming impression people get from Africa is the one fostered by the journalist/NGO nexus that it is a Dark Continent of unremitting misery and suffering and will continue to be so without more aid dollars.

There are some reasons for wondering if current positive trends will continue. After all, after decades of stagnation and decline, many poor African countries started to enjoy rapid rates of growth in the 1990s thanks to a global rise in commodity prices, but these then crashed.

However, the advent of the mobile phone has had startling economic effects all around the continent, massively boosting trade and commerce. (The investor Miles Morland has written that: 'the mobile is to Africa what the railway was to Europe and America'.) Areas that have long lacked roads and telecommunications[8] are now connected, without the help of aid agencies or governments. (In Kenya a vibrant new credit and banking system that reaches poor and remote villages has been enabled by mobile technology.) The phenomenon has revealed African entrepreneurs to be far more effective than aid agencies, NGOs or African governments ever expected. Even Somalia, with no functioning state and a minimal foreign aid presence, has three functioning, profitable mobile phone networks that provide it with what one expert describes as being 'among the continent's best cellphone communications systems'.[9]

Chinese economic activity and increased foreign investment from other countries taking advantage of newly opened markets also seem to be achieving what successive 'big pushes' of aid failed to do.

These same statistics indicating an increase in economic activity are, of course, those that aid critics rely on to show that Africa does not need more aid, and indeed has made progress *in spite of* aid and its ravages. A diminution or pauses in conflict may have played a key role in what progress has been made, as may an increase in the number of states that are at least nominally democracies. The key fact, however, is there seems to be little evidence that aid has played much of a positive role in the good news from

Africa, except insofar as the much condemned strictures of the World Bank and IMF may have made the continent friendlier to foreign direct investment.

PART 3

Aid and its Contradictions

7. The Nomenclatural Fallacy

What I call the Nomenclatural Fallacy is an all too common phenomenon in the aid world. It is one of the key reasons why so much foreign aid does not work in the way it should. (It has also hamstrung allied security efforts in places like Afghanistan.)

The term refers to the way that aid officials and other foreigners often make the naïve mistake of assuming that officials in poorer/developing country officials who possess titles such as 'policeman', 'judge' or 'minister' have the same function as officials who bear those titles in their home countries. This is sometimes a matter of cultural arrogance; at other times it reflects the triumph of politically correct piety over experience. It is an error that is understandable in Third World neophytes because the 'policemen' wear uniforms, the 'judge' may even wear a wig or robes like an English one, the 'minister' or 'civil servant' may wear a suit, operate in an office with a computer and have a degree on the wall from a Western university, next to the picture of the President.

In fact, in many, many countries from Equatorial Guinea to India, a 'policeman' is essentially a licensed and uniformed bandit; a 'judge' may be a judicial entrepreneur rather than a dispenser of justice; and the 'civil servant' and 'minister' are different sized cogs in machines designed for predation on the public.

In most Middle Eastern, African and South Asian countries, men pay large amounts of money, often going into significant debt, in order to purchase such potentially lucrative positions. The positions are only lucrative if they can, from the 'Northern' or 'Western' or 'Anglo-Saxon' perspective, be abused: so that the policeman can extort small bribes from the public and that the minister can take his share of the many extorted bribes. Those who purchase official positions in aid-recipient countries – and there are few if any aid-recipient countries where official positions are not for sale – do so not necessarily because they are bad people with criminal inclinations but because government in those countries is a form of enterprise, albeit one parasitic on the rest of society and on the aid given by foreign donors.

In many societies in Africa (this also true in much of South Asia), corrupt and extortionate behaviour by officials is all but *necessitated* by cultural demands placed on members of extended families. If you are able to secure a government job of any kind, you will be expected to support the educational, health and other needs of many, many relatives. A man who fails to do so is often considered to be moral reprobate.

A Westerner involved with a gorilla reserve in Congo Brazzaville told me that the guards he employed to protect the animals from poachers asked him to ensure that they were paid on an irregular basis. He could not understand why they did not want to be paid on a more regular, Western-style basis. They explained to him that if they were paid in that conventional way all their distant relatives would move from their rural homes and become permanent dependents.

To a remarkable, indeed unconscionable degree, Western aid agencies and NGOs have taken little or no account of anthropological patterns like this. Like the imperialists and missionaries before them, members of the aid community have tended to assume that the people they are allegedly serving have the same attitudes to family, money and work that they do.

This failure to recognise the social and cultural realities that lie beneath the adoption of Western forms of government in many underdeveloped countries is at the root of many aid failures throughout the Third World. The refusal by Westerners and their local staff to admit that, in country 'x', elected members of government see their primary loyalty as being to extended family or tribe rather than to the country as a whole, and that the state is really a mechanism for predation and rent-seeking, can turn development efforts into a kind of black comedy. Yet one of the constants in the five or six decade history of official aid is the expression of official surprise when stories break that reflect this reality.

They come along on a fairly regular basis. In July 2010, for instance, it was reported that Afghan officials were stuffing suitcases with aid cash and flying out of the country. A report by USAID (the American equivalent of DfID) the previous year admitted that massive aid inflows had contributed to corruption in the country (which went from the 42nd most corrupt state in the world in 2005 to the 2nd most in 2009 in Transparency International's rankings) and that USAID-funded anti-corruption efforts had themselves become 'a critical part of the corruption syndrome'. (Afghanistan is, of course, not only a recipient of British aid for obvious strategic reasons, it is also an example of the kind of country that Development Secretary Andrew Mitchell said he wanted more British aid to flow into, in that it is a 'fragile state' and also 'in conflict'.)

8. Perverse Incentives and the Aid Industry

In theory, development and humanitarian aid workers, like other members of helping professions, are working to eliminate their own jobs. If they and their agencies were successful, they would 'make poverty history' as the slogan goes (and as Jeffrey Sachs predicts could happen by 2025). Poor countries would then be free from famine, the terrible illnesses that still scourge Africa and Asia would be defeated, refugees would be resettled somewhere appropriate, and all people would be living if not above the poverty line, then in conditions that allow them life, health, dignity and opportunity.

However, one of the things that becomes obvious if you spend much time in South Asia and Africa, and the parts of the world where refugee camps dot the desert or sit outside the cities, is that even the least utopian goals of aid are hardly ever met. The refugee camps rarely if ever close. The only times the armies of young aid workers and their fleets of white landcruisers seem to 'finish' their tasks and disappear is when they leave for places where the need is more urgent or where the crisis has captured the attention of the world's media.

This is partly because underlying political conditions do not change: the Darfur crisis for example has no end in sight. Therefore the Darfuri refugees in their vast camps in Eastern Chad are too frightened of government and militia violence to go home to Sudan, and many of their menfolk continue to defy the UNHCR and other agencies and use those very camps as bases for raids across the border.

Unfortunately, in those camps, as in so many camps for refugees and internally displaced persons (IDPs) around the world, the people do not work and become increasingly dependent on aid agencies.

On the other hand, you do not have to be a Marxist to see the economic and professional benefits that perpetual crisis offers those who make their careers in foreign aid. Nor do you have to go as far as the social thinker Ivan Illich who developed a whole theory about the way 'helping professions' – which he mocked as 'disabling professions' – generated 'needs' for their members to minister to.

However, it is surely not surprising that NGO marketing materials almost invariably claim success and simultaneously the need for more funds to finish the job. A cynic would watch for goal posts being moved so that the expats can continue with their sweet, servanted existence, the senior officials can continue flying from one aid effectiveness conference to another, and the equivalents of Andrew Mitchell and David Cameron can bask in the glow of their own goodness.

There are some 100,000 expatriate aid workers engaged in sub-Saharan Africa,[1] a staggering number that greatly exceeds the number of foreign administrators engaged by the former colonial powers at the height of the imperial era. It is telling that, despite tremendous increases in literacy and improvements in education all around the Third World, the aid community still prefers to hire white Westerners to work in poor countries even though they are vastly more expensive and often less able than local alternatives.[2]

In some places where DfID works, such as Afghanistan, to employ a foreign aid worker costs between £500,000 and £1 million a year, while extra local employees cost as little as £5,000 per year including training and salary, meaning that DfID and other agencies could employ 200 more local employees for the price of a single expat.[3]

Indeed there is an argument that the aid industry's primary economic function is as a system of 'outdoor relief', or rather high-status employment, for members of the upper and middle classes in Britain and elsewhere*. Clare Lockhart, co-author of *Fixing Failed States*, likens the aid industry to the Victorian Church of England, a prestigious institution in which third sons of élite families could work without soiling their hands in trade or industry.[4] Today, for university educated, idealistic young people (who may not have many marketable skills at home and whose background is no longer a guarantee of a fulfilling job at home), aid work offers prestige, moral glamour, adventure, foreign travel and, for some, a good living.

---

*In many Third World and aid-recipient countries, the aid industry plays a near-analogous role, providing high-status, and also high-income employment for the offspring of the well connected and powerful. Unfortunately these privileged folk tend not to be the kind of local employees who would make useful substitutes for expatriates.

PART 4

UK Aid Targets and Goals

9. Magic Numbers, Foolish Commitments

The 0.7 per cent solution

There is little or no integrity to the claim that poverty could be cured if countries gave 0.7 per cent of their budgets to foreign aid.

Any coherent and honest attempt to measure the amount needed to cure poverty would be based on an estimate of the costs of actual projects, not on a proportion of rich country spending. A real effort to 'cure' poverty might well cost radically more – or less – than 0.7 per cent, but any serious estimate would be based on output rather aid input.

Contrary to what you might expect from the pronouncements of the economist Jeffrey Sachs (who after inspiring disastrous shock therapy in Poland and elsewhere, rehabilitated himself by advocating lavish aid budgets), the 0.7 per cent number has its origin not in economic research but 60-year-old policy debates.

It was the World Council of Churches in the 1950s that first came up with the idea that Western countries should give one per cent of their GDP to foreign aid – that round number perhaps seeming like a reasonable 'tithe' and being approximately double the amount of contemporary public and private capital flows into the developing world.[1] Back of the envelope calculations furthered the idea that this sum would be enough for developing countries to fill the so-called 'financing gap' – a then fashionable explanation for underdevelopment. The notion was taken up by the UN General Assembly in 1960, though the number was revised down to 0.7 per cent after a report by the Pearson Commission on International Development in 1969.

Since then 0.7 per cent of GDP has achieved totemic significance even as changes in the relative wealth of nations have made the original calculations less relevant than ever. (More recently the UN itself has calculated that 0.44 per cent of the national income of rich countries would be sufficient) By the mid 2000s, media claims that the 'International Community' had 'committed' to 0.7 per cent together with 0.7 per cent campaigns by organisations such as ActionAid and British Overseas NGOs for Development (BOND) had turned the number into a politically powerful symbol.

Nevertheless, none of the other major Western countries that supposedly committed to the 0.7 per cent target during the wave of public altruism that accompanied the 2005 G8 summit and Live 8 concerts have reached that target or are likely to. Most have quietly dropped it as a goal. Even wealthy, internationalist Germany only contributes 0.38% of its national income to foreign aid. And even before the UK's planned aid increase, it gives twice as much money to aid as Japan.

Even before the Cameron-Clegg government committed to increase aid, DfID's ability to distribute aid efficiently and to monitor its effectiveness was compromised by a growing aid budget and diminishing staff. As Margaret Hodge MP has pointed out, this problem has deepened and will continue to do so as more millions flow in and out of the department.

The Tory-LibDem increase to 0.7 per cent may also exacerbate another problem that advocates for increased aid tend to overlook, namely the ability of recipient states and bodies to absorb aid. A low 'absorptive capacity' is particularly a problem in many African countries with their 'shortage of qualified bureaucrats, lack of institutional experience, and the absence of many of the legal checks and balances required by Western partners'.[2] Linda Polman quotes a representative of the European Commission confessing in Sierra Leone that 'in this country it's simply impossible to think up enough viable projects to spend all our money on'.[3] One of the great unspoken truths about foreign aid is that in many places the problem is not too little money for aid, it is too much.

Much to the discomfort of the Cameron government, in March of this year, the House of Lords Economic Affairs Committee urged the governmment to abandon the 0.7 per cent target. The committee said that reaching the target and the 37 per cent real-terms increase in aid spending it would amount to would:

- Wrongly prioritise the amount spent rather than results achieved

- Make the achievement of the target more important than the overall effectiveness of the programme

- Risk reducing the quality, value for money, and accountability of the programme

- Increase the risk of a corrosive effect on political systems in recipient countries[4]

The recent enthusiasm for the magical 0.7 per cent number is only the latest manifestation of the Aid World's belief in the ability of a 'Big Push' that will lead to 'Take Off' (to use Rostow's term from the 1960s) or even, in Sachs's words 'end poverty'. Faith in the transformative power of a 'big push' is significantly more common in the 'international development community' in Western capitals than it is in Africa or the poorer parts of Asia. As the left-wing critic of aid Jonathan Glennie writes: 'African analysts appear not to believe that huge aid increases are the way to achieve growth and development. Many explicitly reject the idea, and it is *hard to find a single example of an African NGO that is actively campaigning for aid increases*'[5] (emphasis added).

Indeed in the debates on foreign aid, the advocates for maintaining or increasing current aid levels are invariably white and Western; the only black or non-white faces are to be found on the other side.

The Zambian economist and banker Dambisa Moyo is perhaps the best known African critic of foreign development aid. But there are other increasingly well-known critics like Ghana's George Ayittey, the founder of the Free Africa Foundation, and Uganda's Andrew Mwenda,[6] editor of the Kampala *Independent*, who have in recent years made their voices heard in international debates about aid to the continent that remains the target of most of the world's charitable efforts.*

For institutions like DfID and Oxfam, unaccustomed to outside scrutiny let alone criticism, the recent attacks on aid and the aid industry from African intellectuals and some African leaders like Rwanda's Paul Kagame, seem to have come as a shock. Part of the standard response in the past to critics asserting that aid might do as much harm as good, or even more harm than good, has been to claim that ordinary Africans were part of the constituency for ever greater amounts of foreign aid.

If it is African governments and African officialdom (rather than ordinary African people, African intellectuals or African business people) who tend to be most enthusiastic at the prospect of aid increases, this would not surprise anyone with even a modest familiarity with patterns of 'governance' on the continent. Journalists,

---

In a letter to the *Daily Telegraph*, six African intellectuals pointed out that instead of increased aid: 'A real offer from the British people to help our development would consist of the abolition of the Common Agricultural Policy, which keeps African agricultural exports out of the European marketplace... It is that egregious policy, combined with the weight of regulations, bad laws and stifling bureaucracy, subsidised by five decades of development aid, which prevents Africans from lifting themselves out of poverty.' 'What is the Best Way to Help the World's Deserving Poor?' (2010) *The Telegraph*, 22 August.

grassroots community organisations and civil society groups in Africa, on the other hand, are all too aware of the ways in which foreign subsidies and aid dependence tend to make their voices, and those of ordinary citizens, less influential and less important.

The Millennium Development Goals

The Millennium Development Goals (MDGs) were signed by rich and poor countries at a UN Summit in September 2000. World leaders pledged to:

1. Eradicate extreme poverty and hunger

2. Achieve universal primary education

3. Promote gender equality and empower women

4. Reduce child mortality rates by two thirds

5. Improve maternal health

6. Combat HIV/AIDS, malaria and other diseases

7. Ensure environmental sustainability

8. Develop a global partnership for development

and thereby 'end poverty'. This was to be accomplished by the end of 2015.[7]

These eight goals involved 21 quantifiable targets . Goal 1 for instance has three subsets. Target1a is: 'Reduce by half the proportion of people living on less than a dollar a day.' Target 1b is: 'Achieve full and productive employment and decent work for all, including women and young people.' Target 1c is: 'Reduce by half the proportion of people who suffer from hunger.'[8]

The vague-sounding environmental Goal 7 has four targets, the third of which is: 'Halve, by 2015, the proportion of the population without sustainable access to safe drinking water and basic sanitation'; and the fourth of

which is: 'By 2020, to have achieved a significant improvement in the lives of at least 100 million slum-dwellers.'

Uplifting though the latter target may be as aid rhetoric,
its inexactitude is almost laughable. Depending on how
you define 'significant' 'improvement' and 'slum-dweller'
it would be possible for the UNDP, which has taken the
lead in the MDG campaign, to declare that victory has
already been achieved.

Even within the orthodox aid community, there were
questions about the way the MDGs lack any emphasis on
local participation or sustainability. Moreover, even the
public health objectives are hard to measure. UN statistics
on infant mortality, turberculosis cases and malaria are
sketchy at best, and the countries with the highest levels of
maternal mortality, malaria and tuberculosis often have the
least reliable data collection.

William Easterly is deeply sceptical about the way the
MDGs accord collective responsibility for 'fifty-four
different targets to be reached in every country by the year
2015' and points out that both the UN and the World Bank
'have already admitted the MDGs exercise will fail in
Africa, the most aid-intensive region'.

As he also points out, the MDGs 'lead to such
outlandish efforts as the UN Millennium Project's 449-step
comprehensive strategy to reach the MDGs and the World
Bank's elaborate costing exercise as to how much more aid
is needed to reach the MDGs. All such exercises are
seemingly oblivious to the much documented weak link
between spending and results, such as the 30 percent to 70
percent of government-provided medicines that disappeared before reaching patients in surveys of low-income
aid recipients.'

Easterly, Moyo and other development critics and
sceptics see the MDGs as actually harmful to the world's
poor over the past decade. Easterly has written that the

MDGs 'tragically misused the world's goodwill to support failed official aid approaches to global poverty and gave virtually no support to proven approaches.'[9]

Nevertheless since 2000 there have been the inevitable conferences reviewing the progress made in achieving Millennium Development Goals, attended by thousands of aid professionals and activists, and providing much succour to various hotels, airlines and resorts. And of course Britain's DfID continues to cling to the MDGs as if they were inscribed on stone tablets by the God of Aid Himself.

PART 5

Development Aid and its Critics

'Aid is not bad, however, because it is sometimes misused, corrupt, or crass; rather, it is inherently bad, bad to the bone, and utterly beyond reform. As a welfare dole to buy the repulsive loyalty of whining, idle and malevolent governments, or as a hidden, inefficient and inadequately regulated subsidy for Western business, it is possibly the most formidable obstacle to the productive endeavors of the poor. It is also a denial of their potential, and a patronising insult to their unique, unrecognised abilities.'

Graham Hancock, *Lords of Poverty* (1994)[1]

'The best kind of help to others, wherever possible, is indirect, and consists in such modifications of the conditions of life, of the general level of subsistence, as enables them independently to help themselves.'

John Dewey in *Ethics* by John Dewey and James Tufts (1908)

Introduction

Aid to sub-Saharan Africa increased massively between 1970 and the end of the twentieth century helping to create a booming aid sector in the West, while per capita income dropped and many African countries went into negative growth. This would seem to confirm the view of many aid sceptics that not only has development aid failed to produce economic growth but that there may be a negative correlation between the two. Whether there is a *causative* relationship is harder to prove, but there is a growing consensus that foreign aid has subsidised political and social developments that are inconducive to growth. It is significant that the most sceptical voices concerning development aid come from sub-Saharan Africa itself, where pro-aid opinion has become harder and harder to find outside of groups which benefit directly from it.

That development aid may have largely failed despite the expenditure of vast sums of money should not be a surprise. Even if it were not for factors such as the corrupt ways that aid has often been tied to trade, the naivety and foolishness of so many aid deliverers, the impacts of war and natural disaster, the sometimes destructive impact of great power rivalries, and the incompetence, greed and general malignity of many recipient governments, development aid would surely have been a gamble. What after all could be more complicated and difficult than the development of an entire society?

To make an impoverished or damaged society wealthier, better-educated, more technologically sophisticated, happier, more stable and all the other goals implicit in development is surely a task way beyond something like the elimination of smallpox or even the arrangement of a ceasefire between warring states.

To claim, as development aid advocates too often do, that the continued existence of mass poverty and/or the spread of failed states is essentially the product of insufficient benevolence by wealthy states, is not merely an oversimplification but an insult to their own community, and also to anyone who has ever studied economics, history, politics, psychology, anthropology and all the other disciplines that seek to understand 'development'.

10. Aid and Varieties of Actual Harm

How to undermine the states you are helping

Like many national aid agencies, DfID believes in supplementing poor country government budgets in fields like healthcare. In real life however, or what David Rieff calls the realm of 'actually-existing foreign aid', such budget supplements rarely if ever lead to improvements in services. This is because beneficiary governments use the aid money to cut their own contributions to the relevant sector. A recent study for *The Lancet*[1] documented how aid funding earmarked to supplement healthcare budgets in Africa prompted recipient governments to *decrease* their own contributions. Moreover, 'for every dollar received in aid money earmarked for healthcare, which more than doubled from $8 billion in 1995 to $19 billion in 2006, African governments diverted up to $1.14 to other areas'.[2]

In general, as Clare Lockhart and Ashraf Ghani of the Institute for State Effectiveness put it: 'The aid system as currently configured tends to undermine rather than support state institutions. The thousands of small projects designed to aid a particular school, village or district, end up recruiting the very teachers, administrators and doctors they are designed to support, to work as secretaries and drivers for the international staff.'[3]

Foreign aid can act as a barrier between the state and its citizens and stifle inclinations to reform

To quote Andrew Mwenda, the Ugandan newspaper editor and dissident: 'Foreign aid, which makes up 50 per cent of the Ugandan government's budget, is providing the government with an independent source of "unearned' revenue". That allows the government to avoid accountability to Uganda's citizens. Moreover foreign aid enables the government to pay its bills without having to under-take further necessary reforms.'[4]

As Dambisa Moyo explains: 'In most functioning and healthy economies, the middle class pays taxes in return for government accountability. Foreign aid short-circuits this link. Because the government's financial dependence on its citizens has been reduced, it owes its people nothing.'[5]

In general, moneys contributed to governments like Uganda's increase the patronage and power of those individuals and groups who control the levers of state, and tend to preserve their dominance of key institutions. (In the past, highly aided governments have often exploited their foreign subsidies to restrict foreign equity investment that might threaten the economic dominance of their key supporters.) This raises the political stakes and makes control of the state by particular groups all the more valuable, and all the more worth cheating for or fighting for or killing for. In other words, foreign aid can actually make civil wars and coups d'etat more rather than less likely; it certainly served to encourage gang and clan violence in Somalia in the 1990s.

'Native assistants' and the NGO brain drain

As in colonial times, foreigners, or 'internationals' as expat aid workers tend to be called today, employ an élite cadre of locals to assist them. This cadre gets access to many goods including high-tech, high-status tools like the latest laptops and mobile phones, and sometimes visas to countries that would otherwise be hard for them to visit. Like their predecessors in the imperial era, they have a pronounced but understandable tendency to tell their foreign employers what they want to hear.

In Nepal, one of the world's most aided and poorest countries, it has long been the case that the children of the country's élite work in the NGO sector. Foreign or international NGOs have the highest status as well as paying the highest salaries in the land and offering rich opportunities for graft. The élite youth are theoretically desirable employees for such organisations because of their political and social connections and their (often foreign) university degrees. In practice, they tend to be a burden, because they often assume that their positions, like the better and more expensive government jobs, are high-status sinecures.

The situation is similar in India and Pakistan, though there are more opportunities in both countries for profitable private sector employment. All over South Asia, NGOs often find themselves under pressure from local bigwigs to employ relatives or the children of other powerful families. The presence in an NGO office of the offspring of powerful politicians, senior police officers and civil servants politicians (assuming they turn up to the job), rarely leads to greater effectiveness and can often hinder the work that an NGO is trying to do. Unfortunately, the fact that so many people in the aid community come from élite backgrounds at home often seems to prejudice them in favour of hiring people from roughly analogous back-grounds in the countries where they are working.

Both this tendency combined with political pressure to hire from the local élite makes it less likely that aid agencies and NGOs will hire from the disadvantaged communities they are supposed to be serving, even though it is the development and training of such people that makes genuine sustainability possible. This is not to say that the poor in aid recipient countries are necessarily or invariably less corrupt and more able than their social and economic superiors – certainly no one who has worked in a conflict zone and seen how desperate, cynical and greedy even good people can become would make that assumption. However, when local hires are drawn from local communities not just from the capital city of the host country, they are likely to care more about the notional beneficiaries of an NGO and also to have a better understanding of local cultures and local needs.

In many African countries, the presence of a large, rich NGO sector has a more negative effect. As Michela Wrong says of Kenya: 'If you have a good degree are you going to go into business with it or politics? No you go into the aid world because that's where the fancy cars are and the titles.'[6] Indeed, in many developing and highly aided countries, any rational entrepreneur would choose a career in relief and development work either in a foreign NGO or one funded by wealthy foreigners. (Aid agencies are always looking for 'sexy' local NGOs to fund.[7])

And of course, as Linda Polman puts it, 'when the aid circus arrives, officials quickly turn all their energy and attention to the search for opportunities to attach themselves to INGOs'[8] because 'a civil servant or local chief attached to an INGO project as an advisor of supervisor can earn a salary dozens of times higher than normal'.

The sucking of talented, entrepreneurial people into the aid world and away from arguably more productive endeavours is arguably a human resource variant of 'Dutch Disease', the economic phenomenon whereby, when a country suddenly discovers a rich natural resource like oil or gas, its other industries such as manufacturing go into decline.

Aid, Dutch Disease and the 'curse of resources'

Critics like Easterly have pointed out that a large influx of foreign aid can have precisely the same ultimately destructive economic effects as a natural resource boom, and send other economic sectors into decline. Economists call this Dutch Disease after the financial crisis in the Netherlands in the 1960s following the discovery of natural gas reserves in the North Sea. The term refers to the way the country's sudden wealth made its exports less competitive and caused other problems. The mechanism is partly financial, because, as with any sudden increase in wealth a large influx of foreign aid can cause a recipient country's currency to go through the roof. IMF scholars found that aid inflows had a particularly damaging effect on labour-intensive industries in developing countries, therefore creating unemployment.[9]

Tim Harford and Michael Klein of the World Bank explain the phenomenon succinctly using the example of a 'resource curse' rather than aid:

> Natural resource exports may damage economies in several ways. First, they create volatility in government revenues that, if poorly managed, will lead to inflation and boom-and-bust cycles in government spending. Second, they produce foreign currency earnings that, if not neutralised by monetary policy, will raise the real exchange rate, undermining the competitiveness of other sectors. Third, they can damage institutions (including governance and the legal system) indirectly–by removing incentives to reform, improve infrastructure, or even establish a well-functioning tax bureaucracy–as well as directly–by provoking a fight to control resource rents. Although research is inconclusive, there is growing evidence that the third effect is the most problematic.[10]

There is a more dramatic description of the way the natural resource curse – or its aid analogue – can work economic harm in Jerry Useem's 2003 *Fortune* article 'The Devil's Excrement', about Venezuela and its impoverishment by oil riches:

> The economy can't absorb the sudden influx of money, causing wages and prices to inflate and the nation's currency to appreciate (by an average of 50 per cent, according to a World Bank economist's study). That makes it harder for local manufacturers to compete. Incentives, meanwhile, become wildly distorted. When free money is flowing out of the ground, people who might otherwise start a business or do something innovative instead busy themselves

angling for a share of the spoils. Why slog it out in a low-margin industry when steering some oil business toward a contact could make you a millionaire? Thus a doubly deadly dynamic: a ballooning public sector, a withering private one.[11]

As Useem goes on to point out, nations whose economies are unbalanced and distorted by such resource booms can end up like sixteenth century Spain whose inflated, gold-dependent economy withered once the ships stopped coming.

Some analysts believe that the 'curse of aid'[12] can actually have an *even more* negative impact than the famous 'curse of oil' and other natural resources.[13]

Dutch Disease (according to which the arrival of external subsidies raise the real rate of exchange in the recipient country and affect its export competitiveness) is only one unfortunate financial side effect of aid. Large influxes of foreign aid into developing societies ill-prepared to absorb such inflows can also reduce domestic savings and investment.

Aid and corruption

Experience has shown that when foreign aid is the primary source of financial resources for a government, it can become an engine of corruption in the same way as a natural resource windfall like the discovery of oil. Both money flows are susceptible to theft by those who control the reins of the state.

It is also worth noting that aid agencies themselves become involved in corruption. In India, currently the largest recipient of UK aid, all active NGOs necessarily pay bribes to get the many licences and permissions that are required for them to function. Like medium-sized and large companies in India, they generally do not do so directly but through their lawyers. It is a fact that everyone knows but which never appears in any report. No NGO would want the pensioner putting a pound in the bucket to worry that a significant proportion of that is going to bribe an Indian official. Fortunately for all the NGOs large and small, who work with or for DfId or which are independent, NGOs are thus far not scrutinised for taking part in corruption in the same way as businesses. This is especially the case in the field of humanitarian aid: arguably every major British aid agency that took part in the early stages Sri Lanka tsunami relief effort committed acts that would today be violations of the 2010 Bribery Act because it was impossible to function without doing so.[14]

Aid as condescension

The aid critic Dambisa Moyo is convinced that most foreign aid is based on the 'largely unspoken and insidious view' that its beneficiaries are quasi-children who cannot 'improve their own lot in life without foreign guidance and help'. She points out that even the 'development' metaphor is a biological one and that aid industry paternalism can feel and sound a lot like colonial paternalism. Her concern, however, is that the 'aid-dependency model' fostered by the aid industry over five or six decades requires that Africa be 'fundamentally kept in its perpetual child-like state'. It is perhaps telling that so much aid industry marketing, whether by NGOs or in DfID's public relations materials, features photographs of children. As David Rieff likes to point out: 'there are two groups of people who like to be photographed with children: dictators and aid officials'.[15]

Greater vulnerability to famine

Alex de Waal argues in his book *Famine Crimes* that 'international humanitarianism is an obstacle rather than an aid to conquering famine in Africa' because of its political consequences. For him 'the rapid growth in the power of the 'Humanitarian International'[14] is one of the three main reasons why post Cold-War hopes for the end of famine turned out to be premature. He defines 'humanitarian international' as 'the cosmopolitan élite of relief workers, officials of donor agencies, consultant academics and the like, and the institutions for which they work. By extension [it] includes journalists and editors who faithfully propagate the humanitarian worldview.' Although 'the humanitarian international is avowedly dedicated to fighting famine [it] does not in fact operate in a way that enables this to be achieved. There are successes and failures but… its power is exercised and its resources dispensed at the cost of weakening the forms of political accountability that underlie the prevention of famine.'[17]

Who Really Benefits from aid?

Though the visual symbol of foreign aid is a black or South Asian child, it is arguable that the main beneficiaries of official development aid are wealthy white people from Western countries.* This is increasingly the point of view of African activists who have lived through decades of development aid. Chukwu-Emeka Chikezie, a co-founder of the African Foundation for Development, condemns the aid industry in forthright terms: 'the increasing aid flows to Africa that this industry advocates will, at least, make "northern-NGO poverty history". Who else, after all, will implement all the new projects that will come? This conflict of interest, in which those arguing most loudly for increased aid flows are the aid's biggest beneficiaries is inherently corrupt and corrupting.'[18] Uganda's Andrew Mwenda puts it another way: 'Foreign aid enriches politicians, bureaucrats and aid workers… whose consumption fuels inflation.'[19]

---

*Moyo estimates that much of the pressure to give aid comes from the fact that the aid business employs some 500,000 people, 'the population of Swaziland', working in institutions ranging from the World Bank to small private charities. Moyo, D., *Dead Aid*, p.54.

11. The History of Foreign Aid

The birth of foreign aid

What the aid analysts Clare Lockhart and Ashraf Ghani, in their pathbreaking book *Fixing Failed States*, called 'the aid complex'[1] first came into being after World War II and evolved through a series of historical contingencies. One of its first major manifestations was the Marshall Plan, according to which the United States pledged almost one per cent of its 1948 GDP to the reconstruction of Europe. Most of the $13 billion paid by the USA went to rebuilding infrastructure. It was well used because the European states that were the beneficiaries of Marshall aid already had functioning and effective states, the rule of law and abundant human capital in the form of 'a highly skilled and disciplined population living among the rubble'.[2] The problems that the Plan was designed to address in Europe were therefore very different to those that aid advocates who have called for a 'Marshall Plan for Africa'[3] are hoping to solve. Unlike some of the foreign aid that was to go to Third World countries in the 1980s and after, the recipient governments of Marshall Aid were trusted to make good use of the money – which they were given without imposed plans or conditions – and most of them did so.

When aid began to be given systematically to the developing world in the 1950s, it tended to take different forms and to be a tool of Cold War power politics. As Lockhart and Ghani point out: 'aid quickly became a means of rewarding rulers on the basis of whether their foreign policies supported or opposed one of the superpowers – rather than whether they were pursuing any particular developmental agenda. For its first 45 years the global aid system did not even regard good governance as part of its agenda. Indeed, both the West and the Soviet bloc actually preferred to work with dictatorial regimes.' The World Bank, the IMF and the various development banks explicitly 'placed politics and security outside of their purview' though later they shifted emphasis from funding infrastructure to governance.[4]

It seems hard to believe now, but largely because of the example of Marshall Aid, when the World Bank and other organisations funded infrastructure projects in the Third World such as dams, railways and roads, they rarely considered how these projects would be managed, operated or maintained.[5]

During those early days of development aid, Western aid advocates justified aid according to theories of a 'poverty trap'. The basic idea was that underdeveloped (the euphemisms and politically correct labels for poor countries have changed over the years) states lacked the saved capital to invest in growth-promoting infrastructure like dams and roads and that development aid would 'fill the gap.' A few sceptical voices like that of Peter Bauer pointed out in the mid-1960s that all developed societies had emerged from similar or worse underdevelopment and poverty, including several recently poor states, and questioned the existence of such a trap.[6] However it remained orthodoxy for the next five decades and conditioned post-colonial élites to believe that rich country aid and indifference to its real results were the way of the world.

Indeed until the early years of the twenty-first century, informed scepticism about foreign aid was mostly the province of free-market or libertarian think-tanks like the International Policy Network.[7] They argued that factors such as the rule of law, property rights, government size and effectiveness, and openness to trade and foreign investment were more determinative of economic growth than ever greater amounts of aid.[8] However, since then sceptics have also emerged on the left.

In the 1960s the emphasis of Western foreign aid began to shift to health, education and the promotion of 'human capital', a term derived from Adam Smith, who defined it as the 'acquired and useful abilities of all the inhabitants or members of the society'. Mostly, the money was directed towards primary education, though some critics pointed out that poor countries also needed investment in higher education to create effective managers and leaders and foster the development of a middle class. At the same time, many within the aid community were drawn to 'appropriate development' which was based on so-called 'intermediate technology' (sometimes known as 'people's technology', 'indigenous technology' or even 'community technology') and which appealed to development workers who had become suspicious of, if not hostile to, economic growth.

Meanwhile there was a growing groundswell of complaints from within and outside the aid community about the 'tying' of development aid. Tied aid is aid that must be spent on goods or services from the donor country. In 1968 the Pearson Commission condemned the practice as reducing the overall value of aid. Ever since then, the inequities of tied aid have been an obsession among aid advocates on the left and have been cited as the prime reason for the disappointing results of bilateral development aid.

Clearly there have been many cases when market-distorting tied aid ensured that developing countries got much less for their grants or loans than they should have done, and the aid amounted to little more than disguised domestic industrial subsidy by the donor country. (This seems to have been the case with Britain's notorious Pergau dam project in Malaysia, as a result of which the Labour government's International Development Act made tied aid illegal.)

However, the products and services bought with tied aid are not necessarily inferior or overpriced, and there is an argument that countries have a right to benefit their own workers and companies whilst being altruistic. Indeed, it could be argued that if development aid is more or less destined to fail as a means of encouraging sustained economic growth, then it might as well fail while helping to keep some of the donor countries' workers employed.

Every few years the aid industry discovers new and necessary approaches that are in fact the same. As Easterly points out, aid professionals first called for donor co-ordination in the late 1940s to avoid inefficient duplication and competition. Then, in the early 1980s, a World Bank report pronounced that 'aid coordination...has been recognised as increasingly important.' Twenty years later, another World Bank report found that to be effective donors would have to 'ensure better coordination'.

Another buzzword that is rediscovered every few years, as if part of a profound set of new insights, is 'selectivity'. The *Economist* newspaper reported in 2002 that 'new research' had revealed that 'foreign aid tends to work well–that is, it helps to reduce poverty–in countries with good economic policies. In countries with bad policies, it is ineffective at best.'[9] However, no less a person than John F. Kennedy himself had pronounced *in 1963* that the primary of objective US foreign aid would be 'to apply stricter standards of selectivity... in aiding developing countries'.[10] Likewise there was a new emphasis on 'poverty reduction' at the agenda-setting World Bank, the globe's biggest aid agency, where it was announced in 1973, again in 1990 and again in 2001, and on 'country ownership' in 1969, 1981 and 2001.

Similarly, a doubling of foreign aid was said to be essential in 1973 by the then President of the World Bank Robert McNamara, and in 2001 his successor James Wolfenson said the same thing. (In 2005, British Chancellor Gordon Brown, an ardent supporter of the G8 plan to double international development aid to $100 billion per year, actually claimed that doubling such aid would halve poverty, a calculation presumably based on the Hogwarts curriculum rather than that of the University of Edinburgh.)

As Easterly pithily puts it: 'The lack of historical memory in the aid community inhibits people from learning from mistakes.'[11]

Infrastructure vs institution building

China is praised by some analysts of aid, including Dambisa Moyo, for its willingness to pay for grand infrastructure projects in contemporary Africa. Until the 1970s, foreign development from the West was also focused on building roads, bridges and other forms of infrastructure that help or are necessary for economic development and trade. (The West, however, even during the height of its Cold War assistance to allied Third World countries, was not as generous as modern China when it comes to building stadiums, palaces and military academies for the gratification of African dictators.[12])

As critics like Collier and Easterly have pointed out, the donors did not always budget for the maintenance of their new roads and bridges, and even where local governments were minded to maintain their gleaming gifts, they often lacked the skilled human capital to do so. As a result, Africa is littered with collapsed infrastructure projects. It seems likely that a similar fate will meet some of the much vaunted Chinese projects, many of which are poorly designed and badly constructed, even when the Chinese import their own Stakhanovite labourers.

Infrastructure went out of fashion in Western development aid circles in the 1970s and 1980s. This was partly a matter of cost, partly a matter of a new focus on *building institutions*. However, given the claims made by David Cameron and Andrew Mitchell about the effectiveness of aid as a means of winning goodwill and influence for Britain, it is worth noting that compared to infrastructure projects, institution-building or human-capital projects tend to go largely unnoticed and unremembered by the peoples and leaders of developing countries. By contrast, Somalis referred to 'The Chinese Road' three decades after it was built, and you frequently hear other poor Africans and South Asians expressing gratitude for similarly transformative projects.

There is little question that better communications can give vast economic boosts: the arrival of the mobile phone, and with it a new form of branchless banking*, is transforming economic life in much of Africa and India. If Western aid agencies such as DfID were to get back into the business of subsidising transportation infrastructure, it would be most effective and efficient for everyone if those agencies brokered agreements that allowed for multi-country, regional projects. It seems likely that such projects, if maintained, could genuinely foster economic growth.

Development without aid?

Implicit in the marketing rhetoric of international NGOs, aid agencies and government aid departments like DfID, is the notion that without their efforts and your money things would get much, much worse. As the Brandt Commission's famous 1980 report claimed: 'For the poorest countries, aid is essential to survival.' The aid critics and sceptics, on the other hand, are convinced that this is not the case and that poor or 'developing' societies can thrive without foreign aid. (One of the earliest and most effective proponents of this argument and one of the earliest critics of modern development aid was the development

---

*A development for which DfID may claim some credit, given its support for the Vodafone project that lead to the groundbreaking M-pesa phone banking system in Kenya.

economist Peter Bauer, best known to the general public for his formulation that foreign aid is 'an excellent method for the transfer of money from poor people in rich countries to rich people in poor countries'.)[13]

There are a few cases of poor societies that for one reason or another have been denied foreign aid but have flourished nevertheless. Although these theoretically might provide a control group for empirical inquiry into the effectiveness of aid in general, the usual problem of causation and correlation applies here as it does elsewhere in the aid debate.

Nicaragua, for instance, was cut off from most foreign development aid after the collapse of the Somoza regime in 1979. Nevertheless, during the 1980s, the Government of National Reconstruction was supposedly able to reduce adult illiteracy from 53 to 13 per cent and to triple access to basic healthcare.[14]

Another example is the Somaliland Republic. This small state is not recognised by the UK and other Western governments despite its achievement in bringing peace and stability to the north of what was for 30 years united Somalia; it therefore receives little or no aid. It is flourishing[15] nevertheless.[16]

Pro-aid narratives and many academic examinations of aid by the likes of Paul Collier and others tend to pay remarkably little attention to the real-life processes by which wealthy nations achieved their development. It is perhaps understandable that they choose not to look at how industrialisation took place two centuries ago in Britain, France and the United States or the particular way that development was connected to factors such as the rule of law, the growth of effective state institutions, and the evolution of democratic or quasi-democratic institutions. However, they also tend to take little account of the great development success stories of the modern era.

The emergence of countries like Singapore, South Korea and Taiwan should be particularly instructive, as should the more recent economic success of the so-called BRIC countries – Brazil, Russia, India, China.

India has for decades been the chief beneficiary of British overseas development aid and indeed received a disproportionate amount of all foreign aid. Nevertheless, poverty rates and overall underdevelopment in India remained obstinately high until the government began to liberalise the Indian economy and open markets to limited foreign investment, beginning in 1989. During the last twenty years of growth, on the other hand, development aid has played a minimal role in the Indian economy. (Many problems remain, thanks largely to irresponsible decisions by a ruling élite that prefers to spend capital on prestige projects like a space programme to investing in education or infrastructure, and which has benefited from an ineffective and corrupt taxation system. This élite seems happy to have foreign aid supply some of the more squalid deficiencies in its education and medical provision for the poor.)

On the other hand, libertarian and free market critics of aid tend to underplay the extent to which East Asian Tigers and other Third World success stories protected nascent industries from foreign competitions and their currencies from capital flight. Moreover South East countries like South Korea were at one time the beneficiaries of large amounts of foreign aid. Whether or not such countries would have become as prosperous as they are without such aid is a matter of genuine debate.

12. Alternatives to Development Aid

Aid vs trade reform as a key to development

'The development lobbies themselves, notably the big Western NGO charities, often just don't understand trade. It is complicated and doesn't appeal to their publics, so they take the populist line.'

Paul Collier, *The Bottom Billion*

Many critics of development aid argue that a 'fair' or fairer trade system would help bring about much or all of what development assistance is supposed to achieve. There is no question that European and American agricultural subsidies have made things much worse for African farmers. (Some have argued that the removal of the EU's subsidies and trade barriers would increase the GDP of sub-Saharan Africa by as much as five per cent.) Even though such subsidies have sometimes successfully promoted other notional goods, such as keeping alive a traditional and attractive way of life in the French countryside, there is a powerful moral case for establishing genuine free trade in agriculture and for the UK to use its influence to make that happen.

On the other hand, despite the well-known success of Kenyan bean exports to the UK, there is evidence that even if African farmers were not being undercut by EU and US subsidies, they would still not be able to compete effectively in the international markets because there is so little industrial scale farming on the continent and transport infrastructure is so inadequate.

Similarly, although Paul Collier and others have advocated low-cost manufacturing as the solution to African and other 'bottom billion' poverty, countries like South Africa that have tried this have found it impossible to compete with poor but growing Asian countries like Bangladesh.[1] The latter have equally low labour costs thanks to their vast populations and migrations from rural areas, but superior access to both efficient transport hubs and capital. (A better alternative, as Alex de Waal suggests, might be integration of Africa into a global service economy along the pattern of Mauritius's successful call-centre industry.)

On the other hand, contemporary left critiques of aid often call for protectionism as part of their rejection of the free market 'Washington Consensus'. Much of this seems to grow out of a kind of ignorant nostalgia for African socialism. For decades, import restrictions enriched mainly those officials who controlled customs facilities and those who smuggled luxuries to ruling élites. Even today, existing tariff barriers in Africa make money for government officials but cripple the regional trade that could and should offer opportunities for growth and prosperity.

Nevertheless, it is an article of faith among some aid critics on the left that aid 'conditionality' requiring free market reforms and privatisation has brought economic catastrophe to African and South American countries. It is an argument that ignores the fact that some countries (like Kenya) agreed to carry out such reforms but never really did, or carried them out corruptly so that government officials and their cronies were able to steal valuable economic assets. The widespread belief in much of the Third World that poverty is the result of World Bank-led free market reforms is a result of such governments failing to explain privatisation and other reforms or blaming economic stress on non-existent reforms.

Arguably DfID should be pushing hard for African governments to *eliminate regional barriers to trade*. Restrictions on capital flow are a different matter, and there are strong arguments that free trade fundamentalism with regard to the latter does indeed damage the potential of vulnerable underdeveloped economies.

Another alternative to development aid pushed by

former advocates is to close down the foreign boltholes where irresponsible Third World élites and kleptocrats put their money. Some 60 per cent of Africa's private wealth is said to be abroad in bank accounts in Switzerland (or even the UK). That $40 billion (the sum could be as high as $150 billion) is double the amount of money that the continent recieves in aid. The UK certainly could accompany a re-evaluation of its development aid budget with a more serious effort to combat the movement of such moneys. (It was only with the greatest difficulty that the Nigerian government was able to recover some of the billions stolen by the former dictator General Sani Abacha.)

Another way in which the UK could help development in Africa and South Asia without spending more money on aid projects that are all too often wasteful, misconceived or counterproductive, would be to make it easier for immigrant and migrant workers in the UK to send home *remittances*. As Dambisa Moyo, Chukwu-Emeka Chikezie and others have pointed out, such remittances have played a vital role in boosting the economies of many Third World countries from Africa to South East Asia. If the UK applied tax relief to such remittances it would massively increase the flow of capital into poor countries and put it into the hands of ordinary people at a much lower cost than any conceivable form of bilateral aid.

The UK could also make better and more frequent use – as the US does – of personal and family sanctions against corrupt officials and politicians, including travel bans. Depriving the wives and families of such officials of the opportunity to shop at Harrods is by far the most effective way of showing disapproval of and actively dissuading official corruption. The more the UK government were to engage in such practice, the less damage would be done by the DfID aid programmes whose continuation in places like Zimbabwe inevitably sends the message that Britain does not really care about corruption and tyranny.

Aiding democracy and governance to help development?

> 'Countries are not poor because they lack roads, schools or health clinics. They lack these things because they are poor – and they are poor because they lack the institutions of the free society, which create the underlying conditions for economic development. Aid has it upside down.'
>
> Fredrik Erixon, ECIPE

It is often said in the aid world that China's economic rise to greatness means that the West must reconsider its core assumptions about the route to development and the necessity or desirability of democratic institutions for growth. However, China's rise is hardly the first time that a politically repressive, relatively unfree society has enjoyed rapid economic and technological development. South Korea, Taiwan in the 1960s, 70s and 80s, and Malaysia and Indonesia more recently enjoyed rapid development and economic growth while being ruled by dictatorships and authoritarian regimes.

Although experts like Amartya Sen and William Easterly rightly stress the economic benefits that democratic institutions can bring, it is possible that authoritarian systems may find it easier to impose austerity measures and other forms of economic restructuring necessary to turn around underperforming economies. In the 1930s, several democracies foundered under severe economic pressure and it is not clear at the time of writing that contemporary European democracies will be able to carry out economic measures vital for their continued prosperity.

One of the practical and philosophical problems with the democratic conditions on aid sometimes imposed by Western donors including DfID in the last two decades, is that greater democracy, freedom and accountability could conceivably make some Third World governments *less likely* to take measures, such as cutting bloated and corrupted state sectors, that would foster growth and development. This is especially likely, and indeed has already happened in countries (especially in South America) where ruling élites have failed to tell their electorates the truth about indebtedness and other financial problems.

Moreover, while the calls from democratic activists, foreign political observers, and international humanitarians for democratic conditions on British aid have great moral force, and would probably be favoured by the British public if it were given more of a say in British aid policy, there is a plausible argument that only governments that resemble those of 1970s South East Asia are likely to make much development headway in Africa.

On the other hand, until recently most dictatorial – and for that matter most 'democratic' – post-colonial African regimes have been kleptocratic, irresponsible and incompetent. It seems unarguable that lack of effective legal or democratic checks and balances has prompted or enabled authoritarian rulers to govern in ways that have poisoned growth and undermined development. That said, the regime in sub-Saharan Africa that is perhaps the most disliked by the aid community (in particular by humanitarian organisations), seems to be successfully following the South East Asian, or more controversially, the Pinochet model of economically responsible authoritarianism. That government is Paul Kagame's Rwanda.

A major beneficiary of UK aid, a favourite destination for Tory and Coalition ministers, the nation shattered by the attempted genocide of 1994 is now the most efficient and one of the most rapidly developing countries in Africa. The Kagame government may well have been responsible for the murder of a dissident general in South Africa and it has certainly disappointed those who hoped it would be a beacon of political freedom on the continent. On the other hand, its repressiveness is arguably not exceptional by the low standards of the region, and indeed seems minimal compared to the mass-murderous political, economic and tribal policies of the Mugabe regime in Zimbabwe, a regime that would likely have fallen if it were not for emergency foreign food aid, especially from the UK.[2]

Empowerment rhetoric but top-down delivery

An essential part of the rhetoric of official development aid from its very beginnings has been the assertion that such aid is intended and designed to help people to help themselves. Almost everyone involved in the aid business theoretically subscribes to the idea underlying the Chinese saying that if you give a man a fish, you feed him for a day; if you teach him how to fish, he will feed himself for a lifetime. Ideally, development aid would provide impoverished countries or peoples with 'the capability and know-how to satisfy [their own] needs'.[3] Nevertheless, every few years a 'new' way of delivering aid comes to the fore that is said to represent a fundamental change from an old, discredited, top-down paradigm.

In other words, despite all the fads in the fields of development economics, the shifts from infrastructure to governance, from large-scale to small-scale projects, the seizing on capital, education, institutions or even climate as a 'key factor' in development, it continues to be the case that much of our 'help' is unhelpful and has made its intended beneficiaries even less capable of self-help than they were before.*

---

*The Palestinian Territories, whose people are amongst the world's most aided, present an interesting example. From 1999 to 2006, while foreign aid more than doubled, GDP shrank by half, prompting James Prince, a consultant to the Palestinian Investment Fund, to say that 'many of the donor programmes have not only been ineffective, they have harmed the economy'. Sterngold, J., 'Expert Says Palestinians Don't Need Financial Aid / Ex-International Monetary Fund Official Says Investments, Not Donations, Needed More to Rebuild Economy of Territories' (2005) *San Francisco Chronicle*, 5 September.

This reflects the fact that, however desirable and morally right it is to provide aid in poor countries, it is actually difficult to do so effectively, and much easier and more convenient for aid agencies, NGOs and governments to deliver aid in ways that are top down, centralised, and disrespectful of the needs, desires and autonomy of notional beneficiaries.

It also reflects the fact that the early decades of development aid were dominated by an essentially socialist mindset informed by the Great Depression. In an unpublished article, William Easterly cites Gunner Myrdal as saying in 1956 that: 'special advisers to underdeveloped countries who have taken the time and trouble to acquaint themselves with the problem... all recommend central planning as the first condition of progress'.[4] The result was white elephants like the Ajaokuta steel plant in Nigeria that cost $6 billion but never produced a single bar of steel, and the transformation of countries like Ghana and Tanzania from relatively wealthy exporters to economic basket-cases.

Since then, thinkers like Amartya Sen have rightly emphasised the importance of freedom and autonomy as simultaneously goals and means of development. This has not necessarily affected attitudes within the aid industry – especially the humanitarian aid sector, which is one reason why experts like Clare Lockhart believe that 'the humanitarian aid mentality is bad for development work'.

(It is telling that the aid community remains largely oblivious to the ideas and work of Hernando de Soto. He is the Peruvian economist who has argued that merely giving poor Third Worlders legal title and property rights to land they live or work on would give them access to the legal system, to credit, to legal markets and other goods essential for prosperity.[5])

However, it is worth considering, as the philosopher and former World Bank economic adviser David Ellerman[6] points out, that 'autonomy cannot be externally supplied'.[7] In other words, if you entice, cajole, persuade, bribe, blackmail or frighten someone into doing something that will be good for them, they are not really helping themselves.

Easterly's paradigm of 'searchers' and 'planners'

Professor William Easterly, the best known of academia's aid critics, believes that much development aid has failed because it has been designed and carried out by 'planners' rather than 'searchers'. Planners have good intentions and offer solutions but never have to bear the consequences of their failures.

Two quotations summarise Easterly's broad critique, the first from 'The White Man's Burden', his controversially titled bestseller:

> In foreign aid, Planners announce good intentions but don't motivate anyone to carry them out; Searchers find things that work and get some reward. Planners raise expectations but take no responsibility for meeting them; Searchers accept responsibility for their actions. Planners determine what to supply; Searchers find out what is in demand. Planners apply global blueprints; Searchers adapt to local conditions. Planners at the top lack knowledge of the bottom; Searchers find out what the reality is at the bottom. Planners never hear whether the planned got what it needed; Searchers find out whether the customer is satisfied.

The second is from an online debate and puts the class aspect of the Searcher/Planner in perspective:

> To oversimplify by a couple of gigawatts, the needs of the rich get met because the rich give feedback to political and economic Searchers, and they can hold the Searchers accountable for following through with specific actions. The needs of the poor don't get met because the poor have little money or political power with which to make their needs known and they cannot hold anyone accountable to meet those needs. They are stuck with Planners.

Easterly's work goes far beyond this insight. He is the pioneer of the (shockingly) new field of assessing aid empirically for genuine effectiveness and his 'Aid Watch'[8] blog and project at New York University has been an invaluable tool for people within the aid community who are struggling for more honesty and accountability.

Moreover, contrary to the image of Easterly held by many people in positions of power within the aid industry, he does not believe that the rich have no obligation to the poor, or that the poor should be abandoned to their own devices; he merely opposes the imposition of grand designs by outsiders. Nor is it true that Easterly is some kind of dogmatic free marketeer: the IMF comes in for severe criticism in 'White Man's Burden' for unthinkingly 'imposing comprehensive reforms on...fragile political systems' and helping various states collapse. (Although Easterly also rightly points out that, contrary to the left critique of the allegedly destructive role of 'the Washington consensus' in conditional development aid, many of the countries where the IMF is blamed for economic dislocation never in fact carried IMF reforms or fulfilled conditions supposedly necessary for future bailouts.)[9]

Easterly's prescriptions are necessarily vague. He prefers piecemeal interventions and comments favourably on the Mexican programme once called Progresa, now Opportunitades. This programme through which poor Mexican families are paid small amounts of cash in return for the regular attendance of children in school (an incentive to keep them in school rather than put them to work), health clinic visits etc., has apparently had good effects in that country, though it is not a foreign-designed or funded programme. Easterly also proposes the issuance of 'development vouchers' which would allow poor people to choose which public goods they want and which aid agency they want to get them from. Characteristically he says that: 'Giving vouchers to the poor may the stupidest idea ever, except for all the ideas that have already failed in foreign aid.'[10]

One possible problem with Easterly's view is not his celebration of 'searchers' as opposed to 'planners', but his faith in the ability of the world's poor to help themselves. At one point in his vital book he wonders if it might not be best simply to hand out cash to individuals and let them spend as they know best. Of course, as a general rule the people who live in the more benighted parts of the world do have a better sense of their own needs than the consultants and aid professionals who flit from one UN Conference to another and whose on-the-ground experience is little more than rushed landcruiser expeditions to impoverished villages. But you do not have to buy into any of the self-justifying shibboleths of the aid establishment to find something utopian in his insistence that if you let the intended beneficiaries say what they want, that good outcomes will result. Indeed it only takes a relatively short time on the ground in Africa or South Asia to discover instances of astonishing bloody-mindedness and self-destructiveness on the part of the poor and oppressed.

I once visited a valley in North West Pakistan where the administrator of a European aid project had given a significant cash sum to every family so they could educate their children.[11] Most of the beneficiaries used the money not for their children's schooling but to buy land, pay off debts or buy high status electronic goods that could rarely be run on the valley's feeble and uncertain electricity supply.

It may generally be the case that critics of foreign aid follies like Easterly put excessive faith in the abilities of local people in poor countries to decide where aid funds should go. The truth is that local people – including elected village leaders – can be almost as irresponsible or greedy or foolish as government bureaucrats or Western volunteers. I remember in Kashmir in 2006, after the great earthquake, how a local businessman turned NGO operator allocated aid contributions from the UK to the construction of mosques rather than homes in villages flattened by the quake, and how he gave money only to Sunnis rather than Shias.

Moral hazard

It is telling about the state of discourse within the aid community that you rarely if ever hear the theorists and practitioners of aid talking about moral hazard. This is a term used by economists and philosophers to describe the way a party to a transaction may be induced to behave badly if he knows that the other bears all the risk of the transaction going wrong.

Questions of moral hazard have inevitably been raised in the wider society's debates about development aid because of the long battle over Third World debt forgiveness. Some aid critics like Jonathan Glennie argue that it is one of the most important alternatives to conventional development aid, along with fair trade and the suppression of international tax havens for corrupt officials. While charities such as Oxfam, Save the Children and much of the political left have long argued for debt forgiveness for various African states, opponents have pointed out that this would be unfair to poor countries in Latin America that paid off their debts to the World Bank and other agencies.

However, moral hazard is also a danger in emergency and humanitarian aid. As David Ellerman points out: 'the world is awash with disaster situations that call for various forms of short-term disaster relief'. The problem is that, over a longer term, such relief 'creates a dependency relationship. Charity corrupts; long-term charity corrupts long-term.'[12]

Aid and unaccountability

As David Ellerman argues, 'the availability of large amounts of money to developing countries [by which he presumably means their governments] overrides their other motivations and redirects their attention to playing whatever game is necessary to get the money'.[13]

Andrew Mwenda, describing Uganda, is more specific: 'foreign aid, which makes up 50 percent of the Ugandan government's budget, is providing the government with an independent source of 'unearned' revenue. That allows the government to avoid accountability to Uganda's citizens. Moreover, foreign aid enables the government to pay its bills without having to undertake further necessary economic reforms.'[14] In other words, the easy cash that aid represents means that bad governments are accountable to absolutely no one, except, nominally, their aid donors[15]. This is not an easy problem to solve short of cutting off aid entirely or pushing harder for democratic and anti-corruption reform by insisting on and enforcing aid conditionality. And indeed, greater use of conditionality to promote more responsible behaviour by aided governments may be the most effective form of intervention.

However the aid industry, including DfID, generally prefers to promote so-called 'country ownership' and 'civil society' which often means Western-founded local NGOs that can perform invaluable functions but which some would argue are too dependent on foreign funding and leadership to be sustainable and which arguably drain talent out of local politics.

Aid critiques from the Left

One of the critics of foreign aid from the Left is Jonathan Glennie, a former campaigner for several charities and author of an important 2008 book titled *The Trouble With Aid – Why Less Could Mean More for Africa*. Glennie is an advocate of what he calls 'aid realism' which he says 'means not getting swept away by the ethical clamour to "do something" when a proper analysis shows that what is being done is ineffective or harmful'.

He is accordingly sceptical about the so-called 'Better Aid' agenda propagated originally at the Rome Conference on Aid Harmonisation in February 2003. 'Its rhetoric is similar to previous eras, with promises to double aid, to ensure country ownership, to reach a group of internationally agreed targets and, this time, to end poverty for good. To the untrained ear these appear to be signs of hope that aid giving is undergoing a transformation that will make it more effective than before. But more seasoned observers remember similar calls in past aid eras, since the 1950's.'[16] He believes however that 'there is one characteristic that is fundamentally different in this new aid era: short term aid support has turned into long term dependency'.

Glennie believes that: 'If the first reason to stop campaigning for aid increases is that aid may be doing more harm than good in some countries, the second is that all the emphasis on aid is obscuring the far more important policies the West should be adopting to help Africans out of poverty'.

Glennie argues primarily for 'plugging the leaks' of money out of Africa in the forms of 'capital flight, investment abroad [and] debt repayments'. He acknowledges briefly that corruption in Africa is a problem but points out that there are many flourishing but corrupt countries in the world. He believes that 'the problem is not corruption per se' but the fact that it flows abroad rather than being invested at home 'as it was in nineteenth century Britain'.

One problem with this argument is historical. Eighteenth century Britain was extremely corrupt, but nineteenth century Britain was actually notable for the way it developed an overwhelming culture of anti-corruption.

If anything, the Victorians had even more opportunities for overseas investment than contemporary African élites – hence the role of British businessmen in economic development around the world.

It is one reason to doubt whether the closing of tax havens (Glennie believes this has not happened because of 'pressure from big businesses and banks who are making billions from the system') might not be as effective a panacea for underdevelpment as some would hope. In general, Glennie's analysis takes too little note of awkward political and cultural realities in the Third World.

Dambisa Moyo's aid critique

Moyo is one of the aid sceptics who believe that there are less harmful alternatives to conventional development aid that are more likely to foster growth and prosperity. She differs from others in arguing that the states of sub-Saharan Africa would be better off raising money the same way emerging Asian countries did – through international financial markets – and that microfinance projects offer similar hope to the peoples of the continent. She also calls for Western countries to stop subsidising their farmers, and to make it easier for emigrants to send remittances home. She believes that Africans could generate their own prosperity if, as suggested by the Peruvian economist Hernando de Soto, shanty town dwellers and poor farmers were given title to long-occupied property. Moyo and others believe that free trade in the form of genuinely open Europe and American markets for African agricultural products and textiles will achieve more good than aid ever could.

Problems with Moyo's critque arguably include an underestimation of historically positive effects of capital controls for developing societies, a somewhat naïve enthusiasm for China's quasi-colonial investment activities in Africa, and a failure to grapple with impressive growth rates in corrupt societies like India, China and their predecessors in South East Asia.

13. The Expansion of the Aid Industry

One of the global changes that has complicated the overall picture of development aid and the decisions that must be made by those who run organisations like DfID is the enormous growth in the number of aid donors. There are now more than two hundred multilateral aid agencies and thousands of private aid agencies, large and small, including some 18,000 international NGOs.[1] (The former includes the new specialised multilateral agencies like the Global Fund to Fight Aids and Malaria.) Poor and underdeveloped countries now have hundreds of foreign aid groups working with their governments and their own NGOs. Corporate philanthropy has grown as has the influence of vast new private charitable foundations like that of Bill and Melinda Gates. As the number of donors per country has increased, the average size of aid projects has shrunk. All this means that the likelihood of wasteful duplication or triplication of work is very high and that aid agencies compete with each other for attention, funds and government cooperation.

Moreover, as one aid critic has put it, 'an unintended side effect of the increased activity of NGO issue lobbies has been to expand even further the set of goals that foreign assistance is trying to achieve. Since no [single] issue lobbby takes into account the effect on other issue lobbies of its demands on the scarce aid and administrative resources of agencies, each lobby overemphasises its goals.'[2] Because aid agencies are rewarded for setting goals rather than reaching them, this leads to a version of what economists and environmentalists call 'the tragedy of the commons'.*

---

*'The tragedy of the commons' refers to situations in which multiple individuals, acting on their own self-interest, exhaust a commonly held resource, as when too many farmers send their flocks to graze on a piece of common land. The phrase comes from the title of a famous 1968 article in *Science* magazine by the ecologist Garrett Hardin.

Awareness of the need for greater harmonisation in aid delivery was the inspiration behind the 2005 Paris Declaration on Aid Effectiveness. This grew out of one of those conferences that have become so notorious among aid critics for the public money that gets spent at five-star hotels, expensive restaurants and business or first class airline tickets – all of which are standard perks for those in the upper reaches of the aid industry. There have been subsequent conferences on the same subject, most recently at Busan in South Korea.

However, harmonisation in aid delivery in the face of vast numbers of players and 'stakeholders' would not be an unalloyed good. It is often the smallest NGOs – even the tiny MONGOs ('my own NGO') mocked by critics like Linda Polman – that come up with the most creative and effective programmes. I have seen a number of small low-budget foreigner-created NGOs in South Asia that achieved remarkable results while eschewing what might be called the standard 'landcruiser model' with its fancy offices and highly paid local and foreign staffs[3]. Operating on very small budgets, these organisations[4] achieve genuine sustainability by fostering ownership and by recruiting and training truly local people from outside the political and NGO-working Indian, Nepali and Pakistani élite. (In the bigger aid agencies, the expats are often not really that keen to train locals to do their jobs, because if they do so successfully they will lose theirs. With these mini-NGOs, on the other hand, the founder is genuinely happy to leave behind a functioning organisation so he or she can start one somewhere else.)

All too often, foreign aid officials make the mistake of thinking that 'local' means from the same country: they are then mystified when villagers in, say, a remote part of Afghanistan or Nepal treat builders and contractors from the capital as 'foreigners' and outsiders. The Central Asia

Institute (CAI)[5] that was able to build highly functional earthquake-resistant schools in Pakistan and Afghanistan for a tenth the cost of those put up by USAID did so precisely because it appreciated this.

CAI built its schools on land donated by local villagers and used local labour wherever possible. It supplied only certain materials and skilled labour. Understanding that no teacher from the provincial let alone the national capital would consider living in a remote village – though they might be happy to take the job and salary and never turn up – CAI turned for its teachers to local secondary school graduates. This met with the disapproval of larger aid agencies and government officials who said that teachers should be fully qualified graduates, despite the unlikelihood of such graduates taking and performing such a job. Throughout the projects, moneys for construction were given out in cash at meetings attended by the entire village so that there was no possibility of the headman or mayor or another person taking and misusing the funds.

For all the debates that go on within the aid industry about how to make aid more efficient and effective, most of them couched in industry or academic jargon,[6] there are few that concern the harm that can be done by aid or that confront the point that if poverty really were eliminated as per the Millennium Development Goals, then the aid industry would then be morally obliged to abolish itself.

Private and NGO aid has become more popular with the British and other publics as scepticism about government and multilateral agencies like the World Bank has grown. Unfortunately, some of the small NGOs with whom DfID has contracts are less than honest in their all-important reporting – the reporting that is the basis for DfID's grand claims about saving, educating or curing millions of people.* Some duplicate the work of other contractors. Many are structurally unable or unwilling to see the bigger picture and assume that their aspect of development is paramount and sacrosanct.

---

*DfID PR is replete with such claims. A typical example was Nick Clegg's boast in September 2010 that UK aid 'will save the lives of at least 50,000 women in pregnancy and childbirth, save 250,000 newborn babies and enable 10 million couples to access modern methods of family planning'. See DFID, 'UK Hails Plan to Save 16 Million Women and Children' (2010) *Department for International Development*, 22 September.

PART 6

'Masters in Mufti' – Humanitarian Aid and Its Critics

International relief for the poor, starving population is an inexhaustible source of profit to the warlords. From each transport they take as many sacks of wheat and litres of oil as they need. For the law in force here is this: whoever has weapons eats first. The hungry may take only that which remains. The dilemma faced by the international organisations? If the robbers are not given their cut, they will not let the shipment of aid get through, and the starving will die. Therefore you give the chieftains what they want, in the hope that at least the leftovers will reach those suffering from hunger. The warlords are at once the cause and the product of the crisis in which many of the continent's countries found themselves in the post-colonial era.

Ryszard Kapuscinski, *The Shadow of the Sun*

When one goes to a poor country where the humanitarian role is vital, the colonial atmosphere is unmistakeable. Humanitarians live in houses previously occupied by cabinet ministers or at least by the richest person in the village. Their user-friendly democratic attitudes can do nothing to disguise their power. Whether they are in sandals or old jeans or not, the reality is the same. And the youthquake clothing only makes them masters in mufti.

David Rieff, *A Bed for the Night*[1]

14. Emergency Aid and the NGO Sector

It is customary in the aid industry and in analyses of it to refer to private charities and non-government organisations as belonging to the emergency or humanitarian aid sector. Of course, many of these myriad organisations are also engaged in development aid or in activities such as healthcare that are included by DfID and others in the category of development aid. Many others that enjoy inclusion in the 'humanitarian' category are wholly or partly political advocacy organisations; their classification as 'humanitarian' secures for them both the moral glamour of 'humanitarianism' and its traditional association with neutrality. (The positive image of the charity worker abroad as a heroic or even saintly figure is deeply entrenched in Western societies, especially in the UK.)

Emergency aid has not come under the same systematic sceptical scrutiny as development aid. There are as yet no Easterlys or Moyos for that sector, (although whistleblowing books by the likes of Linda Polman are beginning to make inroads on public consciousness and David Rieff's *A Bed for the Night* brilliantly anatomises the inherent contradictions of humanitarian action). This is partly because the sums raised and disbursed by humanitarian organisations are dwarfed by the sums raised and disbursed by governments. They are, however, far from insignificant. The humanitarian sector has expanded exponentially over the past three decades. There are now thousands of humanitarian aid agencies, some as small as a single activist, others the size of large corporations. As Lindsey Hillsum wrote in 1995, the 'emergency aid business' has grown from 'a small element in the larger package of development into a giant, global, unregulated industry worth [then] £2.5 billion a year. Most of that money is provided by governments, the European Union and the United Nations.'[1] The US remains the world's largest donor of humanitarian aid, giving some $3.8 billion a year, followed by the EU with $1.9 billion and the UK with $1.1 billion. Not only is this industry funded by official aid bodies, it also wields enormous influence over official aid policy.

Although the mega-charities like Oxfam and Care have grown in power and influence, they undergo little or no independent scrutiny, especially in the UK.

Contrary to popular impression, much of the money that little old ladies give to Oxfam (or that is made from Oxfam's growing quasi-monopoly of the second-hand book business) does not necessarily go to feeding the hungry. A journalist who examined the accounts of Oxfam Ireland found that of its 'total resources expended' last year – some 16 million euros – only six million was spent on its overseas programme, but one million went on 'campaigns and advocacy'.[2]

In Britain it is normal for aid NGOs, especially the more powerful, corporate-sized private humanitarian agencies like Oxfam and Save the Children (both of which receive large grants from DfID) to lobby for particular foreign aid policy goals and spending levels.[3]

For instance when DfId and British aid policy were the object of criticism by the Telegraph newspaper for the amount of UK aid money 'wasted' by EU aid, it led to a typical joint letter[4] to the paper from Cafod, Oxfam GB, One and Unicef GB insisting that 'European aid makes a positive and real difference to the poorest children in the world', that in the six years to 2009, EU aid gave more than nine million children a primary education, and claiming even more dubiously that 'Britain's investment in the EU aid budget ensures that other European governments contribute towards poverty reduction efforts'.

Recently the announcement by DfID that it would be cutting down on the number of countries to which the UK gives aid prompted a rare flurry of criticism from the NGO sector.[5] But such criticism is the exception. In general, whenever DfID has to defend its priorities and policies it can usually count on stout support from the major NGOs. Such encouragement may be related to the way that DfID often seems to take its 'line' from the hard-line elements within the industry, and because the department is acutely conscious of aid industry opinion. In fact it often seems much more concerned with NGO opinion than with that of the public, as if the wider aid community were its clients rather than British voters.

This may sound cynical but it would be foolish to ignore the role played by individual and institutional self-interest in the establishment of aid policy. As the former aid worker Michael Maren puts it, for aid agencies: 'famine is a growth opportunity'. And indeed as he points out, you can be in a room or tent in a famine area and look around at a group of professionals every one of whom – the technical experts, the diplomats, and aid workers – are making a good living from the crisis. This expresses an uncomfortable truth about humanitarian and emergency aid. But it is only one among several. Much humanitarian aid has been disastrous, though its failures rarely reach public notice.

For instance few people in the West are aware that the standard operating procedure of the 'humanitarian aid community' for dealing with famines through the 1980s made current famines worse and future famines more likely. Aid agencies would set up camps and give out aid from them. Large numbers of people would then flee the famine area and settle near the food distribution points. As a result, there would be no planting in the famine area for the next season, and the temporary settlements became long term ones, and also petri dishes for epidemic diseases, social breakdown and crime. Nowadays, aid agencies have learned to distribute emergency food aid in situ. But it is a lesson learned at the cost of thousands of lives.

The unfortunate truth is that while humanitarian/ emergency aid has tended to be a less quixotic and vastly more valuable enterprise than development aid, its real history is rather more chequered than the public has been led to believe. Caroline Cox of the Humanitarian Assistance Relief Trust recalls landing at a remote South Sudanese in the midst of a famine, and being shocked to see tribespeople throwing stones at the UN plane that had dropped her off. When she asked them why she was told that the previous week the villagers had rushed to a container dropped by a previous UN flight only to find that it was filled with blackboard chalk.[6]

An aid worker from the Central Asia Institute was in Pakistan-controlled Kashmir after the earthquake when foreign emergency relief agencies turned up to the refugee camps with truck loads of goretex rain jackets. Most of the jackets ended up being burned. The earthquake victims were in desperate need of firewood to cook food and stay warm.[7]

This kind of anecdote is not unrepresentative of the kind of cultural errors that are frequently made by even experienced aid agencies. A Pakistani aid worker told me how during the same crisis as that described by Mortenson, many refugees were injured in fires because they cooked their meals inside the expensive and highly flammable nylon camping tents contributed by foreign agencies: what worked better for such village people were the old fashioned, high-ceilinged canvas army tents supplied by local agencies.

Justine Hardy, who was working with earthquake victims on the other side of the border, cited the problems caused by high-tech nylon sport clothing supplied by foreign aid agencies. 'The people in the camps didn't have washing facilities for themselves or the nylon clothing. They would sweat in the heat and develop terrible fungal infections. A simple request for woollen blankets was all that was required.'[8]

She also witnessed a more common emergency aid error. A large international aid agency had hired lorries and drivers in the state capital to deliver food packages to the worst-affected districts. When these drivers arrived at these remote villages, they were mobbed by locals, as often happens in the delivery of humanitarian relief. (In some cases youths were paid by local corruption lords to elbow villagers out of the way and take the food so it could then be sold at a premium.) The drivers had not been trained in the techniques of safe delivery in such circumstances and were badly frightened by the experience. They started to ditch their payloads, tossing desperately needed food supplies into thick forests or on the side of the highway. The drivers were paid a bonus for fast delivery on each journey, and the agency was not checking if supplies actually reached the villages, so the drivers already had an incentive to speed up their trips. As a result, some of the worst hit villages never received the food that aid agency later claimed to have delivered.

Anyone who has worked in the aid industry or who has covered it as a journalist could come up with scores of similar anecdotes. The dirty little secret of emergency aid is that it is often carried out in ways that are astonishingly wasteful, incompetent or even harmful to its intended beneficiaries. There are various reasons for this, including the tendency of agencies to hire young Westerners with few real practical skills and insufficient inexperience. But probably the most significant factors are the way the aid industry is insulated from the kind of scrutiny that is par for the course in other forms of public and private enterprise, and the widespread belief within the aid community that altruistic motivation is not only more important than results, but renders criticism of any kind both moot and offensive.

It is, of course, also true that hundreds of thousands of people, perhaps millions, are alive today thanks to the efforts of dedicated, skilled and courageous humanitarian aid workers. However, the sometimes lethal gap between the claims of the humanitarian aid sector and its accomplishments is not a problem that the sector will ever address unless the general public is made aware of it.

15. Problems with Emergency and Humanitarian Aid

The Goma Syndrome

In late 1994 and early1995, after the genocide in Rwanda, the world's humanitarian aid legions descended on Goma in neighbouring Congo. Goma had a long airstrip usable by large transport aircraft and was therefore an ideal base for helping the refugees that the international news networks had shown fleeing from Rwanda. The refugees were not fleeing from the genocide that had been carried out by the government-sponsored Interhamwe militia. They were the Interhamwe militia, together with their families, many of whom had also taken part in the mass slaughter. They and the Hutu government had been confronted with defeat by a Tutsi exile army (the RPF) invading from Uganda. (Complete rout had been avoided thanks to military intervention by France on behalf of the Hutu 'genocidaires' and regional Francophony in the now notorious Operation Turquoise.)

Some 750,000 people turned up in Goma to be greeted by camera crews who sent home images of exhausted humanity. As so often when large numbers of poor, underfed people flee and gather in a small place, disease broke out. Very quickly, NGOs initiated a PR campaign to help the cholera victims. More and more NGOs turned up, until there were some 250 agencies operating in Goma and many more journalists. The UNHCR held daily press conferences at which the NGOs made heartrending appeals. As Richard Dowden later told the LSE: 'Each one would give a higher death toll, because each one would know that the man with the highest death toll would get on the nine o'clock news that night. And being on the nine o'clock news meant you got money.'[1]

More than $1.5 billion was collected very quickly and 25 refugee camps were established around Goma. As Linda Polman recalled, some eight UN departments, twenty donor governments and 'an untold number of local aid organisations funded by foreign donors' set up shop. The various organisations engaged in fierce competition for publicity. As David Rieff has written: 'the struggle to stamp out cholera, get the shelters built, and dig the pit latrines was simultaneously a struggle for market share'.[2]

Meanwhile, across the border in Rwanda itself, where the Tutsi population was reeling from the attempt to exterminate it, there was hardly any foreign aid presence at all. If that were not bad enough, inside the increasingly permanent-looking Goma camps, furnished with goods stolen from Rwanda, the militias and the extremist Hutu government now in exile recruited squads of rested and well-nourished young men to raid into Rwanda and murder more Tutsis. They extorted a war tax from the camp residents and rooted out dissidents. Markets grew up in donated supplies. Criminals ruled the night and stole warehouses full of goods from the NGOs who chose not to report or complain about the overall lack of security lest it bring bad publicity and undermine donations.

This dark circus flourished for two years thanks to the donations of foreign governments and charitable Westerners. It only came to an end, to the economic disadvantage of the 'international humanitarian community', when Rwandan Tutsi forces, fed up with attacks mounted from the camps, invaded Congo and overran Goma.

As David Rieff points out, if in 1944 200,000 SS soldiers had taken their families out of Nazi Europe as it fell to the allies and fled to some neutral country, they too would have humanitarian needs, but the rest of the world might have found it hard to ignore the political and moral context of their presence. They would have found it even harder, if the SS troops had used refugee camps as bases for attacks on those who had survived their genocidal efforts. Yet that is almost exactly what happened in 1995, when the world's aid agencies and NGOs landed at the Goma airstrip and made a vast effort to succour, house and feed the defeated Hutu forces and their families.

The humanitarian needs of these mass murderers and their families were genuine, though of necessity the media and the aid world presented them inaccurately as innocent victims. In a grim irony they received much more help – thanks to the proximity of their camps to the Goma airstrip and the international town that grew around it – than the population of genocide survivors who were struggling to get back on their feet in Rwanda.

As Rieff explains: 'In the humanitarian story … victims are always innocent, always deserving of the world's sympathy, its moral concern, and beyond that, its protection… Reality is elsewhere.' He goes on to point out that 'the first and greatest humanitarian trap' is not prolonging wars or giving great powers an excuse for either intervention or non-intervention, but 'this need to simplify, if not actually lie about the way things are in the crisis zones, in order to make the story more morally and psychologically palatable…'

It would be fortunate if the Goma example of a humanitarian aid effort being based on a misleading media/NGO picture and helping the wrong people were unique. However that is far from the case. Refugee camps have all too often become places of refuge and R&R for guerrilla armies or launching pads for terrorist attacks because the presence of foreign humanitarian NGOs works as a human shield, protecting the perpetrators from counter-attack. And relief organisations have all too frequently found themselves discreetly tithing to or otherwise subsidising brutal warlords, rebels, bandits and militias, and thereby prolonging or worsening the very conflicts whose effect they are trying to meliorate.

The phenomenon is deftly anatomised in *Condemned to Repeat* by Fiona Terry[3], a book that is essential reading for anyone who wants to understand the grim and complicated moral dilemmas that face aid agencies in war zones. Terry was in charge of the French section of Médecins Sans Frontières when it pulled out of the Rwandan refugee camps in Tanzania and Zaire at the end of 1994 – an action of integrity and courage all too rare in such a context.

She recalls how 'the genocide against the Tutsi and those who were seen as supporting them had continued in the camps, and bodies were frequently dragged from the lake. In the MSF hospital we strongly suspected that Tutsi children were given minimal care, or left to die, when we were not around to supervise. We wondered how many of our Rwandan staff – working the feeding centre, the hospital, even in our house – had blood on their hands.'[4] This resulted a debate between the various MSF sections about whether MSF's 'participation in the aid system implicated us in all its outcomes [and] everything from our presence in the camps to the resources we lost from theft made us direct accomplices in whatever harmful acts ensued'. In the end, of all the various MSF sections, only the French one departed.

It is often asserted by aid industry apologists that what happened in the Hutu refugee camps was unprecedented. But in *Condemned to Repeat*, Terry examines the phenomenon of 'refugee warriors' by analysing in detail several other cases of 'militarised refugee camps' that preceded the Rwandan genocide. Her examples include the Afghan refugee camps in Pakistan that grew up following the Soviet invasion, the Salvadoran and Nicaraguan refugee camps in Honduras during the 1980s, and the much-aided Cambodian refugee camps in

Thailand from which the remnants of the Khmer Rouge regime continued to operate after 1979.

She also cites the 'refugee warrior communities' hosted by Tunisia and Morocco during France's Algerian war, the Ugandan refugee camps where the Tutsi RPF army was born, the Eritrean refugee camps cum bases in Sudan during the 60s,70s and 80s, 'the refugees from East Pakistan who were trained and equipped in India before their victorious return to form Bangladesh in 1971, the bases maintained by SWAPO right next to Namibian refugee camps in Angola, and the refugee camps that have long formed bases for Burmese minority armies in Western Thailand.

The most notorious military activity from refugee camps – some of which are so long-established they feel more like cities or army bases than anything resembling a 'camp' – has been in the Palestinian camps in Lebanon, Jordan and Gaza, activity that has been indirectly subsidised by UN bodies and by foreign charities.

At the time of writing, 'refugee warrior' rebels are mounting attacks on Sudanese government forces from camps in Darfur and across the border in Chad. It is behaviour that is theoretically forbidden by the UNHCR and the other organisations that run the camps, but they have neither the paramilitary means nor the legal mandate to stop such behaviour or even to keep order in the camps they run. (Understandably many of the expatriates who work in the camps feel ambivalent about or even sympathetic to the militias they are housing: these are, after all people who have been driven from their homes by the murderous Janjaweed militia and the Sudanese armed forces.[5])

Terry points out that: 'Humanitarian sanctuaries created by the international refugee regime provide... major advantages to guerrilla factions over purely military sanctuaries'. For one thing humanitarian assistance 'provides guerrillas with an economic resource independent of external patrons'. That is because once the inevitable 'myriad of NGOs and specialized UN agencies' are present, 'guerrillas can appropriate food and medical supplies for military use and raise revenue from a variety of sources including taxes on the salaries of refugees employed by international organisations'. Worse still, 'refugee camp structures provide mechanisms through which a guerrilla movement can control the civilian population and legitimise its leadership'.[6]

Basically the aid agencies are always looking for 'leaders' to act on behalf of the refugees; once recognised as a refugee leader your influence is legitimised and your power grows, even if your only real qualification is the ability physically to intimidate your fellow refugees. This can of course lead to some very nasty outcomes. But it is not a problem that aid agencies and NGOs like to talk about in public. While the difficulties and dilemmas inherent in dealing with militarised or semi-militarised refugee camps are discussed within the aid community and in academic literature, they remain largely unknown to the public, thanks to fundraising-driven disingenuousness and secretiveness.

Moreover, much of the discussion, even in well-regarded books such as *Do No Harm*[7] by the aid consultant Mary B Anderson, tends to be unreasonably optimistic about the ability of relief organisations to learn from past errors and avoid empowering the wrong people. Anderson, like many in the aid community seems to believe that even if aid does harm it is always better to give it than not – abstention is never an option. And in practice, apart from the ICRC and some branches of MSF, few aid agencies seem able to set themselves limits or draw lines in the sand when it comes to compromising with killers or enabling violence. The discussion also tends to be too ready to relieve aid agencies of their moral accountability when harm does take place. As Fiona Terry points out: 'emphasising the complexity of crises has become a convenient way of deflecting responsibility for the negative consequences of humanitarian action'.[8]

Even in refugee crises where no refugee-warrior or refugee-bandit emerges, the altruistically motivated behaviour of the aid agencies and NGOs running refugee camps can cause many varieties of harm. None of the brochures or advertisements that aid agencies use to encourage donation are open about the problematic way their operations can subvert or upend fragile hierarchies in refugee communities: the way English speakers suddenly become petty princes, benign or malign, or the way some factions gain prestige and power by grabbing control of distribution chains, or the epidemics of rape and other crimes by young men in cheek-by-jowl tent cities where there are no police and tribal elders have lost all influence. Nor do relief agencies make public the staggering amount of aid that gets pillaged, diverted or extorted in conflict zones. One historian of the Balkan wars estimated that half of all the aid delivered to former Yugoslavia ended up being diverted to militias and armies. Alex de Waal's Somali sources believed that half of the food distributed by Red Cross in Somalia was looted or extorted.[9] In the Liberian civil wars, the scores of trucks and the communications equipment stolen from aid agencies made an important contribution to the combat effectiveness of various factions.

The real history of humanitarian and emergency aid is very different from the official ones.

Aid lies and compromises and the Ethiopian famine of the mid-1980s

In 2010 the British public was given a rare insight into the more complicated realities behind aid industry fables when the BBC World Service ran a programme[10] asserting that, during the 1984 famine crisis, some Live Aid funds had been diverted by Ethiopian rebel groups to buy weapons. The investigation met with furious denials from Bob Geldof and some NGO officials, but given the available evidence, and how frequently aid money gets extorted by government and rebel groups in Africa, the programme seems to have been on target.

If anything, the real story of Live Aid, the international aid community and the Ethiopian famine may be darker than anything the BBC programme suggested. Contrary to the reports broadcast at the time by the BBC's Michael Buerk, the starving children of Ethiopia were not so much the victims of drought but of politics in the form of civil war and ethnic cleansing. (The rebels also used hunger and food as weapons, and their leader, Meles Zenawi, who eventually became President, proved almost as ruthless a manipulator of foreign aid efforts – especially from Britain – as his predecessor.)

The food crisis in Ethiopia was in part the result of the usual cyclical drought in the Sahel, but it was mostly the product of the forced resettlement programme of 600,000 people from the rebel North and the 'villagisation' of two million others. Buerk's impassioned reports about a 'famine of biblical proportions' then played a key role in bringing hundreds of millions of dollars to Ethiopia's murderous Marxist regime, ensuring that it could feed its core constituency and its army and subsidising its campaigns of Soviet-style forced collectivisation and population transfer.

Buerk's simplified account of what was really happening in Ethiopia[11] and the vast often morally-compromised aid effort that followed, went unquestioned for many years, partly thanks to the tremendous moral prestige of Band Aid and Live Aid. Buerk's simplifications, the fundraising efforts of celebrities like Bob Geldof and the efforts of the aid agencies were all motivated by admirable compassion and horror at human suffering, but as so often in the history of aid, they may have caused almost as much harm as they prevented.

While it is all too common in the emergency aid world for NGOs to pay off bandits, guerrilla forces and armies with a cut of food or cash, the compromises made by aid agencies during the Ethiopian famine were even more problematic – and more lethal. As the Mengistu regime, like so many aid-recipient governments, became ever more skilled at manipulating the all-too-willing Live-Aid-funded NGOs and the media, the latter in effect became accomplices to the use of starvation as a weapon of war and oppression.[12] As Fiona Terry, the Director of Research at Médecins Sans Frontières puts it: 'Aid was the bait' in the government's resettlement plan designed to deprive opposition movements of their base of support, 'and the presence of international NGOs gave the programme an element of legitimacy'.[13] Lorries from Save the Children and several other agencies[14] actually took Mengistu's victims out of refugee camps to the new government villages – which some compared to concentration camps.[15] Of all the major NGOs, only the French chapter of Médecins Sans Frontières refused to cooperate with the Mengistu regime's forced population transfers. After MSF was duly expelled from the country, its president rightly denounced 'the biggest deportation since the Khmer Rouge genocide'.[16]

It is worth noting that neighbouring Somalia and the NGOs working there at that time collaborated in exaggerating the size of refugee problem during the Ethiopian famine – habitually claiming that one to two million Ethiopians had crossed the border – though in reality they believed the number might be around 750,000 – in order to ensure large grants from the UN High Commission for Refugees (UNHCR).[17]

Famine lies and distortions today: Somalia

There are similar distortions at play today in the NGO-fed reporting about the current 'famine' in the Horn of Africa. News reports along with appeals for charitable donation claim that the region is suffering the 'worst drought in sixty years'.[18] Although this datum is repeated everywhere, it is one of those headline-worthy numbers that seems to come from nowhere: everyone repeats it without attributing a source. It may well have no empirical basis whatsoever: someone said it to a journalist in an informal briefing and it has become a pseudo-fact, one that is too dramatic and too useful to check.

However, according to some genuinely disinterested and well-informed Africa experts,[19] there is in fact no exceptional drought in the region – merely the usual cyclical drought that takes place every three years. Moreover, famine conditions only exist in a very small part of Somalia. People are starving in large numbers not because of an overall shortage of food and water in the country but because misrule by militias, warlords and Somali politicians makes it hard for food to travel from areas of plenty to those in need. (Modern studies of famine, especially the work of Amartya Sen, make a convincing case that famines are generally created by governments.)

The food shortages in southern Somalia are blamed by some on the Al Shabaab Islamist militia which recently expelled the World Food Programme along with other foreign aid agencies.[20] However, for all Al Shabaab's malefactions and al Qaeda links, it could possibly have had a point when it gave the reasons for that expulsion: its leaders complained that the WFP's food donations were undermining the incomes of local farmers and disincentivising planting for coming seasons.[21]

Economic distortions and the subsidising of bad regimes by humanitarian aid

When the aid agencies and INGO's[22] arrive in a crisis area with their need for interpreters and drivers, their willingness to pay First World salaries, their requirements for food and petrol, and their desire for relatively luxurious housing, local prices rise dramatically. This brings benefits to some local businesspeople but catastrophe for many other local inhabitants. If this distortion is recognised at all by the aid workers, it tends to be viewed as mere collateral damage, subordinate to the more important task of saving lives.

In some places, the effects of the aid presence are even more politically and morally problematic. As Linda Polman points out, in Sudan, whose ruler Omar Hassan al-Bashir is wanted for war crimes committed in Darfur, 'the INGOs...are the milch cows for Bashir's state apparatus'. Polman quotes an aid agency worker who explains that: 'it is an open secret among donors, UN organisations and INGO's that the government earns several million dollars a quarter on visas, travel permits, work permits for humanitarians and permit extensions... to visit or work in any location outside of Khartoum you need a permit.... To set up an INGO you need approval from the Humanitarian Affairs Ministry. The minister is Ahmad Harun, indicted by the ICC for crimes against humanity. Registering an INGO costs money and at every stage of the application process you pay again. Every INGO oils the wheel of the regime with cash and gifts. One gift that is much in demand is that you give someone a job.'[23]

The regime also benefits handsomely from income tax, fees for the use of government internet and satellite networks and import duties on all of the expensive gear that NGOs need from generator and car batteries to laptops and printers. For the most part, the many foreign NGOs here as in many other countries rent their landcruisers and lorries from companies owned by associates of the regime at very high prices. (The aid workers aren't paying these extortionate fees and prices themselves, distant donors are, so there is little incentive to push back, especially since being seen as difficult in any way might lead to permit refusal or expulsion and therefore a loss of contracts for the organisation.)

Sri Lanka, Sierra Leone and the lethal side-effects of the aid industry/media nexus

A few days after the 2004 Tsunami struck Sri Lanka, the British public was bombarded by the major aid agencies with urgent appeals for more and bigger donations. Help was not getting to the villages, the appeals said, more money was needed right away. It was true that aid was not leaving Colombo and getting to many of the places devastated by the giant wave. But the reason for this was that emergency medical supplies and other aid agency materials were sitting on the tarmac at Colombo airport. There they were being held hostage by Sri Lankan customs officials who demanded that special 'duty' be paid on every item, including non-dutiable medical supplies. To bring in a Land Rover or equivalent vehicle, the agency had to pay a duty of 100 per cent of its value, in cash. None of the agencies had enough cash on hand to pay both ordinary unloading bribes and the extortionate require-ments of the customs officers. Hence the delay while the agencies gathered millions of dollars in ready cash, and hence the anguished appeals.[24]

If a single one of these agencies – and they included powerful international organisations like Oxfam – had gone public with the illegal and morally monstrous demands by the Sri Lankan customs officials, the roadblock would have been cleared instantly with an embarrassed Sri Lankan government putting out a statement saying there had been an unwitting mistake and of course there was no official policy of holding emergency aid hostage until duty was paid. However, not one agency dared to blow the whistle.

To have done so might have been the right thing and might have saved thousands of lives, but it would also have introduced a profoundly unwelcome element into the aid agency marketing narrative and threatened fund-raising. The agencies apparently felt that they could not take the risk of alerting the thousands of ordinary, often not-very-well-off Britons who had given to the Tsunami appeal to the fact that their contribution might have gone to pay bribes to customs officials rather than to help the island's victims.

If the aid agencies' deceit was cynical, wasteful, self-serving and unfortunately all too typical, the fact that the whole scandal went unreported was equally so. But then every major journalist working on the Tsunami was dependent on the aid agencies for stories, access and transport. As a result there was no mention at all of what had gone on until months later. *The Daily Telegraph* and then the BBC ran shock-horror stories about Oxfam having to pay a 300% import tax on jeeps it wanted to bring into Sri Lanka for Tsunami relief *half-a-year after the fact*[25] – by which time there was no danger that Oxfam's massive fundraising might be harmed by the revelation.)

This kind of mutual dependency is all too common, as is the distorted and hagiographical media coverage that it inevitably leads to. In 1992, the BBC TV correspondent George Alagiah gave a rare insider's explanation of the symbiotic, reality-distorting relationship of media organisations and NGOs: 'Relief agencies depend upon us for publicity and we need them to tell us where the stories are. There's an unspoken understanding between us, a sort of code. We try not to ask the question too bluntly: "Where will we find the starving babies?" and they never answer explicitly. We get the pictures just the same.'[26]

Since then, media dependence on NGOs has deepened because the latter increasingly pay for the transport and housing of journalists as well as providing them with images and stories that the NGOs select carefully so as to further their policy or fundraising agendas.*

As David Rieff put it in 1997: 'there is no use denying that for the press corps, with the exception of the richest newspapers and television networks that can hire their own vehicles and translators, the international aid organisations have shaped coverage of their own stories. Whether it was in Mogadishu, Sarajevo, or Goma, more often than not print and television journalists turned to a member of a humanitarian NGO for the story on the ground – not to mention transportation, lodging and companionship. *The situation is not all that different from the American media and the US military in the early days in Vietnam before the reporters turned against the war.'*[27] (Emphasis added.)

This of course means that public perceptions of far-off crises, where aid is needed, and therefore government aid policy, are shaped by NGOs with a political and financial interest in those perceptions. It also, just as troublingly, means that groups on the ground, including civil war combatants, change their behaviour in ways that they know may bring more aid money into their countries. (One of the things that the aid community persistently underestimates is the extent to which entrepreneurial energy and ability in Africa and South Asia gets applied to the manipulation of foreign aid workers and journalists.)

---

*For a typically subjective news story about hunger and aid that uncritically repeats statistics from aid agencies and NGOs see the report in the London Times from August 2011 entitled '400,00 children could starve'. The main aid agency quoted without a trace of due scepticism is DfID in the form of Andrew Mitchell himself. McConnell, T., '400,000 Children Could Starve, Warns Aid Minister' (2011) *The Times*, 18 August.

Linda Polman's book *War Games* details the way both NGOs and the international media searched for the most shocking images of amputation and mutilation in Sierra Leone and Liberia, and how local people then changed their behaviour in destructive ways to get attention and money.

According to Polman, during the Sierra Leone civil war there was a secret meeting between rebels and government troops at which both sides noted that they only received coverage from the BBC when people they had mutilated emerged from the jungle.

In other words, the NGO-media nexus made the civil war there much worse and actually increased the practice of arm and hand chopping.

Shaking hands with other devils

When international agencies were still active in Somalia, the various tribal militias and criminal gangs grew rich on 'taxes', protection fees and moneys charged for food aid to enter their territories. During the Liberian civil war both sides demanded a percentage of the value of aid that foreign agencies brought into the country.

In Sri Lanka, after the Tsunami the Dutch arm of the international Christian charity Caritas wanted to build emergency housing in the North of the country. Doing so meant paying 25% over the odds, mostly in 'taxes' imposed by the ruthless Tamil Tiger rebel movement, which was then able to buy more weapons and prolong its doomed struggle against the central government.[28] During the Balkan wars it was said that UNHCR gave almost a third of its aid supplies to Serb militias as a price of using certain highways.

As Linda Polman put it: 'Once inside a war zone, it's essential [for an NGO] to have a blind spot for matters of ethics. Warlords... deluge INGOs with taxes, often invented on the spot: import duties on aid supplies, fees for visas and work permits, harbour and airport taxes, income taxes, road taxes and permits for cars and trucks. The proceeds go straight into their war chests.'[29] Of course, these groups and individuals are merely mirroring the cynical and ruthless practices of many well-established Third World governments in the midst of humanitarian crises. But the fact that aid agencies may be subsidising the very conflicts whose harms they exist to reduce, should surely prompt rather more questioning and reticence than it has. Especially as in some cases the vehicles and fuel and food taken by or handed over to militia groups have spelt the difference between victory and defeat, war and peace.

The problem of 'shaking hands with the devil' has had more publicity than other troubling compromises demanded of aid agencies; it even formed a key plot point in *Beyond Borders*, the Angelina Jolie/Clive Owen film about heroic aid workers. However, it is still something that agencies don't like to talk about, along with the amount of money they lose to theft, bribery and their own mismanagement.

The multiplication of aid agencies and NGOs has arguably made this problem worse. When there were only a handful of international agencies, it was theoretically possible for them to unite and resist extortionate demands. Now that there is such fierce competition to gain access to disaster areas and conflict zones, and now that some of the major donors come from places like China, and the Gulf states, there are ever greater incentives for agencies to just shut up and pay up.

AID, NGOs and neutrality

As Polman persuasively argues in *War Games*, in several of the most deadly post-Cold-War conflicts the much vaunted neutrality of the international NGOs (INGOs) and some of the UN agencies has made them de facto accomplices to aggression, rapine and attempted genocide. At the same time, competition for public generosity and government funding makes NGOs less likely to admit to their failings or to the misuse of their aid by armies and militias. However there is a powerful argument that humanitarian neutrality is itself morally and politically problematic. And though one of the two great humanitarian traditions – that inspired by the Henri Dunant and the Red Cross – is steeped in neutrality; the other, largely inspired by the anti-slavery movements, tends to reject it. The neutralist tendency has been stronger for a long time and predominates in the aid industry despite the conversion to the cause of humanitarian military intervention of figures like Bernard Kouchner. It has increasing influence on, and some might argue distorts, the priorities even of national agencies like DfID.

This can be seen in aid community discourse concerning the role of aid agencies in places like Iraq and Afghanistan. The targeting of aid workers, especially in the latter, where humanitarian and development work has been part of the hearts-and-minds effort by the US-led coalition, has inspired what seems to be a neutralist reaction. Allegedly, the outsourcing to NGOs of nation-building efforts by Western militaries inevitably means that the Taliban and others will see all aid workers as part of the enemy war machine. It would be better, the argument goes, if the aid community separated itself from the US-led coalition and the Kabul government and went back to to the traditional strict neutrality practiced by the International Committee of the Red Cross.

It is rarely if ever pointed out in such discussions of aid and war that 'hearts-and-minds' work of a similar kind is carried out *by the other side* in these and other conflicts. Indeed, Islamist militant groups in the Middle East and in South Asia have developed long running, successful social programmes and simultaneously made up for the failings of weak and corrupt state institutions by providing relatively efficient forms of law and justice.

This assertion of neutrality amounts to a rejection of a more politicised approach to humanitarian aid work that became especially influential during and after the Biafra war, when several major NGOs and aid agencies including Oxfam took sides against a government they believed was committing genocide. The promotion of human rights and political freedoms was seen as not just appropriate but essential for humanitarian organisations, especially given the role of malign governments in causing famine. In Europe this approach was largely led by Bernard Kouchner, (co-founder of Médecins Sans Frontières) and other veterans of the 1968 left-wing movements. It reflected the migration of thousands of disillusioned *soixant-huitards* from political activism into NGO and humanitarian work, and also a consciousness of the historic failures of humanitarian neutrality, in particular the role of the ICRC as passive abetters of the Nazi Holocaust.

In the UK, many of the major charities engaged in emergency aid were already highly politicised and had been part of the *tiersmondiste* or 'Third Worldist' movement when that was fashionable. Oxfam, founded by Quakers as the Oxford Committee for Famine Relief, began life as a campaign against the Royal Navy's blockade of Axis-occupied Greece in World War II. Its focus shifted from famine relief to 'development' in the 1950s and after adopting the slogan 'Oxfam: Working for a fairer world' it supported various Third World 'liberation' movements. In accordance with its socialist ideological orientation, it developed strong links to the anti-American Campaign for Nuclear Disarmament.[30] Since the 1990s Oxfam has become even more involved in political activism and lobbying, taking strong stances on issues like anthropogenic climate change and intervention in Iraq, though it is continues to be treated by the British media as a neutral organisation of the on-the-ground aid workers.

Save the Children was founded in 1919 to campaign against the ongoing blockade of Germany and Austria, where children – and presumably adults too – were believed to be starving. It has recently been criticised for putting 'shameless political campaigning' before actually helping the needy.[31] And War on Want, founded in 1951, actually has as its slogan 'poverty is political'.

War on Want consistently aligned itself with revolutionary movements beginning in the 1980s[32] and its general secretary from 1983 to 1987 was the controversial activist and politician George Galloway.

It claims to be concerned with 'the root causes of global poverty, inequality and injustice. Such an emphasis on root causes apparently justifies the amount of money it spends on lobbying and campaigning.[33] In 2005 War on Want was warned by the Charities Commission that its campaign for the suspension of a trade treaty between Israel and the EU was problematic and that it must demonstrate 'a reasonable expectation' that its political activities will 'further its charitable purposes'.[34]

It should perhaps be noted for foreign readers and others that the UK Charities Commission does not forbid political activities or campaigning by organisations that enjoy charitable status, whether they be NGOs, think tanks, or educational institutions; only such activity on behalf of a political party.[35]

In the United States, on the other hand, there has been a stronger tradition of politically motivated humanitarian aid. The International Rescue Committee, for example, was founded by anti-Nazis to get Jews out of Vichy France and later became involved with Hungarian refugees after the

1956 uprising. Much US foreign aid was and is carried out by organisations that never embraced the ICRC doctrine of neutrality and which were happy to work alongside the US government and military, although there were some left-oriented charitable organisations on the Oxfam model like the American Friends Committee.

The involvement of NGOs like Oxfam and Save the Children in both humanitarian and development activities, and their relationships as subcontractors, partners and suppliers of personnel to DfID, means that their political cultures are both relevant and highly problematic.

PART 7

DfID Policies and Problems

'My ambition is that over the next four years people will come to think across our country of Britain's fantastic development work around the poorest parts of the world with the same pride and satisfaction that they see in some of our great institutions like the Armed Forces and the monarchy.'[1]

Andrew Mitchell, UK Secretary of International Development

16. The Latest Reforms

The establishment of ICAI (Independent Commission for Aid Impact)

ICAI, unlike previous official institutions designed to measure aid effectiveness here and in other countries, is genuinely independent of the organisation it scrutinises. (It reports not to DfID but to Parliament's International Development Committee.) It has four commissioners, one of whom is the celebrated Kenyan anti-corruption campaigner John Githongo, and a four-person secretariat. Its scrutiny of all British overseas development assistance (ODA) is intended to 'maximise the impact and effectiveness of the UK aid budget for recipients and the delivery of value for money for the UK taxpayer'.

The establishment of ICAI in May 2011 is a giant step in the right direction, even if its remit could be wider. However, it is obviously not possible for eight people to scrutinise all the programmes funded by DfID. These include thousands of projects around the world run by multilateral organisations like the World Bank, private aid agencies like Oxfam, international and local NGOs, as well as those run by DfID's own staff. Although ICAI's staff do make trips to recipient countries to see DfID offices and projects for themselves – and they make a point of flying economy class, unlike DfID staff – the bulk of ICAI's work is subcontracted to a team of consultants. This in practice carries with it problems of conflict of interest, given that some of the consultants that ICAI contracts with, are also contractors of DfID.[1]

That said, ICAI has already discomfited DfID and the Secretary of State for international development with its report in May 2012 on the department's support of education programmes in East Africa.[2] The report essentially said that DfID's staff in Ethiopia, Rwanda and Tanzania only checked to see if students or teachers attended primary schools on the first day of term but not subsequently, and if that weren't inadequate or misleading enough, DfID staff then neglected to check on the actual quality of education allegedly provided. The report observed that: 'The quality of education being provided to most children in these countries is so low that it seriously detracts from the development impact of DfID's educational assistance... To achieve near-universal primary enrolment but with a large majority of pupils failing to attain basic levels of literacy or numeracy is not, in our view, a successful development result. It represents poor value for money both for the UK's assistance and for national budgets.'[3]

It is a credit to ICAI's staff, and perhaps a reflection of the inclusion of Mr Kithongo on the commission, that it understands the deceptive nature of statistics relied on in the past as evidence of aid success: 'The assumption that has underpinned past donor support to education – that a simple focus on enrolment would translate into learning – stands disproved.'

Other reforms

To his credit, Development Secretary Andrew Mitchell reined in some of the more egregious DfID marketing excesses and indulgences that were endemic during the last Labour government, and which indicated just how extreme the department's NGO-influenced culture had become. The department no longer spends quite such a large amount of taxpayer money trying to sell its mission to a sceptical public. There will apparently be no more DfID stalls at summer music festivals, and the department will no longer spend £46 million over five years on 'development awareness' propaganda projects in the UK such as teaching 'global citizenship' to three-year-old children in Devon; the establishment of Brazilian dance classes in East London; and photography exhibitions, run by the Brighton Peace and Environment Centre and backed by Oxfam, designed to raise awareness of climate change and world poverty.[4]

However, despite Coalition promises to eliminate such programmes entirely, the department still spends some £3 million a year – that could go on medicines, mosquito nets or World Service broadcasts – on UK 'consciousness-raising', i.e. marketing, through a scheme called 'Global Community Links' or GCL.[5]

Mr Mitchell also claimed that a 'full value-for-money review' and elimination of £100 million worth of 'low priority projects' will change the system whereby, according to the Department's own reports, fully a quarter of DfID's projects do not 'achieve' or even 'largely achieve' their stated aims.[6] He seemed to believe that the department's new aid transparency guarantee and the practice of listing all spending on the department's vast website will ensure that DfID will be 'able to look the hard-pressed taxpayer in the eye, so that we can reassure them that they are getting 100p of value for every pound spent on development'.[7]

This rhetoric, unfortunately, was telling in its incoherence and apparent disingenuousness. Given that up to a third of DfID's projects fail according to its own dubious self-assessment procedures, and given the inherent uncertainties of development aid, hitting a 100 per cent success rates seems highly unlikely. In any case, the 'value' of money spent on 'development' – a term that includes multitudes – is inherently difficult to measure. Moreover, given the time it takes to foster economic growth and other goods, it is not necessarily even a good idea to look for an immediate measurable outcome. All of this should be obvious to any aid agency head with either experience in the field or a reasonable understanding of how development works on the ground; for all his other qualifications, Mr Mitchell (like his successor Justine Greening MP), seemed to lack both of these.

Mr Mitchell's attempts to make DfID culture less hostile to free markets or business seem almost as confused. According to one report, they involved paying multi-national corporations like Diageo and Unilever to behave more 'sustainably' in the Third World.[8] They also included having DfID give money to private companies in Pakistan which offer banking services over mobile phones.[9] Such services have been a huge success in Kenya[10] in the form of M-Pesa – a money transfer service run by IBM for Safaricom, a joint venture between Vodafone and Telkom Kenya. Though it was partly based on a DfID-sponsored pilot project designed for microfinance repayments – a project which may well have be been DfID's most important contribution to development – M-Pesa is fundamentally a private sector initiative that flourished because customers wanted it.

Changing DfID culture

It remains to be seen if either Andrew Mitchell or his successor Justine Greening have had the wherewithal to change troubling attitudes endemic within their department.

In both Iraq and Afghanistan, DfID officials[11] were perceived by senior UK military and security officials as being unwilling or unable to support UK government efforts to win hearts and minds for various reasons, including personal opposition to those wars, overly strict health and safety rules, or the ideological conviction that all aid workers must be neutral even if working for the UK government.

Indeed, in Iraq the refusal of DfID staff to assist the

military mission and their inability or unwillingness to spend the money allocated for reconstruction may have played an important role in the frustration of British efforts in the South.[12] In Afghanistan, the failure of DfID staff to move into Helmand province when British troops were deployed there caused a severe rift between DfID and the NATO command.[13] It also meant that DfID relied so excessively on unsupervised local subcontractors that large amounts of British aid funds were wasted or simply disappeared.[14]

Additional anecdotal evidence from Afghanistan includes the now notorious story of the Gereshk hospital washing machine[15] in which DfID staff refused to allow British paratroops to connect a washing machine in the filthy local hospital but also refused to connect the washing machine themselves,[16] claiming at one point that to do so would create 'a dependency culture among the Afghans' of Helmand, at another time that DfID 'didn't do bricks and mortar' and never bothering to visit the hospital. Together with DfID's funding of the little used and poorly conceived Bolan Leisure Park for Women,[17] these stories cast doubt on DfID's commitment, competence and ability to subcontract projects to appropriate local contractors.

Several of the large private aid organisations with which DfID has contracts are ideologically or culturally hostile to business and free markets and the idea of economic growth as the key to poverty reduction. Others have actively worked to undermine British foreign policy goals. There is no sign that this is changing under the Coalition.

DfID and consultants

Recently DfID's use of consultants and contractors has come under critical scrutiny[18], following an investigation into so called 'poverty barons'[19] by the *Sunday Telegraph*.[20] Perhaps the most disturbing aspect of the *Telegraph*'s revelations is the allegation that 'several of the best paid consultants are former DfID officials who appear to have gained substantial increases in their personal wealth since leaving the department, even though they still doing essentially the same work'. This could imply a troubling conflict of interest at play in the selection of and payment given to consultants.

However, the mere fact of the employment of consultants and contractors is not controversial in itself. It would presumably make economic sense to use contractors if keeping people with equivalent skills on staff at DfID would be more expensive. Nor is it necessarily scandalous that some of the consultants hired by DfID 'earn six, even seven-figure incomes courtesy of the taxpayer'. Some of these are, after all, experts in a highly professional field, and contrary to the *Telegraph*'s assumptions, work in the aid sector does not require a monastic sense of vocation and should not entail a life of relative poverty.

That said, in practice, as various Western militaries have found, it is all too easy for a culture of exploitation and abuse to flourish when the use of private contractors becomes the norm, and when those private contractors are generally former employees of the institution in question. In this regard the *Telegraph*'s discovery that DfID 'spent more than £20 million last year on hotels including many five star ones' is almost as troubling as the fact that DfID paid 'almost £500 million'[21] in 2011 to consultants, and that at least one of them, a former Lancashire police superintendent, was paid £223,683 in 2009 – '£20,000 more than the salary earned by DfID's own permanent secretary'[22] to advise the Jamaican police on matters of corruption.

Fewer countries, more focus?

It is difficult to discern any coherent set of principles underlying DfID's priorities when it comes to the countries to which Britain sends aid. Historical links, absolute need, a sense of guilt or obligation, strategic imperatives and political fetishism all seem to play a role in the allocation of UK aid but are no guide to it. The rhetoric of the Department and its leader would lead one to expect imperial/historical links or absolute need to play the major role. Neither explains why Britain gives so much aid to Ethiopia, or why it contributes so much to the Palestinian territories[23] whose inhabitants are per capita the most aided in the world.[24] The moral justifications given by the Prime Minister for ongoing aid to Afghanistan even after British troops are due to leave sits oddly with the decision to cut off Iraq entirely.

Under the Cameron-Clegg coalition, British foreign aid has commendably become focused on fewer countries. The UK is therefore stopping direct development aid to 16 countries including Russia, China, Vietnam, Serbia, Bosnia and Iraq. In theory this focus on fewer countries should enable UK Aid (as DfID has 'branded' its own efforts) to do more good with the funds it has.

Inevitably, the announcement that DfID would be cutting aid to some countries prompted furious attacks on the Department from more extreme aid absolutists within the industry. Andrew Mitchell was forced to defend himself and the government from charges of 'securitising foreign aid' – because aid to Afghanistan and Somalia would be ongoing while aid to Niger would be cut.[25]

DfID is also ending aid to five countries in Africa: Angola, Burundi, Gambia, Lesotho and Niger. The primary stated reason for this is that those countries lack the infrastructures that would enable them to make reliably good use of aid. (It is not clear why Francophone countries like Niger, which has long been a major recipient of French aid, ever became a focus for UK aid, albeit through multilateral agencies.)

Arguably some of the countries that will continue to receive DfID bounty, including the Democratic Republic of Congo (DRC) and Somalia, are even more lacking in such infrastructure and even less likely to make effective use of UK aid.

At the time of writing, it has been reported[26] that some *two thirds* of bilateral aid to the government Somalia between 2000 and 2010 was stolen or diverted, which if true, would make the UK aid commitment to that country look even more quixotic than previously. If that were not bad enough, there is apparently considerable hostility within Somalia to increased aid from the UK.[27] Somalis are all too aware that much of the money allocated for aid to Somalia is actually spent in Kenya where most regional aid agencies and NGO workers are based. They worry that their country with its growing 'economy without a state' will become dependent on foreigners once again.

It might come as a surprise to many UK taxpayers that Britain had actually been sending official development aid to gas-rich Russia, whose millionaire kleptocrats have bought up choice quarters of central London, or to China at a time when European leaders are begging Beijing for help with the Eurozone crisis.

However there is actually a strong argument for British aid to both Russia and China *if* it goes to genuine, effective and independent civil society organisations that promote democracy and the rule of law, and none of it goes to the government of either. This is not strictly 'development aid' and should probably be funded by the Foreign Office rather than DfID. Indeed it is arguable given the general failure of development aid to bring about economic growth in the underdeveloped world, and given the poor performance of DfID as a backer of governance reform, civil society support and anti-corruption, that more of Britain's aid budget should go via the Foreign Office, and thence to organisations like Freedom House,[28] which promotes democracy and supports democratic activists abroad, and Transparency International,[29] which has been of enormous help to campaigners against corruption. (A similar argument might be made for such aid to other relatively wealthy and technologically advanced countries like India.)

The cancellation of aid to Iraq is especially morally problematic given Britain's recent heavy investment of blood as well as treasure in that country's future, not to mention the responsibility that accompanies any military intervention. It is even harder to justify given David Cameron's promise that high levels of UK aid will continue to go to Afghanistan even after British troops are withdrawn. Iraqis could be forgiven for seeing the cut-off as the final betrayal by a dishonest and craven former colonial power.

It is a decision that seems all the stranger given that the five countries that are getting an increase in their aid budgets include oil-rich Nigeria, chaotic Democratic Republic of Congo, Pakistan with its corruption and sponsorship of anti-Coalition terrorist activity in Afghanistan, and finally Ethiopia – a country with which Britain has few historic or cultural links, and which has been credibly accused of using development aid for state repression.[30]

17. Problematic Choices and Countries for UK Aid

India

India, which has historically been the largest beneficiary of British development aid, is having its budget frozen at 2010 levels. This is not because of any change of policy or culture within DfID but because it has become politically necessary to do so. Even for DfID and David Cameron, it is not easy to sell MPs or the British public on sending £1.5 billion to a regional superpower with ten per cent growth, a space programme, a nuclear missile programme and its own international aid programme, while the UK is in the grip of recession. The justification for ongoing aid to India (and other rich Third World states) is that there are many desperately poor people in that country. India, however, has actually limited the number of countries it allows to provide aid, only accepting applications from a handful of countries (a development virtually unreported by UK media). In the winter of 2010-11, then Development Secretary Andrew Mitchell went to India to beg the Indian Finance Ministry to continue accepting British aid because, as the Financial Times put it,[1] DfID 'derives international credibility from its presence in India.'*

It may be and probably is the case that the Indian state has failed to provide essential goods such as clean water to hundreds of millions of its citizens. However, as a democratic country India has a right to set its own

---

*A year later, in December 2011, when challenged about DfID's planned spend in India (some £1.5billion between 2012 and 2015), Mr Mitchell then claimed that British aid was partly designed to win business Britain a contract for Typhoon jets. However, the aid turned out to be even more inadequate as a bribe than as a development tool when India then chose French fighter planes over the Typhoon in February 2012. Gilligan, A., 'India Tells Britain: We Don't Want Your Aid' (2012) *The Telegraph,* 4 February.

government priorities. For Britain to fill gaps left by those priorities, like education and public health, smacks of missionary condescension. If it is appropriate to send aid to a technologically advanced and wealthy country like India because of the presence of poor people, it would surely be equally justified for DfID to have similar projects in the United States, Canada and Australia – all former colonies with pockets of severe poverty, especially among indigenous tribes.

According to the IMF, India has the eleventh largest economy in the world by nominal GDP (Britain is the sixth largest) and the fourth largest in terms of purchasing power parity. It has three times as many dollar billionaires as the UK. It plans to send its first manned mission into space by 2017 at a cost of at least £1.7 billion. This is only a little more than the £1.4 billion UK will be giving to India in aid over the next few years (an amount equivalent to about one per cent of Britain's 159 billion debts). India is building a third aircraft carrier just as the UK cancels and delays its own.

If it were the case that British aid to India genuinely won the UK influence or friendship in New Delhi, there would be a case for continuing to subsidise the irresponsibility of the Indian political class. However, awareness in India of Britain's aid programme is virtually non-existent. Over years of living in India and reading the Indian press on a daily basis, I never saw a positive reference to British aid in an Indian publication. As a British diplomat told me: 'the UK does have influence in India but it has nothing to do with aid. It is because of historic links, business and relations with the Indian diaspora.'

Just how much influence and goodwill British aid bought when India was the number one beneficiary of UK aid in the 1990s was made clear to the Blair government when India's then Prime Minister IK Gujral reportedly declared that 'Britain is a third-rate power nursing illusions of grandeur of its colonial past'[2]. This belief is even more prevalent in India today[3]. And though Gujral was wrong to call Britain a third-rate power (by almost any measure Britain is world power and one that could depopulate most of the subcontinent with the pressing of an undersea button), there is something in the UK's insistence on aiding India that does indeed smack of delusions of grandeur.

Recently India reduced the number of countries allowed to send it foreign air to four. According to Delhi political insiders. British officials begged their Indian counterparts to allow the UK to be a member of this privileged quartet.[4] This should not be surprising[5]. Early in 2011, the head of India's main opposition party, the BJP, told Lord Desai that India today was in a position to take care of its own problems and that 'Indian states should be able to continue development work without British aid'[6].

Of course, if Britain's unasked-for and grudgingly accepted aid to India were actually doing a great deal for the vast sector of the Indian population that the Indian government has chosen not to succour, there would still be a principled argument for it. However, there is abundant evidence that here, as elsewhere, DfID (or its New Delhi staff) has lacked the competence or will to monitor British aid to prevent it being plundered or wasted.

Following revelations in an independent report on education released by India's Vice President in May 2011,[7] Indian education officials admitted that at least £70 million of the £388 million contributed by DfID to India's Sarva Shiksha Abhiyan ('education for all') programme was stolen or otherwise lost. The country's Comptroller and Auditor general also found that £14 million of British funds for another education programme was embezzled by Indian officials in 2005-6 and never reached any schools. In the way of so much state funding in India, some of the British aid funds were allocated to schools that didn't exist; others went to buy private cars for education officials.[8] In any case, standards and teacher attendance in Indian government schools are often so wretched that large numbers of the poor scrimp to pay for private education. Although the reports concerning diverted or stolen funds came out only five months after DfID participated in a 'Joint Review Mission' with its Indian counterparts, the scandal evidently took Britain's Development Secretary by surprise.[9]

A British investigative journalist who subsequently interviewed a think-tank expert in New Delhi on the matter was told: 'I am surprised that DfID officials work so hard to continue their presence in India. Is it really to help some of the poorest Indians, or is it to justify their own existence?'[10]

The former Dean of Education at Delhi University, Anil Sadgopal, a founder member of India's People Campaign for a Common School System was similarly baffled by DfID's expensively Pollyanna-ish approach to the fate of its education aid. He told an interviewer from Corporate Watch: 'I do not know what your DFID mean when they say, "Sarva Shiksha Abhiyan is proving to be very effective and remarkable progress is being made". What criteria do they use to judge progress?'[11] The professor explained why DfID's claim it had helped 'reduce the number of out-of-school children by five million since 2003' was nonsense: 'enrolment is not equal to attendance... you keep counting children on registers and if you find a number of children on registers you say, "ah they are there".'[12]

Sadgopal later told an interviewer: 'I don't know what the British mean when they say their free school project is "proving very effective and making remarkable progress"... I think the British people should be asking their government why it is funding such bad-value projects out of your public exchequer.'[13]

In February 2012, a furore broke out in the UK press[14] because of the revelation that India's finance minister Pranab Mukerjee had actively sought to terminate British aid to India in 2011 (calling it 'peanuts'[15]), but relented after British officials begged that it be allowed to continue. Apparently, DfID officials pleaded that cancelling the programme would 'cause grave political embarrassment' to the British government.

The revelation, only a week after India rejected a British built warplane in favour of a French one, represents further humiliation for DfID, Andrew Mitchell and the Cameron government with their insistence, against all evidence, that aid such as that to India buys influence and friendship. It should perhaps be pointed out however that in the leaked memo in which India's then foreign minister Nirumpama Rao argued for ending British aid by April 2011, her reason was not that India needed no aid but, essentially, because taking British aid gave a bad impression of India as a country with severe poverty[16] – or as the minister put it, the 'negative publicity of Indian poverty promoted by DfID'*.

In his inevitable PR counter-offensive, then Aid Secretary Andrew Mitchell claimed that: 'Our completely revamped programme is in India's and Britain's national interest… We are changing our approach in India. We will target aid at three of India's poorest states, rather than central government. We will invest more in the private sector, with our programme having some of the characteristics of a sovereign wealth fund. We will not be in India forever, but now is not the time to quit.' Overlooking, if one can, the quasi-colonial arrogance of the last sentence, it is hard to see why the Secretary, assuming he knows anything about Indian local government, would imagine

---

*It is a sad fact that the Indian political elite tends to be more concerned with India's image abroad than with the real-life living conditions of the population.

that helping the governments of 'India's poorest states' would make British aid any less vulnerable to waste and looting. It is even more difficult to understand why he would dispatch British aid into the Indian private sector given that it has exploded and is continuing to boom without state help.

The form of British aid to India that is the most effective, efficient and highly regarded (in India) does not come under DfID's umbrella and the Coalition government planned to eliminate it in 2011. That is the Hindi short-wave service of the BBC's World Service.[17] This reaches at least 11 million listeners, many of them in the poorest and most remote areas,[18] and has been of invaluable use to schools in such areas and also to civil society organisations that (understandably) do not trust the Indian government's media outlets. It costs less than one million a year to run, a miniscule amount of money compared to what DfID spends on projects and activities (including conference-going and giving[19]) of dubious or non-existent effectiveness.

Brazil

Between April 2004 and March 2010, DFID spent around £2.4 million in Brazil under the heading of 'government and civil society' and another three million in economic aid. Though DfID officials have claimed that the aid spigot to Brazil has been turned off, this is apparently untrue, with a British newspaper discovering that there were ongoing payouts of up to £200,000 in both civil society and economic aid in 2011.[20]

As with other 'BRIC' countries, given Brazil's emergence as a major industrial power with its own foreign aid programmes and regular real elections after which Presidents step down, it is hard to justify recent UK aid to Brazil. Unfortunately, UK aid to Brazil seems also to

151

have failed as a method of winning friendship and influence: at the beginning of 2011, Brazil signed a pact with Argentina and Uruguay to bar British ships bearing the Falklands flag from its ports.

One consequence of the lack of accountability and public oversight that generally afflicts British foreign aid policy is that it worsens the tendency to momentum inherent in all government spending programmes. This is the most likely explanation of why Britain continues to aid Brazil today, and also why it continued to give development aid to Argentina even at the height of the Falklands War in 1982 and to Kuwait and Saudi Arabia after the 1973 oil shock.

Of course such anomalies, as Peter Bauer called them, are all too common in the history of Western aid. He noted in particular the provision of Western development aid to certain Third World governments 'hostile to the donors, whom they embarrass and thwart whenever they can. Examples range from Nkrumah's Ghana in the 1950s to Nyere's Tanzania and Mengistu's Ethiopia in the 1980s.'[21]

Ethiopia

In order to circumvent corruption[22] and misuse of aid* by the once lauded but increasingly repressive Meles regime, much UK aid to Ethiopia is given out at a provincial level. Contrary to DfID self-congratulation, this strategy has not removed UK aid from political misuse. Provincial governments have turned out to be equally or even more ruthless and effective than the Addis Ababa authorities in the ruling party's policy of denying state resources to

---

*The fact that Ethiopia ranks 138 out of 179 in the Transparency International rankings, making it a high risk destination for British aid, seems to make it no less of a DfID darling.

supporters of opposition parties and rewarding the loyalty of certain groups and tribes.*

If that were not bad enough, the recent Human Rights Watch report entitled 'Development without Freedom: How Aid Underwrites Repression in Ethiopia',[23] which called for donors including DfID to investigate misuse of aid funds, and which implied that DfID's 250 in-country staff members had failed properly to monitor UK aid, was ignored by the Department. One British commentator summarised the situation thus: 'We have – unforgivably – allowed Zenawi and his thugs to use [Britain's £300 million in aid to Ethiopia] for political manipulation and control. Starving people get told they can only have food if they support the ruling party. Teachers have received donor funds – but only in return for spewing out official propaganda. One British-backed programme, designed to train civil servants, has been adapted to indoctrinate trainees in the loathsome ideology of the ruling party.'[24]

The high level of aid to Ethiopia – a country that was never really colonised and has long had a more effective state than any of the sub-Saharan countries – is also mysterious given a growth-rate that is among the highest in the world.

Sudan

British aid to Sudan will drop to £46 million next year, to be divided between the republic and the new nation of South Sudan. Two years ago, Britain gave the country more than £120 million. It is questionable whether the North should receive any British aid at all. It is already the second most aided country in Africa, receiving some $2 billion a year,

---

*As Michela Wrong puts it: 'DfID ignores the fact that if you want fertiliser etc from the state you have to be a member or supporter of the ruling party.' Interview, Michela Wrong, 5 November 2011.

despite its government's sponsorship of the genocidal Janjaweed campaign in Darfur.

Pakistan

Pakistan is one of the largest recipients of UK aid. Some critics object to the way that the £1.4 billion that Islamabad will be receiving from the UK exchequer over the next three years* effectively underwrites the irresponsible choices of the Pakistani state, and in particular costly and arguably unnecessary acquisitions by a military that is already hugely wealthy thanks to its domination of the country's economy.[25] Others are disturbed by the way the gift may be taken by the ruling élite as a sign that the UK government is not concerned by a number of serious derelictions that affect UK interests. These include the Pakistani state's failure to act against increasing violence against Christians;[26] the Pakistani military's notorious relationship with the Haqqani network of Islamist militants that carries out terrorist attacks in Afghanistan against government and NATO targets; the country's sponsorship of Islamist terrorism in India; the state's mysterious inability to detect the presence of the late Osama bin Laden in Abbottabad; and the state's manifest failure to take effective action against corruption and other factors that feed extremism. On the other side of the argument is the importance of Pakistani intelligence cooperation to counter-terrorist policing in the UK and the hope that DfID's educational efforts will successfully supplant the derelictions of the Pakistani state.

---

*The DfID website represents the commitment thus: 'The UK has outlined its aid plans for Pakistan for the next four years, which includes getting four million more children in to school, preventing 3,600 women's deaths in childbirth, and getting two million more people to vote at the next general election.'

18. DfID and the Two Types of Aid

DfID and bilateral aid

The UK has led Europe in a shift towards 'budget support'. Indeed, in recent years DfID has given 'the largest percentage of direct budget support of any bilateral or multilateral donor'.[1] As William Easterly and Laura Freschi of Aid Watch put it, this amounts to giving aid to poor governments instead of poor people.[2] In the aid industry, though, the conventional line is that budget support is more efficient than giving money to a plethora of donors, and that it builds the capacity of recipient governments to manage their own affairs. The favoured jargon term for this is 'country ownership'. Country ownership sounds good. In an ideal world it would certainly be better for the governments of poor countries to set their own priorities using their superior knowledge and understanding of their people's needs. However, advocates of 'country ownership' necessarily presume the existence of reasonably responsible and benevolent recipient country governments, a presumption that may be unjustified and sometimes belongs to the realm of fantasy. As Easterly and Freschi point out: 'how much 'country ownership' is there when the government is not democratically accountable to the 'country'?' They point out that 11 of the 13 countries to get UK budget support in 2007-8 were not rated as 'free' by the annual Freedom House rankings and that several of them, including Ethiopia, had particularly undemocratic and vicious governments. Budget support is easy to administer and superficially easy to justify, but also morally and politically problematic. By favouring it, DfID is implicitly choosing to favour oppressive and irresponsible governments over their people, all the while exploiting the moral glamour of 'giving'.

As Robert Lugolobi, the Uganda director of Transparency International has said, 'throwing money into a highly corrupt system and pretending you are helping citizens is a waste of public resources'.[3]

Moreover, as DfID's senior officials presumably are aware, bilateral aid is particularly easy to steal; it makes control of the government worth fighting and killing for, therefore undermining political stability; and it tends to undermine domestic saving, investment and economic activity.

DfID and multilateral aid

DfID's multilateral aid spend is inherently problematic, even though multilateral aid has become more rather than less fashionable in the aid world. Jeffrey Sachs, the now-rehabilitated economic theorist behind the disastrous shock therapy attempted in Latin America and Eastern Europe, asserts that multilateral aid is not only less ineffective than bilateral aid, but in the form of organisations like the Global Fund to Fight Aids, TB and Malaria, is the way forward to 'end poverty'.[4]

Given the proportion of DfID's spend that is delivered by multilateral agencies like the World Bank, the claims by David Cameron, Andrew Mitchell and their supporters in the press, that UK aid will buy goodwill and influence for Britain, seem at best disingenuous. After all, few if anyone in beneficiary countries will know that the multilateral agency funds come from the UK.

Moreover the UN system, which includes the largest multilateral agencies to which DfID contributes, is often much less popular in the Third World (apart from among the kleptocratic élites who send their children to work in it) than it is in London salons or Whitehall.

This is partly because Westerners in general and aid community members in particular seem to find it easier to overlook the hypocrisies, absurdities and moral travesties of a UN system in which Gaddafi's Libya was appointed to chair the Human Rights Commission. It is also a matter of the endless series of expensive utopian summits and conferences hosted by UN agencies, the most notorious being the three Durban Conferences on racism. It does not help that UN's Millennium Project Report of 2005 took it as an article of faith that underdevelopment had nothing to do with bad government and everything to do with a 'lack of fiscal resources'. It called for a massive increase in foreign aid to 'potentially well governed' poor countries including Azerbaijan, Bangladesh, Chad, Nigeria and Paraguay, all of which ranked in the top seven of Transparency International's corruption ranking.

Outside the UK and Western European countries, the UN's reputation has been tarnished by the Iraq Oil-for-Food Scandal – during which corrupt senior UN officials enabled Saddam Hussein to take at least $1.7 billion in kickbacks and surcharges at the expense of his own sanction-suffering population – and then the so-called 'sex-for-food' scandals involving UN peacekeeping troops and child prostitution in several African conflict zones including Congo.

DfID's contribution to European aid, is even more problematic, given that the EU's aid efforts are among the least efficient and effective[5] in the world. In 1999 the theft of EU aid funds by EU staff using fraudulent aid contracts in Africa eventually resulted in a scandal that caused the resignation *en masse* of Jacques Santer's European Commission. Another scandal in 2005 prompted the EU's anti-fraud department (OLAF) to investigate 32 EU-funded NGOs working in the Middle East. They were found to have been double billing the EU and either the World Bank or USAid for the same projects, and also, more seriously, to have been diverting supposedly humanitarian aid to radical political campaigns and violent organisations in the Palestinian territories.[6] Whole EU aid programmes, such as the $1 billion given to Russia over seven years to help clean up unsafe nuclear power plants, have essentially disappeared, with EU auditors apparently unable to find out where the money actually went.

In April 2011 a *Sunday Times* investigation revealed several expensive EU boondoggles including a Belgian project teaching citizens of Burkina Faso how to dance and an £8.8 million 'centre for migration information and management' in Mali that had found work for only six people in three years and manifestly failed to persuade Malians not to attempt illegal migration to Europe. According to the report, an EU-funded 20 km bypass outside Kampala cost more than £30 million and took five years to complete, but is already crumbling.[7]

A subsequent investigation by the *Sunday Telegraph*[8] in late summer 2012 found that the EU aid agencies (chiefly EuropeAid and the European Development Fund) that receive a sixth of Britain's aid budget) spend much of it on projects that have little or nothing to do with relieving poverty and in middle income or wealthy countries that are dubious destinations for development aid. The latter include Barbados, Russia, Argentina[9], Turkey and Iceland, and the former include a five-star hotel project in Morocco.

Barbados is wealthier than Portugal, Croatia or Hungary in terms of GDP per capita[10] and today is listed among developed nations, EU Aid to Barbados – understandably a highly desirable 'party' posting for aid officials – goes to projects that include a hospitality management school[11] for training hotel staff.

Other apparently inappropriate EU Aid projects highlighted by the Sunday Telegraph included a £240,000 art project in St Petersburg (Russia got £40 million in EU aid in 2011), a tourism promotion scheme in Iceland, and a

Turkish television station. Perhaps the most egregious example found by the paper was a million euro EuropeAid subsidy for a high-end French tourist resort in Morocco, to improve its 'energy efficiency'.[12] It is a good example of the ability of well connected French companies to influence and direct EuropeAid to their financial benefit, and of the way that heightened environmental priorities have made it even easier to misdirect EU aid to benefit wealthy interests. One might hope that those at DfID whose task it is to monitor Britain's massive contribution to EU aid would be well aware that the latter is very much part of the political spoils system in Brussels, a system almost as open to manipulation and corruption as the governments in Third World countries that DfID was designed to help. And that those officials would monitor EU expenditures carefully and zealously in the interests of the British taxpayer and the world's poor. The fact that it was a British newspaper rather than DfID's supposedly intrepid monitors that discovered and broke this story is not heartening in this regard.

It is worth remembering that the sixth of DfID's budget that goes to European Aid projects in middle income or rich countries counts towards the 0.7% totem, making a further mockery of that number.

19. DfID and NGO Culture and Ideologies

'[A]t every level in the structure of almost all our most important aid-giving organisations, we have installed a tribe of highly paid men and women who are irredeemably out of touch with the day-to-day realities of the ... underdevelopment which they are supposed to be working to alleviate. The over-compensated aid bureaucrats demand – and get – a standard of living often far better than that which they could aspire to if they were working, for example, in industry or commerce in the home countries. At the same time, however, their achievements and performance are in no way subjected to the same exacting and competitive processes of evaluation that are considered normal in business. Precisely because their professional field is 'humanitarianism' rather than, say, 'sales', or 'production' or 'engineering', they are rarely required to demonstrate and validate their worth in quantitative, measurable ways. Surrounding themselves with the mystifying jargon of their trade, these lords of poverty are the druids of the modern era, wielding enormous power that is accountable to no one.'

Graham Hancock, *Lords of Poverty*[1]

Culture Matters. This has become a catchphrase for some critics of Western aid efforts in the Third World. That is because, all too often, like the imperialists and missionaries before them, expat aid workers and their planners at home have failed to understand how and why their beneficiaries might have different attitudes to things like family, honour, honesty, civic duty and corruption. It is not a new idea (in the modern era it goes back at least to Max Weber) and Peter Bauer memorably observed that 'economic achievement depends on a people's attributes, attitudes, mores and political arrangements'.[2] But in terms of the success or failure of foreign aid, the cultures that matter are not just those of aid recipients but also those of the donors and practitioners of aid.

It does not take much time spent with NGO staff in Third World capitals to get a sense of the kind of person who becomes an aid worker. They tend to be young. (David Rieff has likened the humanitarian aid population to a 'children's crusade'.) They tend to be of the Left, with a suspicion of, if not hostility to, markets. Very often the people who go to work for charities and aid agencies abroad feel estranged from their home countries, just as diplomats sometimes come to feel a stronger connection with their opposite numbers than the citizens they theoretically serve. Some are fleeing failure or heartbreak or are seeking to prolong the pleasures of gap year nomadism. Among British expat aid workers, one often hears contempt for the complacency and ignorance of the British public that funds their activities and which has no idea of the misery the aid worker encounters on a daily basis. This is such a prevalent attitude that it is hardly surprising that such workers are not overly concerned about wasting the money of the British taxpayer.

DfID's institutional culture is unique among British government departments. This is partly because it is the only such department that exists for the formal purpose of serving the interests of non-citizens outside the UK. But it is also because of the nature and backgrounds of its staff. DfID is the most sought after department for professional civil servants (while the Ministry of Defence tends to be the bottom choice). Comparatively few of its cadre of able technocrats have a private-sector background, and its recruits tend to have the highest social and economic profile of any government department (including the FCO and the Treasury), ie they come from the most privileged and least economically vulnerable sections of British society. Most significant of all, many of its staff are hired from the aid community.

This is problematic because of the disingenuousness and dishonesty that marks so many aid community interactions with the public and because aid NGO culture is, despite all the rhetoric to the contrary, traditionally hostile to genuine transparency and accountability[3].

Till Bruckner, a former 'aid monitoring coordinator' for Transparency International Georgia, was notoriously[4] confronted by this when he found that ten international NGOs working in the Republic of Georgia refused to publish their project budgets. He filed a Freedom of Information request with USAID, the American equivalent of DfID, which had contracted with these and other organisations. When, after a year, he was given the budgets for which he was asking, it turned out that several of the agencies and NGOs had persuaded USAID to redact large amounts of information lest they suffer 'competitive harm'. Some agencies were worse than others. Save the Children asked USAID to withhold all information pertaining to salaries[5]. World Vision, according to Bruckner, insisted that even the amount it spent on 'visibility items' (t-shirts, caps, publications) to be confidential. Although one of the least open of the big international charities working in Georgia, it is a member of the Humanitarian Accountability Partnership,[6] an international organisation devoted to making humanitarian action accountable to its purported beneficiaries.

The self-righteousness and lack of self-questioning that is such a prevalent characteristic of both field and head-quarters workers in the aid community is all too common within DfID. The latter quality is intensified by the lack of sceptical outside scrutiny which, even more than lack of accountability, has encouraged and enabled poor or counterproductive aid policy. The revolving door between DfID and large agencies like Oxfam and Save the Children ensures that ministry staff below the level of the Secretary and his immediate subordinates are slaves to an NGO-style politically correct unwillingness to confront Third World political realities and cultural impediments to development. Similarly the inability to see the 'bigger picture', common in NGOs working in underdeveloped countries, has its equivalent within DfID.

For instance, one by-product of successful efforts to decrease infant mortality in sub-Saharan Africa is a rapid increase in population. This is because that decrease has not inspired cultural changes that would lead to a decrease in family size, and because population control has been radically unfashionable in the aid community for some years. While growing populations have historically been an economic boon in some Western countries, in Africa ultra-rapid population growth has led to serious social problems including mass starvation. (Nigeria, which had a population of 45 million at independence in 1960, now has 158 million inhabitants and is far from able to feed itself.)

Another unfortunate cultural characteristic that hires from the aid community tend to bring to DfID along with their expertise is an acceptance of or enthusiasm for the five star conference lifestyle. While DfID staff, unlike some of the many consultants hired by the department, are theoretically constrained to travel business rather than first class on long trips, the fact is that the global aid industry spends vast amounts of money on conferences where papers are given, abstractions debated and 'high-level' meetings take place – very often in attractive resort cities with five-star accomodation. Much of this conferencing is of dubious usefulness except as a networking opportunity and perk for Western aid professionals and a status-enhancing holiday for Third World NGO officials.

More disturbing to those who have encountered it in the field is the attitude of many DfID officials and aid workers to those who pay their salaries. The aid-purist culture fostered and exemplified by Clare Short took little note of the interests of the British taxpayer, the opinions of the British public or the national interest. It was and is solely concerned to help the poor of the Third World according to its own conception of helping. This is why, since DfID was created in 1997, its officials have sometimes behaved as if they were not part of Her Majesty's Government but an independent, albeit vastly wealthier, version of Oxfam. This attitude has made for poor relations between DfID and the Foreign and Commonwealth Office in many parts of the world. (Even the IPPR think tank has called for more coordination between the two departments.[7]) In what is in part an overreaction to the sleazy aid-trade deals of the past, DfID's ideological reluctance to take British interests into account in its aid decisions (as to do so would not be altruistically pure), and cultural inclination to humanitarian-style neutrality, has undermined Britain's ability to use aid as a lever for securing influence, goodwill, security, commercial opportunities and other benefits.

It does not help that arrogance, both moral and intellectual, is all too prevalent within DfID's walls. African leaders passing through London invariably make stops at important institutions and think tanks like the Royal United Services Institute and the International Institute of Strategic Studies. Their audiences usually include diplomats, foreign editors from the broadsheets, FCO and MoD officials, academics. But you rarely if ever encounter anyone from DfID. The Department is so secure in its conviction of expertise that it apparently does not need to send its staff to such events. It is an attitude that is equally evident in other aspects of DfID behaviour and in other parts of the world.

There are not many informed analyses of the fascinating, strange culture of the aid community. One of the few knowledgeable explorations is by the American intellectual David Rieff – a frequent participant in debates about foreign aid. In his essential book *A Bed for the Night*, he likens the arguments of aid enthusiasts to the radical comrades of his youth whose belief in the ideal of communism was not diminished by the disappointing reality of 'actually existing communism' in the Soviet Union and elsewhere. For him,

DfID AND NGO CULTURE AND IDEOLOGIES

the ideals of aid are commendable but it is actually existing foreign aid as opposed to those ideals that should be the subject of debate.

20. DfID and Corruption

In October 2011, the House of Commons Public Accounts Committee warned that DfID's new priorities and increased budget would make its already limited ability to control corruption and waste even less impressive. As Margaret Hodge MP put it: 'The department is going to be spending more in fragile and conflict-affected countries and the danger to the taxpayer is that there could be an increase in fraud and corruption. *However, the department could not even give us information as to the expected levels of fraud and corruption and the action they were taking to mitigate it.*' Even more damagingly, Mrs. Hodge said that the department's ability to make decisions on aid programmes abroad was 'undermined by its *poor understanding of levels of fraud and corruption*'.[1] (Emphasis added.) She was drawing attention not only to the apparent naivety displayed by the organisation in the face of flagrant corruption including the theft of DfID's donations in Kenya but also DfID's lack of staff with the financial and legal sophistication to understand complex fraud.

Disinterested observers of graft in Africa and Asia consistently cast doubt on DfID's claims that it can monitor its projects so effectively as to insulate them from endemic corruption. The corruption and development expert Daniel Kauffman, quoted by Michela Wrong, says that 'the idea that donors can immunise their projects in a corrupt country is absurd, it's not what the evidence shows'.[2] Sir Edward Clay believes that as an institution DfID is 'incapable of assessing the risk of aid being misappropriated'.[3]

More disturbingly, it often seems as if DfID officials are simultaneously cynical about corruption – exhibiting the bigotry of low expectations all too common in the aid industry – and naïve about its destructive effects. (By 'corruption' here I do not mean the petty corruption of an underpaid policeman's attempt to extort a small bribe, but the looting and grand theft carried out by politicians and senior officials.)

This tends to be exacerbated by a 'politically correct' discomfort with public discussion of corruption or any other pathology that might be seen as playing into reactionary stereotypes of post-colonial societies. This is often accompanied by a reluctance to acknowledge phenomena such as tribal pressures, the African tradition of the 'Big Man', and other cultural factors that may have thwarted economic growth and good government (while arguably providing other goods) in many underdeveloped societies.

Indeed, in the recent past DfID officials have actually undermined efforts to publicise and combat graft in countries that are beneficiaries of much UK aid, even where there is evidence that local governments are stealing or otherwise misusing that aid. This was certainly the case in Kenya in the mid and late 2000s. There, as revealed by journalist Michela Wrong in her book *It's Our Turn to Eat*, DFID officials were furious with the public stand taken by then British High Commissioner Sir Edward Clay against graft by President Kibaki's kleptocracy.

Clay supported whistleblowers like John Githongo who had discovered the 'Anglo-Leasing' scandal. This concerned the involvement of Kenyan cabinet members in 18 procurement contracts with non-existent companies, many of which had a UK address. Theoretically intended for the purchase of items like a digital communications network for the country's prisons and a new frigate, the $750 million Anglo-Leasing deals actually amounted to a transfer of funds from the Kenyan treasury into the plotters' pockets.

After July 2004, DfID staff in Kenya were reluctant to meet with Clay's staff at the High Commission to discuss a common anti-corruption strategy, while their counterparts in London put pressure on the Foreign Office to monitor and restrain Clay's activities. Clay believed that this was at least in part because DfIDs officials, under pressure to spend as much money as quickly and conveniently as possible, were anxious to defend their relationships, and protect their aim of shifting from project aid to budgetary support. Revelations of endemic, systemic corruption were therefore not helpful.[4]

DfID officials proved to be similarly hostile or indifferent to the import of the Anglo-Leasing revelations in their surprisingly limited dealings with the Kenyan whistleblower John Githongo when he was forced to go into exile in London*.

This bizarrely complacent attitude to corruption enabled the fleecing of the British and Kenyan taxpayer by corrupt Kenyan officials who stole a large chunk of a DfID-funded education programme. Over a million pounds provided by DfID for primary education went missing, along with much bigger sums contributed by other donors. For six years DfID did not even notice that the money had gone. Moreover, DfID officials had dismissed warnings from Clay[5] and others about the obvious risks of funding education programmes overseen by Kenyan politicians heavily implicated in corruption.

While the then Development Secretary Andrew Mitchell boasted that some of the stolen money has been paid back, the fact that DfID's supposedly crack monitoring staff failed to detect the theft was all too revealing of the realities that underly the department's rhetoric, and also its low expectations of African official behaviour.

As one Africa hand commented in an interview, 'the message to the Kenyan electorate from Britain is "steal away – we don't care".'

---

*In a rare example of poetic justice, Mr Githongo is now a Commissioner at ICAI.

DfID's cultural discomfort with issues of graft also manifested in the department's determined lobbying against the World Bank's nascent efforts to establish effective anti-corruption mechanisms under the leadership of Paul Wolfowitz.

The World Bank – through which much British multilateral aid passes – had long been a notorious 'soft touch', its managers largely promoted on the basis of the number of projects they managed to get approved. Despite its professionalism and the justified respect in which its studies of development aid are held, anyone who has observed World Bank projects in Third World countries is likely to have encountered shockingly lax attitudes on the part of non-Western staffers. In Kenya, the World Bank's country representative Makhtar Diop, a former finance minister in Senegal, actually rented his residence from the family of President Kibaki, oblivious to the conflict of interest inherent in such a relationship. Despite the Bank's embarassment five years ago, it has just appointed Diop its Vice President for Africa, betraying the same confidence as Kenyan politicians that time buries memories of past misdemeanours.

DfID, as Michela Wrong points out, 'has huge influence' thanks to its reputation as 'the best organised and least sclerotic'* of the world's major national aid agencies. It ought to use that influence to fight corruption rather than further it by continuing to aid corrupt governments.

---

*Wrong argues for greater conditionality to be attached to British aid, in order to fight corruption, and to ensure more effective delivery. Interview, Michela Wrong, January 2011.

21. DfID and the Use of Aid as a Moral or Political Lever

In October 2011 the Cameron government announced that the UK would slash aid to sub-Saharan African countries that persecute homosexuals. Development Secretary Andrew Mitchell had already cut aid to Malawi by £19 million after that country's courts sentenced two gay men to 14 years of hard labour. Uganda is the prime target of the threat because of a government plan to impose the death penalty on male homosexuals.

This is an example of 'conditionality' par excellence, albeit conditionality employed for a moral and legal goal rather than the more traditional World Bank-inspired ends of economic and governance reform. (Under the Brown government Britain cut its approximately £60 million annual aid to Malawi by £3million after President Bingu wa Mutharika spent £8 million on a presidential jet.)

Conditionality of any kind has long been a source of friction with aid beneficiaries. Both African governments, and perhaps more surprisingly African civil society generally, object to what they see as an infringement of sovereignty, a form of blackmail, and the latest form of arrogant Western missionary activity.

Indeed, even local activists under extreme threat of persecution objected to the UK's measure. Kasha Jaqueline, one of East Africa's leading campaigners for lesbian and gay rights, co-wrote a statement condemning the UK's stance that was signed by fellow activists from around East Africa. They said that the UK's threat to cut the £70 million that Uganda is due to receive in 2011 would prompt a backlash against the already beleaguered gay community. They also objected that: 'Donor sanctions are by their nature coercive and reinforce the disproportionate power dynamics between donor countries and recipients.'[1]

DfID and then Development Secretary Andrew Mitchell did not respond to these objections. Aid sceptics would point out that this was all too in character; the fact that an aid measure might not have its intended result, and indeed might even harm its intended beneficiaries, can be less important than the apparent moral rightness – and righteousness – of the measure, as well as its public relations effect.

Sceptics would argue that the primary function of the proposed measure was never primarily to help beleaguered gays and lesbians of Uganda and other African countries, but to serve a party political purpose at home. After all, the Cameron government's announcement of the policy was made during the week of the Conservative Party's annual conference and in the wake of the Prime Minister's defence of the decision to legalise gay marriage.

The righteous indignation expressed by the threat to cut aid on behalf of persecuted homosexuals seems even less genuine in the light of other forms of misbehaviour by beneficiary governments that provoke no such reaction by the UK government.

This should not be the case, according to DfID whose spokesman declared in the wake of the cut to Malawi's aid: 'We only provide aid directly to governments when we are satisfied that they share our commitments to reduce poverty and respect human rights.'[2]

Zimbabwe received £69 million in official UK aid in 2010, despite the Mugabe regime's persecution of dissidents and support of racist attacks on white farmers. Other oppressive and brutal states that engage in political repression, political murder, the suppression of free speech or torture on a wide scale but nevertheless received generous UK aid included Vietnam (£55 million), Bangladesh (174 million) and Pakistan (£203 million).

The Ethiopian government imprisoned much of the political opposition, though it remains an aid favourite of both Britain and the United States because of its importance in the war against Islamist groups in neighbouring Somalia.

The Rwandan government, though markedly more efficient and public-spirited and less corrupt than many in Africa, may well be responsible for the murder of opposition figures both at home and abroad. (At the time of writing, Rwanda is facing a 'withholding' of a £16 million in UK budget support – out of £116m p.a. – in response to its alleged support of rebel groups fighting in the Democratic Republic of Congo. The action followed suspensions of aid by the US and Netherlands[3].)

In India, the country that received more British aid than any other, security forces were responsible for the shooting of more than a hundred unarmed youths in Kashmir in the summer of 2010. The next year the state government admitted to finding mass graves containing at least 2,000 bodies of people 'disappeared' by the security forces.[4] Human rights groups have lamented the imprisonment without trial and torture of hundreds and perhaps thousands more suspected militants in Kashmir since conflict broke out in 1989, and similar abuses in other rebellion-torn states such as Chhattisgahr and Jharkand.

Yet none of these governments have been publicly threatened with a cut in aid for *their* misdeeds and derelictions.

The selective failure to use moral conditionality against governments whose behaviour would seem to merit a Malawi-style cut is perhaps most marked in the case of Pakistan, where branches of the state, while cooperating with British intelligence on anti-terrorist matters, also engaged in activities that ran directly counter to UK security interests, including the sponsorship of Taliban forces fighting British and allied forces, and the training of British-born Islamist militants.

Hypocrisy in the use of foreign aid conditionality regardless of its impact abroad is only one of the problems with it. Like so many foreign aid debates, moral conditionality raises complicated philosophical issues.

Aid purists and absolutists object to all forms of conditionality just as they object to the use of aid that is even partially designed to benefit the political or economic interests of the donor state.

There is also a powerful argument, implicitly expressed by the Ugandan activists quoted above, that the problems that development aid is intended to solve are of such desperate urgency that they must take priority over other political concerns like persecution and political freedom. Clean drinking water, adequate food, access to basic medical care and education, may trump other arguably less essential human rights. Though this sounds plausible enough, it is a version of the traditional argument used to justify aid to repressive governments. It can sound compassionate – aid should be simply about helping the poor, desperate and weak regardless of the regime they have the misfortune to live under – but it tends to ignore the fact that undemocratic and oppressive regimes are more likely to misuse, steal or waste foreign aid.

Certainly, many Western human rights activists would disagree with the aid purists and the African activists and support the use of morally or politically conditioned aid as a vital instrument for bringing about benign change. There is also a generalised sense among the citizens of donor countries, including the UK, that he who the pays the piper has the right, if not to call the tune, then to at least have a say about the registers in which it is sung.

On the other hand, the case can be made that to condition aid on what we consider 'good behaviour' is a form of demeaning, patronising paternalism redolent of both old-fashioned missionary moralising and the *mission civilizatrice* of European colonial powers. Africans and others should be treated as responsible adults and allowed to make their own mistakes with aid.

Even if you do not consider aid a form of reparation for colonialism or for the imbalance between North and South, First and Third World, as many if not most people in the aid industry do, it is possible to liken the giving of government-to-government aid to the handing of cash to a beggar in the street. In the latter case, it is generally considered demeaning and wrong to enquire of the beggar how he will use the money, to insist that he not use it to buy drink or drugs or to follow him to ensure that he uses it to buy nutritious food.

The issue is particularly difficult in countries like Uganda, Rwanda and Malawi that are (imperfect) democracies but are engaging in illiberal behaviour.

The debate as to whether UK aid should be used to bolster liberal moral crusades, whether selectively and hypocritically, as now, or with more integrity, needs also to be seen in the context of the declining significance of British aid in many beneficiary countries. African states in particular are increasingly in a position to choose autonomy over British aid, thanks to higher rates of growth in many countries and increasing levels of foreign investment, especially from China.

The diminishing effectiveness of UK aid as a lever – moral or otherwise – suggests that the way ahead depends on which of several competing UK government foreign policy priorities should be paramount.

On one hand, if African and other beneficiary countries are either strong enough or morally determined enough to prefer no UK aid to changing political direction, the UK should cut its aid without worrying that a humanitarian crisis will inevitable result.

On the other hand, if the UK wishes to be competitive with China in terms of influence in Africa and elsewhere – and Chinese aid and investment is very much designed to secure UN votes as well raw materials and business opportunities – then it would theoretically make sense to drop almost all conditionality. However, there is little hope of competing with China in this way. Beijing understandably prefers to deal with undemocratic regimes and corrupt élites and vice versa. (The latter prefer Chinese aid because Beijing imposes no requirements for accountability or transparency.) Britain can, on the other hand, compete with China by adopting an aid policy that genuinely refuses to subsidise undemocratic, tyrannical and corrupt governments.[5] As democracy becomes stronger in sub-Saharan Africa – there are now 23 nominal democracies on the continent – this could pay dividends in terms of influence. It also ensures greater development aid success because those studies that do indicate small improvements in growth as a result of aid do so only for countries which already have responsible and competent government.[6]

22. DfID's Own Accountability and Transparency

The establishment of the Independent Commission for Aid Impact (ICAI) is an important milestone in the history of British foreign aid, and perhaps the most important development since the establishment of DfID.

On the other side of the ledger, as Margaret Hodge has pointed out, DfID has a bigger budget to administer and fewer staff. It is hard to see how a smaller DFID can be expected to administer this increased budget efficiently. Moreover, even without a larger budget to administer, the cuts undermine the government's promise that UK aid will be more closely scrutinised than ever before. The decrease in DfID's staff all but guarantees that anti-waste and anti-corruption oversight abroad will become even more notional than it is now.

Government-mandated staff cuts could also result in DfID operations at home becoming more wasteful, or at least more expensive than in the past. This is because constraints on staff and hiring are not matched by constraints on the use of consultants who will perform some of the same people-hours at higher cost.

As it is, there are serious problems with DfID's bookkeeping, according to Mrs Hodge and the House of Commons Public Accounts Committee. As the former pointed out: 'Unfortunately, the Department has not always kept its eye on the financial ball, and in 2010 stopped monitoring its finance plan. That must not happen again and DFID should report publicly on its financial management.'

Finally 'accountability' measures are all too often illusory in that when donor agencies like DfID demand of their partner agencies abroad that the latter file reports and

176

evaluatations in the proper format, all they are really asking is to be given numbers that add up. The partner agencies and NGOs, all of whom have their own differing methods and standards of bookkeeping, know that whatever the truth on the ground may be, their contracts with DfID depend on sending back information that looks and sounds right. Their numbers are unlikely to be checked by DfID's staff: there are simply too many NGOs and subcontractors.

PART 8

What Works and What Doesn't Work in Aid

The current calls for pouring more money into the conventional channels of development assistance are, unfortunately, not a solution and are not even a move in the right direction. Many of the current forms of assistance not only are ineffective but tend to perpetuate if not exacerbate the problems of development.

David Ellerman, *Helping People Help Themselves* (2006)[1]

23. Aid Effectiveness

Sub-Saharan Africa is exhibit 1 for critics of foreign development aid. They point out that, since 1960, foreign transfers to the continent have exceeded $1trillion but GDP per capita has not only *not* grown over those five decades but has actually declined. Some link the lack of growth with the flow of aid, asserting that aid eroded the quality of 'governance' by encouraging corruption and irresponsibility.

Good governance and functioning institutions were not always areas of interest to aid analysts. Indeed, it was for decades politically 'not done' in official aid pronouncements to make any reference at all to corruption and waste by beneficiary states, except to minimize them.

However, *aid effectiveness* has now become as fashionable a subject in the aid industry and its academic satellites as *sustainability* once was. There are now regular large-scale conferences on the subject to which practitioners and consultants are sent. The most recent was in November 2011 at Busan in South Korea. (It hardly needs to be said that five-star hotel accommodation and business-class travel are the norm in such conferences, and that neither public nor private aid agencies make it easy for outsiders to find out how much they spend on such executive luxuries as they battle for the world's poor.)

What is most remarkable about the Paris Declaration on Aid Effectiveness of 2005 and the Accra Agenda for Action of 2008, which preceded the Busan event, is their implicit admission that during the first four-and-a-half decades of large-scale international aid to the Third World, monitorable aid effectiveness was not seen as a priority by either donors or beneficiary countries. These were decades that, as Easterly, Moyo and others have pointed out, saw

181

more than $4 trillion (measured in 2007 dollars) devoted to official development assistance (ODA).

As William Easterly wrote, for many years there have been 'two disgraceful problems' besetting foreign aid. 'The first is that the effectiveness of aid is often not evaluated at all; the second is that, even when aid is evaluated, the methods are often dubious, such as before-and-after analysis that doesn't take into account variables that have nothing to do with the aid itself.'[1]

Measuring the quality and success of aid projects and aid agencies is difficult and sometimes all but impossible, except in certain very discrete areas, such as immunisation. As leading analysts admit in a recent paper: 'there is no disaggregated data available on the impact of aid on the beneficiaries, which would be the most desirable measure of quality of aid'.[2]

It is worth quoting at length from a William Easterly article about the changes he believes are necessary to make foreign aid work:

> In the bureaucratic hall of mirrors that is foreign aid, nobody is individually responsible for any one result. So despite $100 billion in foreign aid in 2005, one million children died from diarrhea due to lack of ten-cent oral rehydration salts and more than one million died from malaria due to lack of medicine that costs twelve cents a dose–and nobody is held accountable for these failures... In the aid world we actually have, genial complacency is not the right response. The right response is to demand accountability from aid agencies for whether aid money actually reaches the poor. The right response is to demand independent evaluation of aid agencies. The right response is to shift the paradigm and the money away from top-down plans by 'experts' to bottom-up searchers–like Nobel Peace Prize winner and microcredit pioneer Mohammad Yunus– who keep experimenting until they find something that works for the poor on the ground. The right response is to get tough on foreign aid, not to eliminate it, but to see that more of the next $2.3 trillion does reach the poor.[3]

Of course, foreign aid is responsible for some successes including various vaccination campaigns and the widespread lifesaving use of oral rehydration therapy to cut child mortality from dysentery. Some foreign aid may even have worked as a means of helping nations lift themselves out of poverty, though it would be hard to prove that there is a causative relationship between the successful development of nations like South Korea and the significant aid they used to receive. As Easterly writes: 'Systematic testing would not just count the alleged "success stories" of aid, but also the larger number that got the same amount of aid as the "success stories" and failed: Guinea-Bissau, Somalia, the Gambia, Mali, Rwanda, Nicaragua, Burundi, Guyana, Zambia, the Central African Republic, Senegal, Suriname, Chad, Niger, Togo, Haiti, and so on.'

Some aid sceptics like Clare Lockhart dislike the language of aid effectiveness as being too focused on money *inputs*, rather than how and why development does or does not take place. She argues that conferences like that in Busan should be about 'development effectiveness' and about how to help aided governments make best use of their budgets and resources. 'If there is one metric that they focus on, it should be revenue!' An emphasis on aid effectiveness, she feels, only serves what is already wrong with an aid system that too often is just 'a subsidy system for third sons and daughters' in wealthy societies.[4]

Alex de Waal also argues that 'the real question is not aid effectiveness but what makes development work, in particular what makes good governance work'. However he also feels that aid effectiveness has been rendered less relevant by the arrival of China as an investor in poor, resource-rich countries: 'the whole debate was premised on European and American aid being the only source and model for aid'.[5]

24. 'Best Practice' in Development Aid

Aid is difficult

Development aid is an inherently difficult and complicated business. An activity as seemingly benign and necessary as digging wells can lead to disaster. One aid expert explains that during the rainy season nomadic or semi-nomadic farmers – (the kind of farmers who were the majority in Africa before colonisation) would benefit from the additional water and increase the size of their herds. But when the dry season came, the nomads would migrate to the new aid-funded wells with those herds, and the land around the wells would become denuded of food for the animals. The distance between eating and watering areas would get greater and greater. (A goat needs to eat and drink every two days; a cow needs to eat and drink every day.) Eventually the herds would start to die. And then the farmers. As Michael Maren puts it: 'Aid organisations were coming in and giving water to nomads, the gift of life, and it was killing them.'[1]

After a few years in the field the more observant and honest aid workers begin to notice some of the less salutary effects of the work: 'Food aid attracts people to refugee camps where they die from dysentery or measles or other diseases they wouldn't have contracted in the bush.' Some wonder if there can truly be said to be 'famines' when those with money – aid workers and rich locals – can buy all the food they need. Others begin to be bothered by the way their efforts enrich local businessmen and/or politicians who lease them their land cruisers and houses or who rent them lorries.

Good ideas often come up against local prejudices and cultural impediments. Some Western aid agencies tried to introduce the cultivation of sorghum in Southern Africa, sorghum being a hardier, more nutritious grain than traditional corn. To get people used to eating sorghum, the aid workers handed out free sorghum in their relief efforts for the very poor and hungry. Unfortunately this gave sorghum a reputation as 'poor people's food' and in the highly status-conscious societies of Southern Africa this meant that it was shunned by everyone who could afford not to eat it.

There are also no easy answers when it comes to delivering aid to countries with corrupt governments, partly because, by and large, those countries suffer from corrupt political cultures that influence the behaviour of even (or especially) low level bureaucrats. When DfID attempted to bypass Ethiopia's central government by handing out aid through provincial governments, the result was that the ruling party gained even more leverage over poor constituents. Bypassing governments entirely also has its dangers: it means undermining the state and establishing a competing parallel system, while enabling governments to avoid their responsibilities, like a teenager subsidised by a soft-touch uncle. It also makes NGOs a target for co-option and exploitation.

Best practice and least worst options

Within the aid industry there is a limited consensus on 'best practice', and the aid researchers William Easterly and Claudia Williamson measured the use of such best practice in a recent paper that attempts to rate the effectiveness of various major aid agencies.[2] Because it is hard to get suitable data on aid impact from beneficiary states, Easterly and Williamson took a more 'indirect approach' and focused on five criteria:

- agency transparency
- overhead costs
- specialisation/fragmentation of aid

- selectivity (i.e. striking a balance between serving the poorest countries and those that are freer and/or less corrupt)

- delivery through more 'effective channels'

Several of these criteria beg certain questions. For instance, Easterly and Williamson assume that technical assistance, food aid and tied aid do not represent 'effective channels', and there are those who would look at the histories of states like South Korea and Singapore and cast doubt on the notion that democracy is vital or even important to make aid an effective tool of development. According to the Easterly and Williamson findings, the Global Fund is the best multilateral and the United Kingdom's DfID is the best among the bilateral agencies, ranking second among all the agencies bilateral and multilateral. The various UN agencies rank very low.

Tried and tested methods

Two invaluable recent books, *Poor Economics* by Abhijit Banerjee and Esther Duflo, and *More than Good Intentions* by Dean Karlan and Jacob Appel, examine recent experiments in genuine evidence-based aid. The former in particular discovered that the task of making aid effective is even more complicated and unpredictable than the authors had previously thought. They describe a clever programme designed to cut down absenteeism at a school in Rajasthan, India: The school set up a system whereby time-stamped photographs were taken of the teachers when they came and left, and the teachers were penalised if absent without permission. The system worked.

However, when a similar system was applied at a clinic, in order to curb nurse absenteeism, it turned out to be a dismal failure. The monitoring equipment was sabotaged and the nurses' supervisors actually increased the number of excused absences for their workshy workers.[3] In other words, time-stamped photography can only work as a mechanism for preventing absenteesim if the officials overseeing those being monitored actually care about effectiveness and are not themselves financially or morally corrupt.

The data gathered in *Poor Economics* also confirms scepticism about microfinance, foolishly touted as a development panacea in the West (and equally foolishly condemned by the anti-free-market left in India and elsewhere as inferior to the old moneylender system with its spectacular interest rates). The authors found that the majority of microloans were not taken out in order to start or foster small businesses but rather to buy consumer goods like televisions or fridges, or to help pay off debts to moneylenders. The former is not a bad outcome – it may even assist general economic growth – but it is not what advocates of microfinance, including those within DfID, have claimed.

Mosquito nets and simple solutions

It is true that insecticide-treated mosquito nets could save a significant portion of the million people who die every year from malaria and the many more who suffer from the debilitating effects of the disease. (They are not by the way a perfect preventative measure as mosquitoes are at their worst at dusk and dawn when many people, especially adults, are not likely to be in bed and under a net.) They cost less than $5 each. However, handing out a free mosquito net to every family living in a malarial zone, as some have advocated, would not wipe out the disease. Dambisa Moyo points out that free nets given out by foreign aid agencies in a particular locality have put out of business local manufacturers, so that when the existing nets wear out and local people need new ones, there is no way of getting them. As William Easterly points out, when aid agencies hand out free nets, they are often 'diverted to the black market . . . or wind up being used as fishing nets or wedding veils.' However there seems to be evidence from an experimental project in Malawi that selling subsidised mosquito nets makes the poor more likely to use them. This would jibe with the belief of some social psychologists that many people attribute less value to things they get for free and more to those they have to pay for.

The Malawian nets were sold by clinics for 50 cents each to new mothers; the same local programme sold identical nets in Malawi's cities for $5 each and used the profit to subsidise its rural activities. According to William Easterly's *White Man's Burden*, the programme increased the nationwide average of children under five sleeping under nets from eight per cent in 2000 to 55 per cent in 2004. . . . A follow-up survey found nearly universal use of the nets by those who paid for them.' A Zambian aid project that handed out free mosquito nets found that only 30 per cent of recipients actually used them.

On the other hand, there is evidence that Africans are more likely to send their children to schools that are free (or which hand out food and other goods) than those which cost money, which would suggest that education, in that particular cultural context, is of such low value compared, say, to the possible benefit of having a child around to help with farming or household chores, that people will only take it if it is free.

Clearly it is difficult to draw large general conclusions from such experiments, but there does seem to be significant benefit to be had from incremental problem-solving that takes proper account of specific local conditions and needs. This would imply that aid should be smaller and more experimental, and in a sense more humble than it has been.

This is the notion that underlies William Easterly's

paradigm about the superiority of 'Searchers' as opposed to 'Planners' as originators and of aid programmes. Feedback is vital in such experimentation, as is competition. Unfortunately most aid programmes get little feedback from their beneficiaries, and the success of aid bureaucrats tends to be measured by how much they give away and whether they spend their entire budgets by the end of the year.

It is tempting to assert that small, private NGOs might be the best vehicle for such evidence-based aid projects and experiments, and it is often the case that small NGOs pioneer the most successful programmes. However it is also possible for small NGOs to be as arrogant and impervious as large ones.

'Helping the heroes'

One of the best ways that DfID could help people in poor developing countries if it had a smaller budget would be to increase its contributions to carefully selected civil society groups and to a small number of politically neutral but highly effective international organisations like Transparency International.[4]

Giving money to local NGOs and activists can of course be a minefield and needs to be carefully monitored. There is a great deal of corruption in Third World NGOs, and DfID has not paid remotely enough attention to corruption in the local NGOs that it funds. There are also political problems. For instance, in East Africa some of the organisations funded by DfID and DfID partners have a strongly anti-free market and anti-capitalist agenda and have arguably undermined efforts to foster growth and development. One such activist group, the Indigenous Movement for Peace Advancement and Conflict (IMPACT), played a key role in lawsuits against the British government alleging rapes by British soldiers training in Kenya. The suits, carried out in partnership with the British lawyer Martyn Day, resulted in significant payoffs by the UK government but turned out to be of dubious merit[5] or based on outright fraud.[6]

On the other hand, one of the most valuable functions of the aid business in Africa and elsewhere is arguably to provide an employment niche and training for dissidents who might otherwise be persecuted or whose skills would go unutilized by local governments.

PART 9

Conclusions and Recommendations

25. General Conclusions

There is an inverse relationship between the simplicity with which aid is discussed and the complex economic, philosophical, political and moral issues that it presents. That complexity is exacerbated by the lack of truly dependable economic statistics from the 'underdeveloped' countries where aid has been directed. (The fact that critics and apologists for development aid are able to claim both revolutionary growth in Africa and its opposite as evidence for their arguments is instructive in this regard.)

While aid enthusiasts and aid absolutists continue to avoid rigorous discussion of aid's real-life effects in favour of moral grandstanding, aid critics probably overstate the benign potential of some aid substitutes such as opening US and European markets to African agricultural products and greater foreign direct investment by China.

In the specifically British context, DfID's admirable efficiency and transparency relative to other international donor bodies amount to little when held against the institution's muddled thinking about priorities, self-deception about the feasibility of checking projects on the ground for waste and corruption, dishonesty about the historical effectiveness of bilateral and multilateral development aid, and cultural inhibitions about using aid in ways that might benefit the United Kingdom and its people.

In general, DfID's operations continue to be informed by an extreme absolutist view of aid that might be tolerable in a private charity but is inappropriate for a taxpayer-funded government department.

British aid continues to be presaged on ideologically conditioned fantasies and delusions about both the behaviour of political élites in underdeveloped countries and the reasons for ongoing poverty. It is also beset by moral blindness concerning the methods, culture and often unjustified expensiveness of aid industry professionals at home and abroad.

Indeed, the ideological and cultural obstacles to genuine self-examination and radical thinking within DfID are such that only re-absorption into the FCO is likely to result in an aid delivery agency able and willing to carry out responsible and reflective aid policy that takes proper account of British interests and puts both the desserts of the British taxpayer and the world's poor before those of the aid industry.

Future foreign aid should be based on realistic or pessimistic assumptions about the likely fate of donations to poor country governments, UN agencies, international bureaucracies, major global charities and local NGOs. DfID 'spends' should take for granted that dishonesty, politicisation, lack of transparency, lack of scrutiny, ideological reluctance to confront cultural factors are the norm rather than the exception.

Cultural reform within DfID

Success in UK foreign aid cannot and should not be measured by how much is spent. Nor should DfID be in the political business of spending taxpayers' money to justify its role and existence.

The dishonest rhetorical fixation on 'doubling' aid or aid results should be dropped along with other non-empirical aid-marketing gambits. These create unrealistic expectations.

DfID should no longer fund first- or business-class travel by its staff or by its hired consultants or by members of partner organisations to or from destinations less than 11 hours from the UK. That includes train travel to the Continent.

Britain's development programmes were a rich

country's indulgence even before the government's recent rhetoric about Britain becoming 'a foreign aid superpower' coincided with the beginnings of a global financial meltdown. Even during the boom years, one of the only certain outcomes of UK aid was the continued state-sponsored flourishing of the UK's small army of high calibre, indeed arguably world-class, aid professionals. (Thousands of such professionals flew business class to five-star conferences around the world, or enjoyed servanted lifestyles of quasi-colonial privilege in cities like Nairobi and New Delhi.)

The adoption by DfID of the cause of anthropogenic climate change has only enabled more confusion and waste in the spending of the UK's aid budget. Of the £900 million spent on climate change linked projects in the year 2010-11 (up from £61 million in 2007-8), much has vanished into vague consciousness-raising or 'leadership' oriented projects that involve the use of highly paid consultants. (DfID has at least 66 climate and environmental advisers on its own books.) This includes a £47 million project to help the government of wealthy Indonesia with 'more effective leadership and management of climate change programming'.[1] The success or failure of such an open-ended, unquantifiable project is almost impossible to assess in any objective way; it is arguably the very opposite of 'evidence-based' aid.

The heartlessness of the heartwarming gesture

Britain's spendthrift approach to foreign aid seems particularly questionable at a time when elderly British citizens face mortal danger from fuel poverty, when libraries are closing and when no funds have been set aside by the NHS or MoD for the expensive long-term support of severely mentally and physically handicapped servicemen injured in Iraq and Afghanistan.

Those who have uncritically supported the increase or even ringfencing of taxpayer-supported UK aid need to ask themselves not just how much the exchequer should be willing to pay to keep this particular industry afloat, but how much of the wellbeing of the weakest and most vulnerable people in the UK they are willing to sacrifice for that end.

At present the rise in British foreign spending could be fairly characterised as an exorbitant and self-indulgent form of public relations for the Tory party. To 'rebrand' or 'detoxify' his party and cement the coalition with the Lib Dems, David Cameron is apparently willing to take advantage of the real generosity of British people and simultaneously make life more miserable for the handicapped, the elderly and the otherwise vulnerable. More jobs will go, British servicemen will wait longer for their third-rate prosthetic limbs, the elderly will suffer not because there is not enough money but because money is being thrown at projects and governments that we know will not use it effectively. It means that a set of policies trumpeted as manifesting generosity is in fact a cynical, ruthless and morally reprehensible con-job pushed by marketing gurus for whom their real-world effects in the underdeveloped world are largely irrelevant.

Understandably concerned to protect a generous ring-fenced budget that has its origins in party political rather than DfID's own demands, Andrew Mitchell was remarkably creative and imaginitive in coming up with justifications for that generous budget, occasionally to the point of absurdity.* It would be a welcome development if Ms Greening and her department were to be even half as

---

*These include claims that as well as 'helping' unfortunates abroad, UK aid will reduce immigration, protect against terrorism and disease, secure massive contracts for British industry, and win tremendous prestige for Britain.

196

imaginitive and creative in rethinking aid policy for the benefit of both British citizens and foreign beneficiaries.

It would be to the benefit of the British public, British interests and poorer societies abroad if someone in the government who is not motivated or constrained by departmental imperatives, were to look at the ways that other government branches serve the various different and sometimes competing real-life objectives of British foreign aid, some of them altruistic, others less so. The BBC's World Service for instance, with its 150 million listeners around the globe, is a far more effective device for both winning influence and promoting good governance than many much more expensive DfID programmes. The UK military, especially when equipped with one or more aircraft carriers, is a far more effective and efficient provider of emergency humanitarian aid than many of the private agencies with which DfID has contracted during crises like the Asian tsunamis. Moreover, it is able to do so without subsidising or otherwise enabling predatory bandits, guerrilla bands and armies.

26. Recommendations

General recommendations

There needs to be an honest and public determination of the primary purposes of British aid, perhaps in the form of a Royal Commission.

After all, whether or not DfID's aid should come with democratic and humanitarian conditions is a political question that depends on the real purpose of British foreign aid. Unfortunately, the marketing crusade for ever greater aid spending and the simplistic, self-righteous and often dishonest rhetoric of Coalition ministers on the subject of foreign aid all but ensure that no proper discussion of the purposes of aid ever takes place.

It is a discussion that is all the more necessary in a world where aid actually buys less and less goodwill or leverage than it did before, thanks to factors such as the arrival of new aid 'players' like China, Brazil and India, politically motivated competition from Islamist charities, and, above all, the emergence of an alternative 'shadow' form of development in the lawless countries like Guinea-Bisseau[1] and Somalia where drug smugglers, counterfeiters and other criminal mafias dominate the economy. The threat that this alternative form of globalisation may eventually present is a good reason for the UK to do what it can to integrate poor African and other countries into the global economy.

The gift of aid can still be a useful tool for achieving various British interests ranging from the promotion of democracy, good governance, and political and personal freedoms, to cooperation in anti-terrorist and anti-extremist operations, and access to industrial resources, just a less powerful one than aid enthusiasts, whether true believers, or mere cogs in the Tory rebranding machine, like to claim.

But perhaps the most important reason for a proper, informed public discussion of the purposes, morality and practicality of foreign aid, is that in real life aid always has bad as well as good effects. Judging whether or not to give it as well as how to give it involves complicated and difficult balancing. This is especially true in situations that are depicted by altruistic extremists as an open and shut case. The perfect example of this is Zimbabwe, where British food aid has kept many people alive, but has also, by preserving the regime, resulted in the deaths of large numbers of people and the destruction of one of Africa's most prosperous, best-educated societies.

In Zimbabwe, where the government has destroyed commercial farming, among other brutal crimes, and employs nationalist anti-British rhetoric to maintain support among key factions and tribes, there would be starvation were it not for British food aid. The argument goes that it would be wrong for Britain not to help poor ordinary Zimbabweans who are not responsible for their Prime Minister's foolish policies; that if we did not feed them we would be victimizing the weak. However, that same food aid removes what would otherwise be an incentive for rebellion and enables the regime to use its financial resources to buy arms, pay its thugs and win elections. Though there is no easy or simple answer to the dilemma posed by Zimbabwe and countries like it (contrary to the urgings of aid maximalists and altruistic extremists), it presents troubling evidence that the aid that seems to be the most purely humanitarian can sometimes be the most pernicious.

The most important change in British aid policy urged by this paper, besides the abandonment of the ludicrous 0.7 per cent GDP target, is therefore that any UK aid body should have embedded in its core mission statement the Hippocratic principle of 'first, do no harm'.[2]

*Structural change No. 1: The BBC World Service Foreign
Language Service should be considered as Overseas
Development Assistance and funded from DfID's budget*

The foreign language service of the BBC is a vastly more
efficient and effective engine for the influence-winning that
the Cameron government has declared is a key goal of
foreign aid. It costs only £272 million per year, less than
DfID contributes to the brutal and corrupt federal and state
governments of Ethiopia.

Funds for the BBC's World Service should be taken from
DfID's overstuffed and unmanageably large budget rather
than from the Foreign Office's much smaller and severely
limited budget. The planned transfer of responsibility for
the World Service from the Foreign Office to the BBC
(where it will be an unwelcome stepchild) scheduled for
2014 should be cancelled.

Planned cuts to the World Service foreign language
services should be reversed, as was the case with the Hindi
service after a public outcry in Spring 2011. These
scheduled cuts include the elimination of Nepali, Swahili,
Kyrgyz, Indonesian and Great Lakes (Burundi and
Rwanda) short wave services, and all radio programming
in Azeri, Chinese, Vietnamese, Russian and Turkish. Many
if not all of these serve peoples whose poverty or
victimisation by conflict mean that they belong to the
category that Secretary Mitchell wishes DfID to concentrate
on. The BBC's proposed substitution of these services with
online internet services reveals ignorance or cynicism on
the part of the proposers:[3] the poor and illiterate tend to
depend on radio (often battery powered) for news and
information rather than on computers and internet services
to which they have little or no access.

At a time of rapid change, uncertainty and multiple
regime collapses around the world, the World Service's

foreign language broadcasts have more utility than ever both as a form of 'soft power,' and as a means of promoting good governance and democratic values. Moreover, its audiences in countries like Burma (where the service may be cut[4]) are actually growing.

Structural Change No. 2: Part of Britain's aid budget should be diverted to the UK military

Emergency relief offers the most value of any kind of foreign aid and, when properly provided with a genuine exit plan in mind, does less harm than good. It is also the kind of relief that the general public (largely unaware of the waste and corruption that often accompanies aid) favours the most. In recent years, some Western militaries, most notably that of the United States, have shown themselves to be the most effective emergency aid organisations on the planet. This was especially the case during the Asian tsunami and the Kashmir earthquake, but it has also been true in cases of political upheaval and societal collapse. At present, while UK military and naval ships and aircraft have taken part in evacuations, food drops and other vital emergency functions, the services are not recompensed for this from the UK foreign aid budget as they should be.

Given the threat to core capacity presented by the Coalition's deep cuts to the Defence budget, it would serve two complementary goals if some of DfID's excessive and unmanageable budget were transferred to the military. These extra funds would enable the UK military to preserve and further develop its already significant humanitarian capabilities. The forces' large helicopters and fixed-wing transport aircraft capable of landing on remote and rough airstrips are assets that can serve both a civil/humanitarian and a military purpose. Funding them through the aid budget offers a dual benefit to the UK and its foreign policy. Just five percent of DfID's budget over the next five years would give the MoD £2.75 billion to spend on dual use equipment such as C-17 transport aircraft and hospital ships.[5]

27. Suggestions

1) The 0.7 per cent of GDP aid target should not be enshrined in law and should be abandoned. Britain's aid budget should be subject to at least the same austerity measures as those essential departments of state upon which the welfare and security of British citizens depend. The 0.7 per cent target, already abandoned by most Western countries, is a mere phenomenon of public relations. If it were a genuine, empirically based altruistic target it would be based on a calculation of Third World needs, not First World GDP.

2) DfID's mission statement and corporate culture should embrace the Hippocratic principle to 'first, do no harm' and all DfID projects – including emergency humanitarian aid – should be evaluated in that context.

3) DfID, or any subsequent body formed after reunion with the FCO, should cut all development aid to countries with a space programme and/or a nuclear weapons programme. Any country with a space programme and or nuclear weapons programme self-evidently has both the money and the technological skills to achieve the goals associated with development aid. This does mean that the very poor and vulnerable people in those countries will no longer be notionally helped by UK aid. However, any state which has significant numbers of people living below the poverty line or without basic goods like clean water or power, while supporting any one of the programmes above, is unlikely to make good or effective use of British aid. Its priorities clearly do not include helping the poor and vulnerable, and its officials are all too likely to steal or waste aid intended for such people. Emergency

humanitarian aid should, of course, be provided to such countries if they request it, and private NGOs are free to fund medical, educational and other projects in areas that such rich country governments choose to neglect.

This means that the DfID's development aid to India should be eliminated. Perhaps more controversially, it means that DfID should also rethink its (increased) aid programme to Pakistan. There are additional powerful reasons for cutting aid to Pakistan that are dealt with in a previous chapter, and this paper argues that they outweigh the government's hopes that increased aid might somehow serve to decrease Islamic radicalism and instability in that country.

4) DfID should cut all development aid to countries with their own foreign aid programme. The reasons for this are the same as for (1). British taxpayers, if they were made aware that their money was going to other rich country governments, would not be happy. There is no fundamental difference between giving aid to benefit poor people in India and giving aid to benefit the poor of the United States or Canada.

5) This overlaps with (4), but the UK should not be in the business of aiding any of the so-called BRIC countries. The acronym stands for Brazil, Russia, India and China but, since it was coined by Goldman Sachs economist Jim O'Neill, it has become a symbol of a shift in global economic power away from G7 countries like Britain to a handful of rapidly developing large countries. The original BRIC thesis imagines these emerging economies dominating the world by 2050.[1] Since the beginning of the recession, it has been predicted that the BRIC countries – all of which currently receive aid from the UK – may overtake the G7 economies by 2027.[2]

6) DfID should rethink all its remaining bilateral government to government development aid as this is known to be the most subject to corruption and waste.

7) DfID should reconsider its recent commitment to focus more on multilateral aid. It should reverse the decision to distribute aid to notoriously inefficient or corrupt multilateral institutions. In particular, the provision of aid to the European Union's aid programmes is little more than a subsidy to European bureaucrats and an unacceptable waste of UK taxpayer money[3].

8) DfID planning and budgeting should take proper note of the growing academic consensus concerning the failure of and negative effects of overseas development aid over the last 40 years and the fact that 'big pushes'and greater accountability have both been tried before.

9) DfID should therefore shift the emphasis of its spending to emergency humanitarian aid. This is a form of aid that is unquestionably necessary, and that for all its pitfalls is less likely to do harm than many forms of overseas development aid.

10) Up to one-third of Britain's foreign aid budget should be diverted to the Ministry of Defence and the armed forces. The armed forces have the capacity to deliver certain key kinds of emergency aid more quickly and more effectively than any NGO or international aid agency. While being able to transport emergency food and medical supplies over large distances and in the most difficult circumstances and terrain, they also have the capacity to maintain order in refugee camps, to defend themselves from predation by bandits, rebel groups and government forces, and to avoid the Goma syndrome in which refugee camps become guerrilla

bases and aid workers become witting or unwitting abettors of war and predation.

11) A greater proportion of British foreign aid should be provided to local branches of Transparency International and other organisations such as Freedom House that genuinely promote the rule of law, democratic accountability and other aspects of good governance in poor developing countries. DfID should increase the resources it devotes to anti-corruption work.

12) At the same time DfID should more carefully monitor the local NGOs it funds for corrupt practices and political extremism. DfID should not be funding NGOs in the Middle East that support terrorism or NGOs in Africa with an anti-development or anti-capitalist ideology.

13) DfID should increase the budget and staff of its Counter-Fraud unit and Internal Audit Department. Both units should recruit staff with appropriate financial forensic skills or borrow them from the Serious Fraud Office.

14) Grants Not Loans. To the extent that the UK continues to give moneys to Third World governments, a practice that should be much more limited than it has been, those moneys should probably be in the form of grants rather than loans. This is because, especially in Africa, aid loans have tended to be grants in disguise – with neither side in the transaction expecting a repayment – and have encouraged irresponsibility and dishonesty.

15) End DfID funding to non-transparent or demonstrably ineffective partners. No DfID money should go to partner NGOs or aid agencies that refuse to submit to

independent evaluation for effectiveness. (Such evaluations have their limits given that they are usually carried out by people from the same cosy community or by consultants with little notion of realities on the ground. But they are better than nothing.) Similarly no DfID money should go to partner agencies or NGOs which are known to be corrupt and inefficient. This would preclude the UK's donations to the EU's aid agency.

16) Foreign aid should not go to utopian projects but only to interventions of genuinely proven effectiveness even if they are less satisfying or glamorous from the point of view of aid professionals and donors. For example:

a) AIDS *prevention* programmes offer much better value for money,[4] and can achieve much more good than AIDS *treatment* programmes, which one critic rightly called 'a gold-plated barn-door'.

b) Family planning programmes, deeply unfashionable in the aid community, for relatively small amounts of money, offer the possibility of many future benefits in poor countries, from decreased likelihood of starvation to better lives for poor women. They are challenging to implement, especially in African cultures where large numbers of children are seen as an unqualified good, and in some Muslim cultures whose men believe they have a duty to increase the numbers of the faithful.

c) Female literacy programmes, though opposed by radical Islamist groups in some countries, have been shown to have remarkable cascading benefits in terms of public health and economic growth.

d) Microfinance, though far from the panacea it was once thought to be, and only effective in certain cultures (it works well in Bangladesh with its matriarchal traditions but not at all in Rajasthan or Pakistan with their fiercely patriarchal and violently misogynistic cultural patterns), seems to offer some genuine hope for increased economic growth and to be worth investment by foreign funds.

17) The British government should offer tax relief for remittances by migrant and immigrant UK residents to their families in poor countries. Remittances have already proved to be an important source of economic growth in many Third World countries; such a measure would instantly increase the amount of capital flowing to Africa and elsewhere at lower cost to the British exchequer than any conceivable form of development aid.

18) The British government should publicly lobby for a diminution of, or even an end to the European agricultural subsidies that serve to undermine and impoverish farmers in the countries which have been and continue to be recipients of UK aid.

19) DfID should assimilate the powerful arguments of Moyo and de Soto concerning land titling and the importance of property rights to development and the world's 'bottom billion'.

20) It would lack the moral glamour and party political benefit of the commitment to give away 0.7% GDP, but if the UK government were to make it much harder for Third World kleptocrats to hide stolen fortunes in UK banks and to restrict travel to the UK by kleptocrats and their high-spending dependents, it could do more for development and good governance than all of DfIDs ODA programmes put together.

Flag up British projects and buy British wherever possible

If a UK development aid project carries with it the possibility of benefiting the UK's image or economy as well as serving an altruistic purpose, then DfID staff should make every effort to ensure it does so. There is no place for altruistic absolutism in official development aid paid for by the UK taxpayer. Anonymous philanthropy has its place and that place is private. Therefore DfID should publicise the British content of all British-funded aid projects, just as the European Union puts flags and symbols across its own.

Pure altruism and anonymous charity have much to recommend them, and it is understandable that many former NGO workers and political activists who have gone to work for DfID may personally prefer such activity. However, all aid distributed by DfID and its subsidiaries and partners comes from the compulsory payments of taxes by citizens. Many of these citizens believe the government rhetoric claiming that foreign aid buys Britain goodwill and gratitude abroad. This may or may not be the case, but there is little or no chance of winning such gratitude if DfID follows the path of anonymous aid. The argument that hiding the origin of foreign aid is necessary for aid worker safety is too often a fig leaf for purist agenda. In a country like Afghanistan, where Britain is a military combatant, hiding the origin of British aid actually undermines the British government's policy goals as well as its overall security strategy.

If the UK is once again to fund infrastructure projects in competition with the Chinese and others – and infrastructure projects are certainly popular in Africa and elsewhere – then this time around DfID should fund the maintenance and operation of any roads or bridges it builds. Such maintenance should be publicised appropriately with signs saying, for example: 'This road is maintained by a grant from the United Kingdom.'

Although one would not like to see a return to the corrupt practices that sometimes characterised the 'aid and trade' era (of which the most enduring symbol was the Pergau Dam project), there should be a prejudice in favour of buying British goods for DfID and DfID sponsored projects abroad. Arguably, this is required by an aid ethos that values the interests of the British public. At a time of severe economic dislocation at home, preferring to buy British tractors or similar is the least that DfID can do for the people who pay for the department's salaries and perquisites. Like the previous recommendation, such a shift would amount to a policy and cultural revolution in DfID and those parts of the British aid community with a conscious or unconscious disdain for Britain and its citizens.

Afterword

Even if DfID were perfect, even if there were no rigorous, compassionate and informed critiques of the whole enterprise of overseas development aid, and even if the 0.7 per cent of GDP were not an arbitrary amount with no proven effect, the 'ring-fencing' of overseas aid would still need to be reconsidered in the light of economic news that is even darker in mid-2012 than when the Prime Minister defended his aid policies at the May 2011 G8 summit.[5] After all, the government has cut police numbers despite significant law and order problems including the worst riots in decades; is cutting the Borders Agency despite heightened security concerns; is cutting defence expenditure despite the country being at war and the military having suffered loss of life because of inadequate equipment; and is arguably risking future prosperity by cuts in British education. In addition, some of the country's most vulnerable people, including the elderly and the severely handicapped, are being made to share the burden of austerity. Yet in this one troubled field the government insists on continuing as if the boom years had not ended. Whatever its political benefits for the Coalition, such a policy cannot be justified on moral or pragmatic grounds and should be ended.

There might be grounds for mild optimism in UK government aid policy, to the extent that the Cameron-Clegg coalition has put on hold its foolish, PR-led but nationally unpopular[6] ambition to enshrine in law its commitment to spend 0.7 per cent of GDP on foreign aid.[7] However this seems to have more to do with parliamentary tactics and the government's desire to spend political capital on other policies unpopular with Conservative backbenchers, such as House of Lords reform.

The conclusion of this paper remains that an effective and moral British aid policy requires a radical re-think. Given the current UK budget crisis, this would necessarily include overall cuts at least commensurate with those affecting other government departments. More important, however, would be the elimination of conventional forms of development aid, and a conscious effort to move away from the complacency, dishonesty, secretiveness and disregard for the opinions and interests of the British public that have plagued and continue to plague DfID's activities up to now.

Britain could and arguably should be a pioneer of a modern, imaginative, and self-critical minimalist approach to foreign aid, one that displays an understanding of economic history and shows respect for the agency and abilities of the people who live in developing countries. It would be an approach that recognises the risks of financial, political and moral corruption inherent in the aid project – both for its providers and its recipients. And it would recognise that neither good intentions nor the moral glamour of aid work are remotely sufficient justification for the harm that has so often been done in the name of foreign aid.

It should be said that none of the criticisms herein of aid industry and NGO culture come out of a lack of respect for the genuine bravery, selflessness and professionalism of individuals working in difficult and dangerous circumstances for the benefit of their fellow human beings. As a journalist, I have had the privilege of meeting many people on several continents who engage in quietly heroic, enterprising and highly effective work that unquestionably makes the world a better place. However, almost all of those individuals, young and old, well-known or (more likely) obscure, are aware of and repelled by the self-righteousness, self-deception and hypocrisy that all too often characterizes the aid industry culture. Indeed they have been key sources and inspiration for this paper, which is accordingly dedicated to them.

Bibliography

Books

Anderson, Mary B., *Do No Harm: How Aid Can Support Peace – Or War* (1999) London: Rienner

Ayittey, G., *Africa in Chaos* (1999) Basingstoke: Palgrave MacMillan

Banerjee, A.V & Duflo, E., *Poor Economics* (2011) New York: Public Affairs

Bauer, P., *Economic Analysis and Policy in Underdeveloped Countries* (1957) Durham, NC: Duke University Press

Bauer, P., *Equality, The Third World and Economic Delusion* (1981) Bristol: Arrowsmith Ltd

Bauer, P., *Reality and Rhetoric – Studies in the Economics of Development* (1984) London: Weidenfield and Nicolson

Bauer, P., *The Development Frontier – Essays in Applied Economics* (1991) Hemel Hempstead: Harvester Wheatsheaf

Peter Bauer, *From Subsistence to Exchange and Other Essays* (2004) Princeton, NJ: Princeton University Press

Bolton, G., *Aid and Other Dirty Business* (2008) London: Ebury

Boo, K., *Behind the Beautiful Forevers – Life, Death and Hope in a Mumbai Slum* (2012) London: Portobello Books Ltd

Calderisi, R., *The Trouble with Africa – Why Foreign Aid Isn't Working* (2006) Basingstoke: Palgrave MacMillan

Collier, P., *The Bottom Billion* (2007) Oxford: Oxford University Press

Dowden, R., *Africa – Altered States, Ordinary Miracles* (2009) New York: Public Affairs

Easterly, W., *The White Man's Burden* (2006) Oxford: Oxford University Press

Ellerman, D., *Helping People Help Themselves* (2005) Ann Arbor, MI: University of Michigan Press

Ghani, A. & Lockhart, C., *Fixing Failed States* (2008) Oxford: Oxford University Press

Glennie, J., *The Trouble with Aid – Why Less Could Mean More for Africa* (2008) London: Zed Books

Hancock, G., *Lords of Poverty* (1989) London: Mandarin Publishing

Harrison, L., *Underdevelopment is a State of Mind – The Latin American Case* (2000) New York: Derrydale Press

Kapuscinski, R., *The Shadow of the Sun: My African Life* (2002) London: Penguin

Maren, M., *The Road to Hell – The Ravaging Effects of Foreign Aid and International Charity* (1997) New York: Free Press

Morris, J., *Sustainable Development* (2002) London: Profile

Moyo, D., *Dead Aid* (2009) London: Penguin

Nutt, S., *Damned Nations – Greed, Guns, Armies and Aid* (2011) New York: Random House

Polman, L., *War Games: The Story of Aid and War in Modern Times* (2010) London: Viking

Rieff, D., *A Bed for the Night* (2003) New York: Simon & Schuster

Schwartz, T., *Travesty in Haiti: A True Account of Christian Missions, Orphanages, Fraud, Food Aid and Drug Trafficking* (2008) Charleston, SC: BookSurge Publishing

Terry, F., *Condemned to Repeat – The Paradox of Humanitarian Action* (2002) Ithica, NY: Cornell University Press

de Waal, A., *Famine Crimes – Politics and the Disaster Relief Industry* (2009) Bloomington, IN: Indiana University Press

Wrong, M., *It's Our Turn to Eat* (2009) London: Fourth Estate

Articles and Papers

Abuzeid, A., 'Foreign Aid and the "Big Push" Theory: Lessons from sub-Saharan Africa' (2009) *Stanford Journal of International Relations*, 14 (1), pp.16-23

AFP, 'Cuts in Aid Putting Lives at Risk Warns Oxfam' (2012) AFP, 7 April. At: http://www.google.com/hostednews/afp/article/ALeqM5jXVhQjPR-OFHkJZIYBl-uZongvnQ?docId=CNG.cf996c196adcad68ef31bfc0abf4d3a4.171 [accessed October 17 2012]

Bauer, P., 'Development Aid – End It or Mend It' (1993) *International Center for Economic Growth*, Occasional Paper 43, San Fransisco, CA: ICS Press. At: http://pdf.usaid.gov/pdf_docs/PNABS408.pdf [accessed September 18 2012]

BBC News, 'EU Aid is a Disgrace Says Short' (2002) BBC News, 31 July. At: http://news.bbc.co.uk/1/hi/uk_politics/2163865.stm [accessed October 17 2012]

Bell, T., 'International Development Department Spent £32,000 Renovating Nepal Place' (2011) *The Telegraph*, 6 September. At: http://www.telegraph.co.uk/news/worldnews/asia/nepal/8740277/International-Development-department-spent-32000-renovating-Nepal-palace.html [accessed September 18 2012]

Birrell, I., 'Ten Great Myths about Foreign Aid: After Cameron Described Critics as "Hard-Hearted", How Your Money is Squandered' (2011) *The Daily Mail*, 7 July. At: http://www.dailymail.co.uk/news/article-2012074/David-Camerons-foreign-aid-How-money-squandered.html [accessed September 18 2012]

Booth, D., 'Aid Effectiveness: Bringing Country Ownership (and Politics) Back In' (2011) *Overseas Development Institute*, Working Paper 336, August. At: http://www.odi.org.uk/resources/docs/6028.pdf [accessed September 18 2012]

Brautigam, D. & Knack, S., 'Foreign Aid, Institutions, and Governance in Sub- Saharan Africa' (2004) *Economic Development and Cultural Change*, 52 (2), pp.255-285

Brennan, Z., 'Sorry Bob Geldof: Band Aid DID Pay for Guns: Charity's Man in Ethiopia Tells his Disturbing Story' (2010) *The Daily Mail*, 19 March. At: http://www.dailymail.co.uk/news/article-1259061/Sorry-Bob-Geldof-Band-Aid-millions-DID-pay-guns.html [accessed September 18 2012]

Boerema, D., 'Foreign Aid Keeps Nepal Going' (2011) *Radio Netherlands Worldwide*, 6 September. At: http://www.rnw.nl/english/article/foreign-aid-keeps-nepal-going [accessed September 18 2012]

Bruckner, T., 'Accountability in International Aid: The Case of Georgia' (2011) *University of Bristol*, PhD Thesis. At: http://www.scribd.com/doc/65675944/Accountability-in-International-Aid-The-Case-of-Georgia-by-Till-Bruckner-2011 [accessed 18 September 2012]

Dejevsky, M., 'Maru Dejevsky: Oxfam is There to Help People, Not to Dabble in Politics' (2009) *The Independent*, 9 January. At: http://www.independent.co.uk/voices/commentators/mary-dejevsky/mary-dejevsky-oxfam-is-there-to-help-people-ndash-not-to-dabble-in-politics-1242499.html [accessed September 18 2012]

Easterly, W., 'How and How Not to Stop AIDS in Africa: Book Review of *The Invisible Cure: Africa, the West and the Fight Against AIDS* by Helen Epstein,' (2007) *New York Review of Books*, 16 August. At: http://www.nybooks.com/articles/archives/2007/aug/16/how-and-how-not-to-stop-aids-in-africa/?pagination=false [accessed September 18 2012]

Eberstadt, N., 'The Global Poverty Paradox' (2010) *Commentary Magazine*, October. At: http://www.commentarymagazine.com/article/the-global-poverty-paradox/ [accessed September 18 2012]

Epstein, H., 'Cruel Ethiopia' (2010) *New York Review of Books*, 13 May. At: http://www.nybooks.com/articles/archives/2010/may/13/cruel-ethiopia/ [accessed 18 September]

Foreman, J., 'Pakistan: Free to Learn' (2008) *The Telegraph*, 16 February. At: http://www.telegraph.co.uk/culture/ books/3671228/Pakistan-Free-to-learn.html [accessed October 17 2012]

Ghimire, L.S., 'Performance and Effective of Foreign Aid in Napal' (2009) *Nepalese Economic Review*, 14 June. At: http://www.ner.com.np/vol-1/issue-2/54-performance-and-effectiveness-of-foreign-aid-in-nepal.html [accessed 18 September]

Gourevitch, P., 'Alms Dealers' (2010) *The New Yorker*, 11 October. At: http://www.newyorker.com/arts/critics/ atlarge/2010/10/11/101011crat_atlarge_gourevitch [accessed September 18 2012]

Groves, J., 'Foreign Aid Budget to Cost Every Family £500: How 17 Foreign Aid Fat Cats are Earning More than £90,000' (2010) *The Daily Mail*, 22 October. At: http://www.dailymail.co.uk/news/article-1322745/Foreign-aid-budget-cost-family-500-Fat-cats-earning-90k.html [accessed September 18 2012]

Hartford, T & Klein, M, 'Aid and the Resource Curse' (2005) *World Bank*, World Bank Note Number 291, April. At: http://rru.worldbank.org/documents/publicpolicyjournal/29 1harford_klein.pdf [accessed October 17 2012]

Hermitage, S., 'Tanzania: Is UK Aid Meeting Its Purpose' (2011) *The African Executive*, 21-28 December. At: http://www.africanexecutive.com/modules/magazine/article s.php?article=6277 [accessed September 18 2012]

Horrocks, P., 'Bob, Band Aid and How the Rebels Bought their Arms' (2010) *BBC News*, 6 March. At: http://www.bbc.co.uk/ blogs/theeditors/2010/03/ethiopia.html [accessed September 18 2012]

House of Commons, 'DfID Financial Management' (2011), *House of Commons Public Accounts Committee*, Fifty-Second Report, 12 Oct. At: http://www.publications.parliament.uk/ pa/cm201012/cmselect/cmpubacc/1398/1398.pdf [accessed September 18 2012]

House of Lords, 'The Economic Impact and Effectiveness of Development Aid' (2012) *House of Lords Economic Affairs Committee*, Sixth Report, 20 March. At: http://www.publications.parliament.uk/pa/ld201012/ldselect/ldeconaf/278/27802.htm [accessed September 18 2012]

Kristof, N., 'Aid – Can it Work?' (2006) *New York Review of Books*, 5 October. At: http://www.nybooks.com/articles/archives/2006/dec/21/how-aid-can-work/?pagination=false [accessed September 18 2012]

Malone, D., 'Nepal Should Not Depend on Foreign Aid, Says Former Envoy' (2010) *The Himalayan Times*, 30 April. At: http://www.thehimalayantimes.com/fullNews.php?headline=Nepal+should+not+depend+on+foreign+aid,+says+former+envoy&NewsID=241939 [accessed 18 September]

Peev, G., 'Why are We Giving £1bn Aid to India? A Nation with Three Times as Many Billionaires as We Have (and its own Space Programme)' (2011), *The Daily Mail*, 15 February. At: http://www.dailymail.co.uk/news/article-1357056/Britains-1bn-aid-India-nation-3-times-billionaires-have.html [accessed September 18 2012]

Rajan, R., & Subramanian, A., 'What Might Prevent Aid from Enhancing Growth' (2005) *International Monetary Fund*, Washington, DC

Reitman, J., 'Beyond Relief – How the World Failed Haiti' (2011) *Rolling Stone*, 4 August. At: http://www.rollingstone.com/politics/news/how-the-world-failed-haiti-20110804 [accessed September 18 2012]

Rieff, D., 'Charity on the Rampage: The Business of Foreign Aid' (1997) *Foreign Affairs*, Jan/Feb 1997. At: http://www.foreignaffairs.com/articles/52653/david-rieff/charity-on-the-rampage-the-business-of-foreign-aid [accessed September 18 2012]

Rieff, D., 'Cruel to be Kind' (2005) *The Guardian*, 24 June. At:
http://www.guardian.co.uk/world/2005/jun/24/g8.debtrelie
f [accessed September 18 2012]

Shipman, T., 'Foreign Aid Millions Wasted on Taxis and Doing
Up the Office (and That Was the ONLY Area to Get Increase
During the Spending Review)' (2010) *The Daily Mail*, 28
October. At: http://www.dailymail.co.uk/news/article-
1324322/Foreign-aid-millions-wasted-taxis-doing-office.html
[accessed September 18 2012]

Sweeney, M., 'Oxfam Climate Change Ad Cleared by
Regulator' (2010) The Guardian, 27 October. At:
http://www.guardian.co.uk/media/2010/oct/27/oxfam-
climate-change-ad-cleared [accessed 17 October 2012]

Wilson, E.B., 'The NGO Culture of Nepal' (2009) *Continuity
Blog*, 29 June. At: http://dpalbeu.blogspot.co.uk/2009/06/
ngo-culture-of-nepal.html [accessed September 18 2012]

Wolf, D., 'What Happened to the F***ing Money' (2009) *The
Spectator*, July 31. At: http://staging.spectator.co.uk/comic/
what-happened-to-the-fing-money/ [accessed September 18
2012]

Video

Johnstone, C., 'The Aid Debate' (2011) *Oslo Freedom Forum*, 9-11
May. At: http://www.oslofreedomforum.com/speakers/
The_Aid_Debate.html [accessed 18 September 2012]

Lehrer, B., 'Aid to Africa Debate. Motion: Aid to Africa is Doing
More Harm Than Good' (2007) *Intelligence Squared*, 4 December.
At: http://www.youtube.com/watch?v=6x7_Ld5bqQY
[accessed 18 September 2012]

Moyo, D., 'Is Aid Killing Africa? Dambisa Moyo talks about
Dead Aid on ABC' (2009) *Dambisamoyo*, 4 May. At:
http://www.youtube.com/watch?v=HIPvlQOCfAQ&feature=
related [accessed 18 September 2012]

Interviews conducted for this book

George Ayittey, economist & President of the Free Africa Foundation, November 2011

Sir Edward Clay, former British diplomat & Africa expert, November 20 2011and subsequently

Baroness Caroline Cox, CEO of the Humanitarian Aid Relief Trust, November 20-21 2010

Alexander Evans, British Diplomatic Service counsellor & Jackson Institute for International Affairs, 16 May 2011

Peter Godwin, author & journalist, January 4 2012

Justine Hardy, Aid worker & founder of Kashmir Lifeline, October 15 2011 & January 6 2012

Malcom Harper, Professor of Enterprise Development, October 18 2011

Mary Harper, BBC World Service Correspondent East Africa, October 18 2011

Lisa Heydlauff, Director of Going to School & Founder of Be! Fund, January 15 2012

Maureen Lines, Hindu Kush Conservation Association (Pakistan), December 2007 & January 2011

Clare Lockhart, CEO of the Institute for State Effectiveness, November 28 2011

Miles Morland, Development Partners International, January 30, 2012

Greg Mortenson, executive director of the Central Asia Institute, December 16-18 2008

Tara O'Connor, Africa Expert & head of Africa Risk Consulting, November 8 2011 & April 17 2012

Rakiya Omaar, Co-Director of Africa Rights, March 11 2010

James Shepherd-Barron, Disaster Response Expert & Contractor for DfID, November 5 2011

Alex de Waal, Executive Director of the World Peace Foundation & Africa expert, December 23 2011

Michela Wrong, journalist & Africa expert, January 2011 & November 5 2011 (and subsequently by phone and email)

Notes

Introduction

1   Relief Web, 'Generosity of British Public Makes East Africa Emergency Appeal Most Successful Ever' (2011) 26 December. At: http://www.reliefweb.int/node/467082 [accessed October 17 2012].

2   For instance, Britain's Prime Minister David Cameron has dismissed as 'hard-hearted' those troubled by his commitment to increased foreign aid at a time of economic crisis. Stratton, A., 'David Cameron Dismisses Critics of International Aid as "Hard-Hearted"' (2011) *The Guardian*, 5 July. At: http://www.guardian.co.uk/global-development/2011/jul/05/david-cameron-dismisses-international-aid-critics [accessed October 17 2012].

3   Flintoff, C., 'Is Aid to Africa Doing More Harm than Good?' (2007) *National Public Radio*, 12 December. At: http://www.npr.org/templates/story/story.php?storyId=17095866 [accessed October 17 2012].

4   William Easterly, *The White Man's Burden: Why the West's Efforts to Aid the Rest Have Done So Much Ill And So Little Good*, p. 4.

5   David Rieff, *A Bed for the Night*, p.275. It is worth giving the full quote: 'It is the aura of sanctity around aid workers – a reputation that had much to do with the image, repeated ad nauseam in the Western media, of the pieta-like image of the Western nurse cradling a black child in her arms – that did so much to enthrone them in the imagination of the Western public.'

6   See e.g. Prime Minister's caricaturing of aid critics: Stratton, A., 'David Cameron Dismisses Critics of International Aid as "Hard-Hearted"' (2011) *The Guardian*, 5 July. At: http://www.guardian.co.uk/global-development/2011/jul/05/david-cameron-dismisses-international-aid-critics [accessed October 17 2012].

7   For definition of these two categories of aid see following.

8   PAC, 'MPs report on Department for International Development Financial Management' (2011) House of Commons Public Accounts Committee, 20 October. At: http://www.parliament.uk/business/committees/committees-a-z/commons-select/public-accounts-committee/news/dfid-financial-report/ [accessed October 17 2012].

9   See especially William Easterly, *White Man's Burden,* p.46, and
    Dambisa Moyo, *Dead Aid*, pp.48-49. Easterly's statistics show
    growth falling in African states as aid accelerated, despite
    successes on specific projects, and that countries with the highest
    aid to GDP ratio have experienced the worst growth rates. Moyo
    posits that from 1970-1998, when aid to Africa was at its height,
    poverty increased by more than 50 per cent, trapping almost two
    thirds of the continent's population.
10 South Korea's economy was about the same size as Jamaica's
    when that subsequently much-aided island nation achieved
    independence in 1962. Jamaica Observer, '50 Years Backward or
    Forward?'(2012) *Jamaica Observer*, 1 April. At:
    http://www.jamaicaobserver.com/columns/50-years-backward-
    and-forward_11052747 [accessed October 17 2012].
11 Dambisa Moyo, *Dead Aid*, p.47. Moyo points out that, after
    decades of aid, her native Zambia ended up with per capita GDP
    that was lower in the late 1990s (about $500) than it had been in
    1960 (p.47).

PART 1: British Aid Basics
1. The Basics of British Foreign Aid

1   DfID's planned £9.4 billion budget for 2015 will also be almost £2
    billion higher than that of the Home Office. 'Foreign Aid Bidget to
    Cost Every Family £500' *Daily Mail*, 22 October 2012.
2   BBC News, 'EU Aid is a Disgrace Says Short' (2002) BBC News,
    31 July. At: http://news.bbc.co.uk/1/hi/uk_politics/2163865.stm
    [accessed October 17 2012].
3   Telegraph View, 'Overseas Aid: One Good Cause Doesn't Justify
    Ever-Rising Spending' (2011) *The Daily Telegraph*, 6 July. At:
    http://www.telegraph.co.uk/comment/telegraph-
    view/8621591/Overseas-aid-One-good-cause-doesnt-justify-ever-
    rising-spending.html [accessed October 17 2012].
4   Interview with emergency aid expert currently working on DfID
    contract in Libya who needs to remain anonymous.
5   As a share of national wealth. See Telegraph View, 'Overseas Aid:
    One Good Cause Doesn't Justify Ever-Rising Spending' (2011) *The
    Telegraph*, 6 July. At: http://www.telegraph.co.uk/comment/
    telegraph-view/8621591/Overseas-aid-One-good-cause-doesnt-
    justify-ever-rising-spending.html [accessed October 17 2012]
6   Kirkup, J., 'Foreign Aid Keeps Us Safe, Insists Andrew Mitchell'
    (2012), *The Telegraph*, 20 January. At: http://www.telegraph.co.uk/
    news/politics/9029330/Foreign-aid-keeps-us-safe-insists-
    Andrew-Mitchell.html [accessed October 17 2012].

7   David Cameron, 'David Cameron: Why We're Right to Ringfence the Aid Budget' (2011) *The Guardian*, 11 June. At: http://www.guardian.co.uk/global-development/2011/jun/11/david-cameron-defends-aid-funding [accessed October 17 2012].

8   Russell, V., 'PAC Slams DFID Financial Management' (2011) *Public Finance*, 20 October. At http://www.publicfinance.co.uk/news/2011/10/pac-slams-dfid-financial-management/ [accessed October 17 2012].

2. UK Aid and Unasked Questions

1   These include Australia, Canada and Japan, as well as near-bankrupt countries like Spain and Greece. AFP, 'Cuts in Aid Putting Lives at Risk Warns Oxfam', 7 April 2012.

2   Rieff, D., 'Charity on the Rampage – The Business of Foreign Aid'.

3   David Rieff, *A Bed for the Night*, p.24.

4   That this is official policy was confirmed by a telephone call to the authority by the author in November 2011.

5   Sweeney, M., 'Oxfam Climate Change Ad Cleared by Regulator' (2010) *The Guardian*, 27 October. At: http://www.guardian.co.uk/media/2010/oct/27/oxfam-climate-change-ad-cleared [accessed October 17 2012]

6   Oxfam, for example, has become a major lobbying organisation, both for higher government aid expenditure – which happens to be good for its own revenues – and for political causes such as global warming measures and opposition to the war to overthrow Saddam Hussein in Iraq.

7   Arguably it reverses the betrayal of Britain's duties to the Commonwealth which began when Britain joined the EEC.

8   Robert Calderisi, *The Trouble With Africa*. An invaluable contribution to the modern literature of aid.

9   Dambisa Moyo, *Dead Aid*.

10   Interview, Mary Harper, Oct 2011.

11   Indeed, it is arguable that he and they should be studying the rise of the BRIC countries and the previous rise of South East Asian tigers as the basis for British aid policy.

12   A reference to the needless, intrusive, ineffective exercises at US airports that critics call 'security theatre'. Bruce Schneier, *Beyond Fear: Thinking Sensibly About Security in an Uncertain World* (2003) New York: Springer Publishing

13   Foreman, J., 'The Terrible Price that is Paid by the Forgotten Casualties of War' (2009) *The Spectator*, 19 August. At: http://www.spectator.co.uk/essays/all/5275928/the-terrible-price-that-is-paid-by-the-forgotten-casualties-of-war.thtml [accessed October 17 2012].

3. Aid Myth and Aid Reality

1   Peter Bauer, *From Subsistence to Exchange and Other Essays*, p.42.
2   Reid, S., 'How India Squanders British Aid: We Give £1.4bn to a Country that Has Its Own Space Programme. In this Damning Investigation, the Mail Reveals How it's Scandalously Wasted' (2011) *The Daily Mail*, 2 December. See for instance the debacle of DfID aid to the Sarva Shiksha Abbiyan education programme in India, examined at http://www.dailymail.co.uk/news/article-2068930/How-India-squanders-British-aid-1-4bn-country-space-programme.html [accessed October 17 2012].
3   Wire, F., 'Daily Rues Pakistan's Ghost Schools' (2012) *First Post*, 21 July. At: http://www.firstpost.com/fwire/daily-rues-pakistans-ghost-schools-386102.html [accessed October 17 2012] and Muhammad, P., 'BECS Ghost Schools: Two Months on, Provincial Authorities Offer No Explanation' (2012) *The Express Tribune*, 24 September. At: http://tribune.com.pk/story/441388/becs-ghost-schools-two-months-on-provincial-authorities-offer-no-explanation/ [accessed October 17 2012]. According to reports quoted in the Pakistani press 'more than half' of the 13,094 schools in the country's Basic Education (BECS) programme 'may be bogus'
4   Interview with Greg Mortenson, December 2007.
5   Foreman, J., 'Pakistan Free to Learn' (2008) *The Telegraph*, 16 February. At: http://www.telegraph.co.uk/culture/books/3671228/Pakistan-Free-to-learn.html [accessed October 17 2012]
6   Interviews with Sir Edward Clay, November 2011. See also: Burgis, T., 'UK Cuts Off Kenyan Education Aid' (2010) *Financial Times*, 16 March. At: http://www.ft.com/cms/s/0/03b07738-311c-11df-8e6f-00144feabdc0.html#axzz29Y4tAzdA [accessed October 17 2012].
7   http://www.ft.com/cms/s/0/03b07738-311c-11df-8e6f-00144feabdc0.html#axzz29Y4tAzdA When the news of this scandal broke, Andrew Mitchell responded that DfID is on the case and that the missing money will be recovered. However Sir Edward Clay (see above) told me that 'there is no reason to think that [similar thefts] could not happen again'.
8   Banerjee, A.V & Duflo, E., *Poor Economics*, p.54. When the aid experts Abhijit Banerjee and Esther Duflo investigated absenteeism in government health clinics in Udaipur, India, they found that at least 56 per cent of the time the facilities were closed and the nurse absent during regular working hours.
9   I have seen schools in Pakistan that were claimed by as many as three different NGOs and appear in the publicity materials of all of them.
10 Linda Polman, *War Games: The Story of Aid and War in Modern Times*, p.177.

11   Rieff, D., 'Charity on the Rampage – The Business of Foreign Aid'
      http://www.foreignaffairs.com/articles/52653/david-
      rieff/charity-on-the-rampage-the-business-of-foreign-aid
12   Aid defenders often imply that there would be no schools or
      clinics without foreign aid, a claim that is unprovable and
      arguably reflects arrogant, even racist condescension, or at the
      very least the bigotry of low expectations.
13   Giles Bolton, *Aid and Other Dirty Business*, p.108. Bolton claims that
      'managing aid is not rocket science…So while it would be plain
      silly to claim every cent of your cash spent … has arrived exactly
      where intended, the large-scale fraud enabled by the Cold War
      lucre-for-loyalty era should be out.'
14   For an introduction to the term and the phenomenon see
      Moelwyn-Hughes, O., 'Global Issues: Aid and Corruption: The
      Wabenzi – Africa's Big Men' (2010) Tutor2U, 14 March. At:
      http://tutor2u.net/blog/index.php/politics/comments/global-
      issues-aid-and-corruption-the-wabenzi-africas-big-men/ [accessed
      October 17 2012].
15   For that matter not everyone in the aid world buys the version of
      development history in which 'socialist' leaders like Tanzania's
      much-lionised Julius Nyere were correct in their nationalisations,
      protectionism, anti-entrepreneurial legislation and doomed efforts
      at autarky – though it often seems so.
16   'Anyone here speak NGOish?' (2011) *The Economist*, 27 January. At:
      http://www.economist.com/node/18014068 [accessed October 17
      2012].
17   Interview, Clare Lockhart, 28 November 2011,
18   Makore, G,. 'NGO-speak Explained' (2011) Gilbert Makore's Blog,
      4 October. At: http://gilbertmakore.wordpress.com/2011/10/04/
19   Polman, *War Games: The Story of Aid and War in Modern Times*, p.181.

Part 2: What Aid Does and Does Not Achieve

1   Rodrik, D., 'Getting it Right on Foreign Aid' (2007) Dani Rodrik's
      weblog, 28 August. At: http://rodrik.typepad.com/dani_rodriks_
      weblog/2007/08/getting-it-righ.html [accessed October 17 2012].

Introduction

2   *Dead Aid*, Dambisa Moyo, p.xix.

4. The Claims of Development Aid

1   See e.g. Moyo, Bauer, Polman etc.
2   'Aid & Somaliland: Mo Money Mo Problems' (2011) *The Economist*,
    24 June. At: http://www.economist.com/blogs/baobab/
    2011/06/aid-and-somaliland
3   Nicholas Eubank, 'Taxation, Political Accountability and Foreign
    Aid: Lessons from Somaliland' (2011) *Journal of Development
    Studies*, 26 March. At: http://papers.ssrn.com/sol3/
    papers.cfm?abstract_id=1621374 [accessed October 17 2012].
4   David Osterfeld, 'The Failures and Fallacies of Foreign Aid' (1990)
    The Freeman Online, 40 (2) February. At:
    http://www.thefreemanonline.org/columns/the-failures-and-
    fallacies-of-foreign-aid/ [accessed October 17 2012].
5   Rajan, R.G. & Subramanian, A., 'Aid and Growth: What Does the
    Cross-Country Evidence Really Show?' (2007) The Peterson
    Institute, July. At: http://www.petersoninstitute.org/
    publications/papers/subramanian0707.pdf [accessed October 17
    2012].
6   Jonathan Glennie, *The Trouble With Aid – Why Less Could Mean
    More for Africa*.
7   Robert Calderisi, *The Trouble with Africa – Why Foreign Aid Isn't
    Working*.
8   Peter Bauer, *From Subsistence to Exchange and Other Essays*, p.46.
9   https://old.intelligencesquared.com/events/foreign-aid-to-poor-
    countries-has-done-more-harm-than-good
10 Some aid defenders also cite global decline in infant mortality and
    the global rise in life expectancy over the last century – though the
    degree to which these are attributable to aid rather than economic
    growth and education is debatable. It is worth noting that problems
    of correlation and causation affect all the critiques on both sides.
    We cannot know if things would have been better without aid,
    would have been just as bad or would have been worse.
11 Forsyth, J., 'Not Aiding the Cause' (2008) *The Spectator*, 20 July. At:
    http://blogs.spectator.co.uk/coffeehouse/2008/07/not-aiding-
    the-cause/ [accessed October 17 2012].
12 Crawford, A., 'UK Paid £3m to Fraud Probe Agency in
    Afghanistan' (2011) BBC News, 20 October. At:
    http://www.bbc.co.uk/news/uk-15376506 [accessed October 17
    2012].
13 'The Department for International Development: Programme
    Controls and Assurance in Afghanistan' (2012) *Independent
    Commission for Aid Impact*, Report 6, March 2012. At:
    http://icai.independent.gov.uk/wp-content/uploads/
    2012/03/ICAI-Afghanistan-Final-Report_P11.pdf [accessed
    October 17 2012].

14 Roopanarine, L., 'UK Aid Projects in Afghanistan Must Be Overseen More Closely, Warns Watchdog' (2012) *The Guardian*, 22 March. At: http://www.guardian.co.uk/global-development/ 2012/mar/22/uk-aid-afghanistan-overseen-more-effectively [accessed October 17 2012].

15 Mayr, W., 'Exotic Birds in a Cage: Criticism Grows of Afghanistan's Bloated NGO Industry' (2010) *Spiegel Online*, 22 September. At: http://www.spiegel.de/international/world/ exotic-birds-in-a-cage-criticism-grows-of-afghanistan-s-bloated-ngo-industry-a-718656.html [accessed October 17 2012].

16 Shepherd, B., 'Want to Stop Foreign Aid Fraud? Scrap Foreign Aid' (2011) Bob Shepherd's Blog, 20 October. At: http://bobshepherdauthor.com/2011/10/20/want-to-stop-foreign-aid-fraud-scrap-foreign-aid/#more-837 [accessed October 17 2012].

17 Deepak.Lal,'In Defence of Empires' (2004) UCLA Economics. At: http://www.econ.ucla.edu/Lal/papers/In%20defense%20of%20e mpires.pdf [accessed October 17 2012].

5. *Assessing the Impact of Aid*

1 Interview with Clare Lockhart, November 28 2011.

2 Peter Bauer, *Equality, the Third World and Economic Delusion*, pp.119-120.

3 Interview, Michela Wrong, 5 November 2011. Acording to Michela Wrong and interviews with former DfID staff members, DfID workers in East African countries spend an average of one day a year away from their bases in the capital cities.

4 Banerjee, A.V & Duflo, E., *Poor Economics*, pp.235-236

5 Interviews, Tara O'Connor, 8 November 2011 & 17 April 2012

6 Evans, A., 'The Most Heavily Aided Place in the World' (2012) *Global Dashboard*, 17 April. At: http://www.globaldashboard.org/2012/04/17/the-most-heavily-aided-place-in-the-world/ [accessed October 17 2012].

7 Eberstadt, N.N., 'The Global Poverty Paradox' (2010) *Commentary Magazine*, October. At: http://www.commentarymagazine.com/ 8 Reitman, J., 'Beyond Relief: How the World Failed Haiti' (2011) *Rolling Stone*, 4 August. At: http://www.rollingstone.com/ politics/news/how-the-world-failed-haiti-20110804 [accessed October 17 2012]

9 Doyle, M., 'UN 'Should Take Blame for Haiti Cholera' – US House members' (2012) BBC News, 20 July. At: http://www.bbc.co.uk/news/world-africa-18928405 [accessed October 17 2012]

NOTES

10 Karunakara, U., 'Haiti: Where Aid Failed' (2010) *The Guardian*, 28 December. At: http://www.guardian.co.uk/commentisfree/2010/dec/28/haiti-cholera-earthquake-aid-agencies-failure [accessed October 17 2012]

11 Maren, M., *The Road to Hell – The Ravaging Effects of Foreign Aid and International Charity*, p.21.

6. Assessing the Impact of Aid on Africa

1 Richard Dowden, 'Can Gordon Save Africa?' (2005) *The Observer*, 9 January. At: http://www.royalafricansociety.org/articles-by-richard-dowden/279.html?Reference=278 [accessed 17 October 2012].

2 Gragnolati, M., Shekar, M., Das Gupta, M., Bredenkamp, C. & Yi-Kyoung, L., 'India's Undernourished Children: A Call for Reform and Action' (2005) *The World Bank*, The International Bank for Reconstruction and Development, Health, Nutrition & Population (HNP) Discussion Paper, Washington, DC 20433. At: http://siteresources.worldbank.org/SOUTHASIAEXT/Resources/223546-1147272668285/IndiaUndernourishedChildrenFinal.pdf [accessed October 17 2012].

3 Sanders, D., 'Amartya Sen Tells me Poverty's Not Really About the Money' (2005) Doug Sanders blog, 18 June. At: http://dougsaunders.net/2005/06/amartya-sen-poverty/ [accessed October 17 2012]. 'The number of people who live below one dollar a day is a figure that has a resilient presence in the poverty literature,' he said..

4 Wahito, M., 'Kenya: Three in Four Kenyans Have a Mobile Phone' (2012) *AllAfrica*, 10 July. At: http://allafrica.com/stories/201207110070.html [accessed October 17 2012].

5 Interview, Michela Wrong, November 5 2011

6 Interview, Miles Morland, 30 January 2012.

7 O'Neill, J., 'How Africa Can Become the Next Bric' (2010) *Financial Times*, 26 August. At: http://www.ft.com/cms/s/0/6c00e950-b153-11df-b899-00144feabdc0.html [accessed October 17 2012].

8 Ten years ago even oil-rich Nigeria had less than 200,000 landlines for a population of 130 million.

9 Smith, D.L., 'Found: A Somalia We Do Not Know' (2012) *Mail & Guardian*, 5 April. At: http://mg.co.za/article/2012-04-05-found-a-somalia-we-do-not-know/ [accessed October 17 2012].

PART 3: Aid and it's Contradictions
8. Perverse Incentives and the Aid Industry

1   Bolton, G., *Aid and Other Dirty Business*, p.115.
2   Interview, Clare Lockhart, 28 November 2011.
3   Interview, Clare Lockhart, 28 November 2011.
4   Interview, Clare Lockhart, November 28 2011

PART 4: UK Aid Targets and Goals
9. Magic Numbers, Foolish Commitments

1   Clemens, M.A., Moss, T.J. & van Gelder, A., 'The Ghost of 0.7%: Origins and Relevance of the International Aid Target' (2010) *International Policy Network*, 3-7 Temple Avenue, London EC4Y 0HP. At: http://www.policynetwork.net/sites/default/files/ghost-zero-point-seven.pdf [accessed October 17 2012].
2   Wrong, M., *It's Our Turn to Eat*, p.208.
3   Polman, L., *War Games: The Story of Aid and War in Modern Times*, p.166.
4   PAC, 'MPs report on Department for International Development Financial Management' (2011) House of Commons Public Accounts Committee, 20 October. At: http://www.parliament.uk/business/committees/committees-a-z/commons-select/public-accounts-committee/news/dfid-financial-report/ [accessed October 17 2012].
5   Jonathan Glennie, *The Trouble with Aid – Why Less Could Mean More for Africa*, p.4.
6   http://www.ted.com/speakers/andrew_mwenda.html and http://andrewmwendasblog.blogspot.com/
7   UN Development Programme, 'The Millennium Development Goals: Eight Goals for 2015' (2012) UN Development Programme. At: http://www.undp.org/mdg/basics.shtml [accessed October 17 2012].
8   UN Development Programme, 'The Millennium Development Goals: Eight Goals for 2015' (2012) UN Development Programme. At: http://www.undp.org/mdg/goal1.shtml [accessed October 17 2012].
9   Easterly, W., 'Guest Post: Only Trade-Fuelled Growth Can Help the World's Poor', *Financial Times*, Beyond Brics, 21 September. At: http://blogs.ft.com/beyond-brics/2010/09/21/guest-post-only-trade-fuelled-growth-can-help-the-worlds-poor/#axzz29YXntQtN [accessed Oct 17 2012].

PART 5: Development Aid and its Critics

1   Hancock, G., *Lords of Poverty*, p.183. Hancock was formerly East
     Africa correspondent of *The Economist*, editor of *New
     Internationalist* magazine and editor of *Africa Guide*. *Lords of
     Poverty*, published in 1989 was the first insider's book to look
     sceptically at the aid industry.

10. Aid and Varieties of Actual Harm

1   Chunling, Lu *et al.*, 'Public Financing of Health in Developing
     Countries' (2010) *The Lancet*, 375 (9723), 1375-1387.
2   Clemens, M.A., Moss, T.J. & van Gelder, A., 'The Ghost of 0.7%:
     Origins and Relevance of the International Aid Target' (2010)
     International Policy Network, 3-7 Temple Avenue, London EC4Y
     0HP. At: http://www.policynetwork.net/sites/default/
     files/ghost-zero-point-seven.pdf [accessed October 17 2012].
3   Ghani, A. & Lockhart, C. *Fixing Failed States*, p.98.
4   Mwenda, A., 'Foreign Aid and the Weakening of Democratic
     Accountability in Uganda' (2006) Foreign Policy Briefing No. 88,
     12 July. At: http://www.cato.org/pub_display.php?pub_id=6463
     [accessed October 17 2012].
5   Moyo, D., *Dead Aid*, p.58.
6   Interview, Michela Wrong, 5 November 2011.
7   For an amusing insider account of this tendency see
     http://stuffexpataidworkerslike.com/2011/03/23/37-sexy-local-
     ngos-slongos/
8   Linda Polman, *War Games: The Story of Aid and War in Modern
     Times*, p.94.
9   Rajan, R. and Subramanian, A. *What Might Prevent Aid from
     Enhancing Growth?*
10   *Viewpoint Policy Journal* (2012) World Bank, Financial & Private
     Sector Development. At: http://rru.worldbank.org/
     PublicPolicyJournal [accessed October 17 2012].
11   Useem, J., 'The Devil's Excrement' (2003) Fortune Magazine,
     2 February. At: http://money.cnn.com/magazines/fortune/
     fortune_archive/2003/02/03/336434/[accessed 17 October 2012].
12   For the argument that countries blessed with natural (especially
     mineral) resources tend to grow more slowly than other countries
     see Richard Auty's *Sustaining Development in Mineral Economies:
     The Resource Curse Thesis* (1993, London: Routledge) or Jeffrey
     Sachs or Andrew Warner's 'The Big Push, Natural Resource
     Booms and Growth' (1999) *Journal of Development Economics*, 59,
     43–76.

13 Djankov, S., Montalvo, J., & Reynal-Querol, M., 'The Curse of Aid' (2005) *Journal of Economic Growth*, 13 (3), September 2008, pp.1835-1865

14 Interviews with Sri Lankan NGO head and aid workers, December 2011.

15 David Rieff, *A Bed for the Night*, p.25.

16 de Waal, A., *Famine Crimes – Politics and the Disaster Relief Industry*, p.3.

17 de Waal, A., *Famine Crimes – Politics and the Disaster Relief Industry*, p.5.

18 Chikezie, C.E, 'African Agency vs The Aid Industry' (2005) *OpenDemocracy*, 6 July. At: http://www.opendemocracy.net/globalization-G8/aid_2650.jsp [accessed September 18 2012].

19 BBC News, 'Africans on Africa: Debt' (2005) BBC News, 7 July. At: http://news.bbc.co.uk/1/hi/world/africa/4657139.stm [accessed October 17 2012].

11. The History of Foreign Aid

1 Lockhart, C., and Ghani, A., *Fixing Failed States*.

2 Richard Dowden, 'Can Gordon Save Africa?' (2005) The Observer, 9 January. At: http://www.royalafricansociety.org/articles-by-richard-dowden/279.html?Reference=278 [accessed 17 October 2012].

3 Richard Dowden, 'Can Gordon Save Africa?' (2005) The Observer, 9 January. At: http://www.royalafricansociety.org/articles-by-richard-dowden/279.html?Reference=278 [accessed 17 October 2012].

4 Moyo, D., *Dead Aid*, p.22: 'good governance was a euphemism for strong and credible institutions, transparent rule of law and economies free of rampant corruption'.

5 Lockhart, C. and Ghani, A., *Fixing Failed States*, p.89.

6 See Peter Bauer's *Economic Analysis and Policy in Underdeveloped Countries* (1957), a refutation of the argument by Samuelson that [the backward nations] 'cannot get their heads above water because their production is so low that they can spare nothing for the capital formation by which their standard of living could be raised'.

7 Erixon, F., 'Aid and Development: Will It Work This Time?' (2005) *Policy Network*, 10 June. At: http://www.policynetwork.net/development/publication/aid-and-development [accessed October 17 2012].

8 Erixon, F., 'New IPN Study Shows Foreign Aid Does More Harm Than Good' (2005) *Policy Network*. At: http://www.policynetwork.net/development/media/new-ipn-study-shows-foreign-aid-does-more-harm-good

9   The Economist, 'Missing the Point' (2002) *The Economist*, 14 March. At: http://www.economist.com/node/1034243 [accessed October 17 2012].

10 William Easterly, *White Man's Burden: Why the West's Efforts to Aid the Rest Have Done So Much Ill And So Little Good*, p.174.

11 William Easterly, *White Man's Burden: Why the West's Efforts to Aid the Rest Have Done So Much Ill And So Little Good*, p.175.

12 See e.g. the new military academy being built by China in Zimbabwe.

13 This much-quoted statement cannot be found in any of Bauer's published work. When questioned about it, he used to say that, although he could not remember either writing or saying the words, he agreed with the sentiment.

14 Graham Hancock, *Lords of Poverty*, p.192.

15 Interview, Mary Harper, 18 October 2011.

16 Birrell, I., 'Somaliland: The Former British Colony That Shows Africa Doesn't Need Our Millions to Flourish' (2011) *The Daily Mail*, 23 July. At: http://www.dailymail.co.uk/news/article-2018055/Somaliland-The-British-colony-shows-Africa-doesnt-need-millions-flourish.html [accessed October 17 2012]

12. *Alternatives to Development Aid*

1   Interview, Peter Godwin, 4 January 2012.

2   Interviews on Zimbabwe and Zanu PF with Peter Godwin, January 4 2012, & Tara O'Connor, December 2011.

3   Ellerman, D., *Helping People Help Themselves*, p.6.

4   Easterly, W., Review of Dambisa Moyo's book *Dead Aid*, (2009) Williameasterly.org, June. At: http://williameasterly.files.wordpress.com/2011/07/moyoreview forlrbjune2009neverpublished.pdf [accessed October 17 2012].

5   See de Soto, H., *The Other Path: The Economic Answer to Terrorism* (2002) New York: Basic Books.

6   http://en.wikipedia.org/wiki/David_Ellerman

7   Ellerman, D., *Helping People Help Themselves*, p.4.

8   http://aidwatchers.com/

9   William Easterly, *White Man's Burden: Why the West's Efforts to Aid the Rest Have Done So Much Ill And So Little Good*, p.199.

10 William Easterly, *White Man's Burden: Why the West's Efforts to Aid the Rest Have Done So Much Ill And So Little Good*, p.379.

11 See Foreman, J., 'Titan of the Kalash' (2007) *The Telegraph*, 28 July. At: http://www.telegraph.co.uk/culture/3666830/Titan-of-the-Kalash.html [accessed October 17 2012]

12 David Ellerman, *Helping People Help Themselves*, p.12

[13] David Ellerman, *Helping People Help Themselves*, p.244. But money, he goes on to say 'is the magnet that sets all compasses wrong; it is the root of much unhelpful help. Decades of experience in Africa and elsewhere have made it crystal clear that money is not the key missing ingredient in institutional development (as it might be in building an airport). The implicit assumption that a development agency should function as a money-moving machine has little to support it and much evidence against it.'

[14] Mwenda, A., 'Foreign Aid and the Weakening of Democratic Accountability in Uganda' (2006) Foreign Policy Briefing No. 88, 12 July. At: http://www.cato.org/pub_display.php?pub_id=6463 [accessed October 17 2012].

[15] Massive humanitarian and development aid to the Palestinian Territories arguably enabled the Palestinian Authority to neglect the economy and also subsidised violence. See Stotsky, S., 'Does Foreign Aid Fuel Palestinian Violence' (2008) *Middle East Quarterly*, Summer 2008, pp.23-30. At: http://www.meforum.org/1926/does-foreign-aid-fuel-palestinian-violence [accessed October 17 2012]

[16] Jonathan Glennie, *The Trouble with Aid – Why Less Could Mean More for Africa*, p.21.

13. The Expansion of the Aid Industry

[1] According to an expert at the Brookings Institution's Wolfenson Center for Development, it is currently estimated that there are somewhere between 6,000 and 30,000 national NGOs in developing countries.

[2] William Easterly, *White Man's Burden: Why the West's Efforts to Aid the Rest Have Done So Much Ill And So Little Good*, p.163.

[3] Foreman, J., 'Pakistan Free to Learn' (2008) *The Telegraph*, 16 February. At: http://www.telegraph.co.uk/culture/books/3671228/Pakistan-Free-to-learn.html [accessed October 17 2012]

[4] Good examples of this include small NGO's like the Healing Kashmir project in Indian-controlled Kashmir http://healingkashmir.org

[5] http://www.ikat.org/

[6] For an an amusing overview of aid industry jargon see: http://williameasterly.org/the-aidspeak-dictionary/ Linda Polman's *War Games* also includes an enlightening glossary of 'aidspeak'.

PART 6: 'Masters in Mufti' – Humanitarian Aid and Its Critics

1 Rieff, *A Bed For the Night*, p.275.

14. Emergency Aid and the NGO Sector

1 Quoted in Michael Maren, *Road to Hell – The Ravaging Effects of Foreign Aid and International Charity*, p.268.
2 Eilis O'Hanlon asks 'how many Somalian bellies could be filled by the money spent on pro-Palestinian agitprop (E332,500 in 2009-10 alone)?'. O'Hanlon, E., 'Aid is Not Only Answer to Third World Problems' (2011) *Independent. Ie*, 24 July. At: http://www.independent.ie/opinion/analysis/aid -is-not-the-only-answer-to-third-world-problems-2829831.html [accessed October 17 2012].
3 Oxfam lobbied against the Iraq War, predicting a vast refugee catastrophe from the invasion. Save the Children and Christian Aid have both campaigned vociferously against economic liberalisation and free market reforms in Africa.
4 'The Whole Foreign Aid Industry Must Face Greater Scrutiny' (2012) *The Telegraph*, 30 September. At http://www.telegraph.co.uk/comment/letters/9574664/The-whole-foreign-aid-industry-must-face-greater-scrutiny.html [accessed October 17 2012].
5 See for instance attacks on DfID's decision to cut down on the number of countries the Department sends aid to. 'Andrew Mitchell Denies Security Claims as UK Axes Foreign Aid' (2011) *Evening Standard*, 1 March. At: http://www.thisislondon.co.uk/standard/article-23927468-andrew-mitchell-denies-security-claims-as-uk-axes-foreign-aid.do [accessed October 17 2012].
6 Interview, Baroness Cox, 22 November 2009.
7 Interview, Greg Mortenson, 22 December 2007
8 Interview, Justine Hardy, 17 April 2012.

15. Problems with Emergency and Humanitarian Aid

1 Polman, L., *War Games: The Story of Aid and War in Modern Times*, p.18.
2 Rieff, D., 'Charity on the Rampage – The Business of Foreign Aid'.
3 Fiona Terry, *Condemned to Repeat – The Paradox of Humanitarian Action*
4 Fiona Terry, *Condemned to Repeat – The Paradox of Humanitarian Action*, p.3.
5 Visits to UNHCR camps in Chad June 2007.

6   Fiona Terry, *Condemned to Repeat – The Paradox of Humanitarian Action*, p.10.
7   Mary B Anderson, *Do No Harm – How Aid Can Support Peace – Or War*.
8   Fiona Terry, *Condemned to Repeat – The Paradox of Humanitarian Action*, p.15.
9   Fiona Terry, *Condemned to Repeat – The Paradox of Humanitarian Action*, p.40.
10 Horrocks, P (2010) 'Bob, Band Aid and How the Rebels Bought Their Arms' (2010) BBC News, 6 March. At: http://www.bbc.co.uk/blogs/theeditors/2010/03/ethiopia.html [accessed October 17 2012]
11 Buerk has admitted that he knowingly simplified the facts of the crisis in Ethiopia in an effort to bring the world's attention to mass starvation, but the presenter of the BBC's Moral Maze has never confronted accusations that he therefore became an unwitting accomplice to the Mengistu regime's population transfers. Wolf, D., 'What Happened to the F***ing Money' (2009) *The Spectator*, July 31. At: http://staging.spectator.co.uk/comic/what-happened-to-the-fing-money/ [accessed September 18 2012].
12 See Alex de Waal's *Famine Crimes*, David Rieff's *A Bed for the Night*, and Rieff's long article in *The Guardian* 'Did Live Aid Do More Harm than Good?' for detailed accounts of this. Rieff, D., 'Cruel to Be Kind' (2005) *The Guardian*, 24 June. At: http://www.guardian.co.uk/world/2005/jun/24/g8.debtrelief [accessed October 17 2012].
13 Fiona Terry, *Condemned to Repeat – The Paradox of Humanitarian Action*, p.48
14 Fiona Terry, *Condemned to Repeat – The Paradox of Humanitarian Action*, p.49. 'Some NGO's and UN agencies even assisted in the deportation process'.
15 Maren, M., *The Road to Hell – The Ravaging Effects of Foreign Aid and International Charity*, p.51.
16 See Rieff, D., 'Cruel to Be Kind' (2005 The Guardian, 23 June. At: http://www.guardian.co.uk/world/2005/jun/24/g8.debtrelief [accessed October 17 2012].
17 Maren, M., *The Road to Hell – The Ravaging Effects of Foreign Aid and International Charity*, p.97.
18 http://www.telegraph.co.uk/news/picturegalleries/worldnews/8630255/Horn-of-Africa-famine-Somalia-Ethiopia-and-Kenya-suffer-worst-drought-in-60-years.html
19 Interviews with Mary Harper, 18 October 2011 & Peter Godwin, 4 January 2012

20 Hartley, A 'Drought Didn't Cause Somalia's Famine' (2011) *The Specator*, 6 August. At: http://www.spectator.co.uk/features/ 7141183/drought-didnt-cause-somalias-famine/ [accessed October 17 2012].

21 Interview, Mary Harper, 18 October 2011

22 An INGO is an international NGO.

23 Polman, L., *War Games: The Story of Aid and War in Modern Times*, p.124

24 Interviews with local NGO officials, February 2005

25 'Sri Lanka Charges Oxfam £500,000 to Allow in Jeeps' (2005) *The Telegraph*, 17 June. At: http://www.telegraph.co.uk/news/ worldnews/asia/srilanka/1492258/Sri-Lanka-charges-Oxfam-500000-to-allow-in-jeeps.html [accessed October 17 2012] and BBC News, 'Oxfam Pays $1m Tsunami Aid Duty' (2005) BBC News, 17 June. At: http://news.bbc.co.uk/2/hi/south_asia/4103054.stm [accessed October 17 2012]. I myself had given the *Telegraph* the story in January, but the then foreign editor declined to follow it up.

26 Quoted in Polman, L., *War Games: The Story of Aid and War in Modern Times*, p.39 and de Waal, A., *Famine Crimes – Politics and the Disaster Relief Industry*, p.83

27 Rieff, D., 'Charity on the Rampage – The Business of Foreign Aid'.

28 Polman, L., *War Games – The Story of Aid and War in Modern Times*, p.90.

29 Polman, L., *War Games – The Story of Aid and War in Modern Times*, p.91.

30 Rieff, D., *A Bed for the Night*, p.81.

31 Kirby, J, 'Spare Some Change for Our New Billboard' (2009) *The Times*, 7 April. At: http://www.thetimes.co.uk/tto/law/ columnists/article2048681.ece [accessed October 17 2012].

32 See Rieff's *Bed for the Night* for more on the ideological and historical roots of humanitarian aid organisations.

33 See e.g. reports on War on Want by NGOMonitor.org

34 Josephs, B., 'Warning to Charity' (2005) NGO Monitor, 5 August. At: http://www.ngo-monitor.org/article/_warning_to_charity_ [accessed October 17 2012].

35 Leather, S. & Younger, S., 'Speaking out: Guidance on Campaigning and Political Activity by Charities (CC9)' (2008) Charity Commission. At: http://www.charity-commission.gov.uk/ Publications/cc9.aspx [accessed October 17 2012].

PART 7: DfID Policies and Problems

1   Groves, J., 'Backlash As Minister Boasts "Be As Proud of Our
     £12bn Foreign Aid Bill As You Are of The Army"' (2011) *The Daily
     Mail*, 6 June. At: http://www.dailymail.co.uk/news/article-
     1395039/Backlash-minister-boasts-Be-proud-12bn-foreign-aid-
     Army.html#ixzz229nJVcjc [accessed October 17 2012].

16. *The Latest Reforms*

1   Provost, C., 'DfID's Spending on Consultants to Come Under
     Increased Scrutiny' (2012) *The Guardian*, 17 September. At:
     http://www.guardian.co.uk/global-development/2012/sep/17/
     dfid-spending-consultants-scrutiny

2   Provost, C., 'UK Aid for Education in East Africa is Failing' (2012)
     The Guardian, 18 May. At: http://www.guardian.co.uk/global-
     development/2012/may/18/uk-aid-education-africa-failing
     [accessed October 17 2012].

3   Independent Commission on Aid Impact, DFID's Education
     Programmes in Three East African Countries (2012) Report 10,
     May. At: http://icai.independent.gov.uk/wp-content/uploads/
     2012/05/DFIDs-Education-Programmes-in-Three-East-African-
     Countries-Final-Report-32.pdf [accessed October 17 2012].

4   Mendick, R., '£50m of Government's International Aid Budget
     Spent in the UK' (2010) *The Telegraph*, 13 February. At:
     http://www.telegraph.co.uk/news/politics/7228534/50m-of-
     Governments-international-aid-budget-spent-in-the-UK.html
     [accessed October 17 2012].

5   Copping, J., 'Where our Overseas Aid Goes: Salsa in Cambridge,
     Coffee in Yorkshire' (2011) *The Telegraph*, 15 January. At:
     http://www.telegraph.co.uk/news/politics/8261809/Where-our-
     overseas-aid-goes-salsa-in-Cambridge-coffee-in-Yorkshire.html
     [accessed October 17 2012].

6   Copping, J., 'Overseas Aid Projects Miss their Targets, DFID Study
     Finds' (2010) *The Telegraph*, 4 July. At:
     http://www.telegraph.co.uk/news/uknews/7870261/Overseas-
     aid-projects-miss-their-targets-DFID-study-finds.html [accessed
     October 17 2012].

7   Copping, J., 'Overseas Aid Projects Miss their Targets, DFID Study
     Finds' (2010) *The Telegraph*, 4 July. At:
     http://www.telegraph.co.uk/news/uknews/7870261/Overseas-
     aid-projects-miss-their-targets-DFID-study-finds.html [accessed
     October 17 2012].

8   Martin, D., 'The Scandal of British Aid Spent on Giving Pakistanis Online Banking' (2011) *The Daily Mail*, 1 June. At: http://www.dailymail.co.uk/news/article-1392840/The-scandal-British-aid-spent-giving-Pakistanis-online-banking.html

9   Martin, D., 'The Scandal of British Aid Spent on Giving Pakistanis Online Banking' (2011) *The Daily Mail*, 1 June. At: http://www.dailymail.co.uk/news/article-1392840/The-scandal-British-aid-spent-giving-Pakistanis-online-banking.html

10   Graham, F., 'M-Pesa: Kenya's Mobile Wallet Revolution' (2010) BBC News, 22 November. At: http://www.bbc.co.uk/news/business-11793290 [accessed October 17 2012]

11   Anthony, L., 'Soldiers and Civilians Fail to Mix on the Ground in Helmand' (2010) *The Times*, 8 January. At: http://www.thetimes.co.uk/tto/news/world/asia/afghanistan/article1843839.ece [accessed October 17 2012].

12   Personal experience of the author in Iraq and interviews with allied military personnel.

13   Author's experience in Afghanistan and interviews with NATO personnel in 2007.

14   Anthony, L., 'Soldiers and Civilians Fail to Mix on the Ground in Helmand' (2010) *The Times*, 8 January. At: http://www.thetimes.co.uk/tto/news/world/asia/afghanistan/article1843839.ece [accessed October 17 2012].

15   Lamb, C., 'Over and Out: Former Para on Why he Quit the Army after Afghanistan' (2008) *The Times*, 20 July. At: http://www.thesundaytimes.co.uk/sto/news/uk_news/article10 7014.ece [accessed October 17 2012].

16   See Col. Stuart Tootal's book *Danger Close* (2009, John Murray Publishing), pp.46-47 and p.112 for this story and a dismaying account of DfID behaviour in Afghanistan; also Patrick Bishop's book *3 Para* (2008, Harper Perennial), pp.43-44 and p.265.

17   'Richard', 'A Paradise Lost?' (2009) EU Referendum, 7 July. At: http://eureferendum.blogspot.com/2009/07/paradise-lost.html [accessed October 17 2012].

18   Rojas, J.P.F, Mason, R., 'Probe Over Millions Spent on Foreign Aid Consultants' (2012) *The Telegraph*, 17 Septemner. At: http://www.telegraph.co.uk/news/politics/9547162/Probe-over-millions-spent-on-foreign-aid-consultants.html [accessed October 17 2012].

19   Gilligan, A., 'Poverty Barons' who Make a Fortune from Taxpayer-funded Aid Budget' (2012) *The Telegraph*, 15 September. At: http://www.telegraph.co.uk/news/politics/9545584/Poverty-barons-who-make-a-fortune-from-taxpayer-funded-aid-budget.html [accessed October 17 2012].

[20] Provost, C., 'DfID's Spending on Consultants to Come Under Increased Scrutiny' (2012) *The Guardian*, 17 September. At: http://www.guardian.co.uk/global-development/2012/sep/17/dfid-spending-consultants-scrutiny.

[21] Gilligan, A., 'Poverty Barons' who Make a Fortune from Taxpayer-funded Aid Budget' (2012) *The Telegraph*, 15 September. At: http://www.telegraph.co.uk/news/politics/9545584/Poverty-barons-who-make-a-fortune-from-taxpayer-funded-aid-budget.html [accessed October 17 2012].

[22] Mendick, A & Gilligan, A., 'Senior Tory Accuses EU of "Squandering" Britain's Aid Budget"' (2012) *The Telegraph*, 29 September. At: http://www.telegraph.co.uk/news/politics/9576399/Senior-Tory-accuses-EU-of-squandering-Britains-aid-budget.html [accessed October 17 2012].

[23] Global Humanitarian Assistance, 'GHA Report 2011' (2011) GHA, Development Initiatives Ltd, Temple Back, Bristol, BS1 6FL. At: http://www.globalhumanitarianassistance.org/wp-content/uploads/2011/07/gha-report-2011.pdf [accessed October 17 2012].

[24] According to the same report, Palestine also receives the second-largest amount of humanitarian aid in absolute terms (after Sudan). Palestinians in the territories received 39 times the amount of aid per person as inhabitants of Congo.

[25] 'Andrew Mitchell Denies Security Claims as UK Axes Foreign Aid' (2011) *The London Evening Standard*, 1 March. At: http://www.thisislondon.co.uk/standard/article-23927468-andrew-mitchell-denies-security-claims-as-uk-axes-foreign-aid.do [accessed October 17 2012].

[26] Warah, R., 'Two-Thirds of Bilateral Aid to Somalia Govt Stolen, Diverted' (2012) *The East African*, 21 July. At: http://www.theeastafrican.co.ke/news/Two+thirds+of+donor+aid+to+Somalia+stolen+/-/2558/1460106/-/5imdrr/-/index.html [accessed October 17 2012].

[27] Hatcher, J., 'Why Britain's Aid Efforts Could be a Victim of Somalia's Spring' (2012) *The Week*, 2 May. At: http://www.theweek.co.uk/africa/46604/why-britains-aid-efforts-could-be-victim-somalias-spring [accessed October 17 2012].

[28] http://www.freedomhouse.org/

[29] http://www.transparency.org/

[30] Human Rights Watch, 'Ethiopia: Donors Should Investigate Misuse of Aid Money' (2010) Human Rights Watch, 17 December. At: http://www.hrw.org/news/2010/12/17/ethiopia-donors-should-investigate-misuse-aid-money [accessed October 17 2012]

17. Problematic Choices and Countries for UK Aid

1   Lamont, J. & Barker, A., 'Future of UK Aid to India to Question' (2010) *Financial Times*, 15 September. At: http://www.ft.com/cms/s/0/80292cc2-c0f7-11df-99c4-00144feab49a.html#axzz1lBaBeXB2 [accessed October 17 2012].

2   Rediff, 'Britain is Third Rate Power Says PM' (1997) Rediff: Information Entertainment Online, 13 October. At: http://www.rediff.com/news/oct/13queen.htm [accessed October 17 2012].

3   Ramesh, R., 'A Washed-up Power Wants its Pound of Flesh' (2012) *Governance Now*, 6 February. At: http://governancenow.com/views/columns/washed-power-wants-its-pound-flesh [accessed October 17 2012]. IndianDefence.com, 'India is Heading for Mars; It Doesn't Need British Aid Money to Pay Bills' (2012), 28 August. At: http://www.indiandefence.com/forums/social-political-issues/21281-india-heading-mars-doesn%92t-need-british-aid-money-pay-bills-6.html [accessed October 17 2012].

4   'If India Doesn't Want Our Aid, Stop it Now, Cameron Told after Country Labels £280m-a-year Donations as 'Peanuts' ' (2012) *The Daily Mail*, 6 February. At: http://www.dailymail.co.uk/news/article-2096628/British-foreign-aid-India-tells-Britain-dont-need-peanuts-offer-us.html#ixzz23tkpPaUM [accessed October 17 2012].

5   BBC News, 'India Debates Whether to Continue Receiving British Aid' (2010) BBC News, 15 September. At: http://www.bbc.co.uk/news/world-south-asia-11318342 [accessed October 17 2012].

6   Zee News, 'Gadkari Questioned on British Aid to India' (2011) Zee News.com, 21 July. At: http://zeenews.india.com/news/nation/gadkari-questioned-on-british-aid-to-india_721178.html [accessed October 17 2012].

7   Peev, G., 'UK's £400m Aid for India Schools "Squandered" After Education Standards FALL' (2011) *The Daily Mail,* 31 May. At: http://www.dailymail.co.uk/news/article-1392552/UK-foreign-aid-Indian-schools-squandered-education-standards-fall.html [accessed October 17 2012].

8   'Education Fund for "Sarva Shiksha Abhiyan" Spent on Babus' Cars, Luxury' (2010) *The Economic Times*, 15 June. At: http://articles.economictimes.indiatimes.com/2010-06-15/news/27628690_1_dfid-british-media-report [accessed October 17 2012].

9   Andrew Mitchell's response to the reports was: 'These are shocking allegations. I have launched an immediate inquiry to ensure British aid money has not been misused.' 'UK Likely to Cut Aid to "Rich" India' (2010) *The Economic Times*, 11 July. At: http://articles.economictimes.indiatimes.com/2010-07-11/news/28465588_1_foreign-aid-british-aid-zero-tolerance

10 Barun Mitra of the Liberty Institute quoted in Reid, S., 'How India Squanders British Aid: We Give £1.4bn to a Country that Has Its Own Space Programme. In this Damning Investigation, the Mail Reveals How it's Scandalously Wasted' (2011) *The Daily Mail*, 2 December. At: http://www.dailymail.co.uk/news/article-2068930/How-India-squanders-British-aid–1-4bn-country-space-programme.html [accessed October 17 2012].

11 'Dodgy Development: DfID in India', *Corporate Watch*, 28 January 2012, http://www.corporatewatch.org/

12 ibid

13 Reid, S., 'How India Squanders British Aid: We Give £1.4bn to a Country that Has Its Own Space Programme. In this Damning Investigation, the Mail Reveals How it's Scandalously Wasted' (2011) *The Daily Mail*, 2 December. At: http://www.dailymail.co.uk/news/article-2068930/How-India-squanders-British-aid–1-4bn-country-space-programme.html [accessed October 17 2012].

14 Gilligan, A., 'India Tells Britain: We Don't Want Your Aid' (2012) *The Telegraph*, 4 February. At: http://www.telegraph.co.uk/news/worldnews/asia/india/9061844/India-tells-Britain-We-dont-want-your-aid.html [accessed October 17 2012].

15 Buncombe, A., 'Andrew Buncombe: If Aid is 'Peanuts' and Not Required, Why Does Britain Continue to Give it to India?' (2012) *The Independent*, 6 February. At: http://www.independent.co.uk/news/world/asia/andrew-buncombe-if-aid-is-peanuts-and-not-required-why-does-britain-continue-to-give-it-to-india-6579562.html

16 'India Rejects Aid from Britain, Says It is Peanuts' (2012) *The Times of India*, 5 February. At: http://articles.timesofindia.indiatimes.com/2012-02-05/uk/31026669_1_british-aid-international-development-secretary-end-aid [accessed October 17 2012].

17 Halliday, J., 'BBC World Service Considers U-turn Over Hindi Cuts' (2011) *The Guardian*, 7 March. At: http://www.guardian.co.uk/media/2011/mar/07/bbc-world-service-hindi [accessed October 17 2012].

18 ConHome, 'Edward Leigh Warns that BBC World Service Cuts May Give Iran and China Opportunity for Soft Power Dominance' (2011) ConservativeHome.com, 15 March. At: http://conservativehome.blogs.com/parliament/2011/03/edward-leigh-warns-that-bbcworldservice-cuts-may-give-iran-and-china-opportunity-for-soft-power-domi.html [accessed October 17 2012].

19 One two-day conference organised in London by DfID in 2009 cost over £500,000. Wardrop, M., 'Anti-Poverty Department Spent More than £500,000 on Single Conference' (2009) *The Telegraph*, 24 March. At: http://www.telegraph.co.uk/news/politics/5040616/ Anti-poverty-department-spent-more-than-500000-on-single-conference.html [accessed October 17 2012].

20 Doughty, S., 'It's Nuts! Britain is STILL Giving Aid to Brazil – Even Though It's Richer than We Are' (2011) *The Daily Mail*, 29 December. At: http://www.dailymail.co.uk/news/article-2079628/Britain-STILL-giving-foreign-aid-A–richer-are.html [accessed October 17 2012].

21 Peter Bauer, *From Subsistence to Exchange and Other Essays*, p.43.

22 According to Helen Epstein, human rights groups have 'for years been alerting the international community to the fact that EPRDF officials frequently deny the benefits of foreign aid programmes– food, fertilisers, training, and so on–to known opposition supporters'. Epstein, H., 'Cruel Ethiopia' (2010) *New York Review of Books*, 14 April, At: http://www.nybooks.com/articles/archives/ 2010/may/13/cruel-ethiopia/?pagination=false [accessed October 17 2012].

23 Human Rights Watch, 'Ethiopia: Donor Aid Supports Repression' (2010) 19 October. At: http://www.hrw.org/en/news/2010/ 10/18/ethiopia-donor-aid-supports-repression [accessed October 17 2012]. See also Human Rights Watch, 'Ethiopia: Donors Should Investigate Misuse Aid Money' (2010) 17 December. At: http://www.hrw.org/news/2010/12/17/ethiopia-donors-should-investigate-misuse-aid-money [accessed October 17 2012].

24 Oborne, P., 'Overseas Aid is Funding Human Rights Abuses' (2010) *Daily Telegraph* blog, 28 October. At: http://blogs.telegraph.co.uk/news/peteroborne/100061337/over seas-aid-is-funding-human-rights-abuses/ [accessed October 17 2012].

25 See Siddiqa, A., *Military Inc. Inside Pakistan's Military Economy* (2007) London: Pluto Press.

26 Mahmood, A., 'UK Govt Under Criticism for Increasing Aid to Pakistan' (2011) The Nation, 16 March. At: http://www.nation.com.pk/pakistan-news-newspaper-daily-english-online/national/16-Mar-2011/UK-govt-under-criticism-for-increasing-aid-to-Pakistan [accessed October 17 2012]

18. DfID and the Two Types of Aid

1   Easterly, W & Freschi, L., 'Why Does British Foreign Aid Prefer
    Poor Governments Over Poor People?' (2009) AidWatch, 20 March.
    At: http://aidwatchers.com/2009/03/why-does-british-foreign-
    aid-prefer-poor-governments-over-poor-people/ [accessed
    October 17 2012].

2   Easterly, W & Freschi, L., 'Why Does British Foreign Aid Prefer
    Poor Governments Over Poor People?' (2009) AidWatch, 20 March.
    At: http://aidwatchers.com/2009/03/why-does-british-foreign-
    aid-prefer-poor-governments-over-poor-people/ [accessed
    October 17 2012].

3   Quoted in Peev, G., 'Dance Lessons in Africa, Jets for Tyrants,
    Derelict Offices...How EU Wastes Aid Billions' (2011) *The Daily
    Mail*, 18 April. At: http://www.dailymail.co.uk/news/article-
    1377837/EU-wastes-aid-billions-dance-lessons-Africa-jets-tyrants-
    derelict-offices.html [accessed October 17 2012].

4   Sachs, J., 'Pool Resources and Reinvent Global Aid' (2010) *Financial
    Times*, 20 September. At: http://www.ft.com/cms/s/0/4c510f34-
    c4fb-11df-9134-00144feab49a.html#axzz1kgOmkXxF [accessed
    October 17 2012].

5   Clare Short herself said in 2002 that: 'The worst offender for highly
    ineffective aid spending is the European Commission'. Short, C.,
    'Reform of EU Aid Programme is Overdue' (2002) *The Guardian*, 29
    July. At: http://www.guardian.co.uk/business/2002/jul/29/
    foreignaffairs.eu [accessed October 17 2012].

6   Brussels refused to name the organisations involved. See Evans-
    Pritchard, A., 'EU Targets Charities in Fraud Enquiry' (2005) *The
    Telegraph*, 29 June. At: http://www.telegraph.co.uk/finance/
    2918151/EU-targets-charities-in-fraud-inquiry.html [accessed
    October 17 2012]

7   Pncevski, B & MacDougall, D., 'Euro Billions Wasted on African
    Failures' (2011) *The Sunday Times*, 17 April. At:
    http://www.thesundaytimes.co.uk/sto/news/world_news/Afric
    a/article606511.ece [accessed October 17 2012].

8   Telegraph View, 'Our Wasteful Aid Betrays the Needy' (2012) *The
    Telegraph*, 30 September. At: http://www.telegraph.co.uk/
    comment/telegraph-view/9576350/Our-wasteful-aid-betrays-the-
    needy.html [accessed October 17 2012].

9   Although a G20 economy, Argentina was earmarked £9.5 million
    in EU Aid in 2011. Mendick, R & Gilligan, A., 'British Still Giving
    Hundreds of Millions of Pounds in Aid to Wealthy Countries'
    (2011) *The Telegraph*, 22 September. At:
    http://www.telegraph.co.uk/news/politics/9560326/British-still-
    giving-hundreds-of-millions-of-pounds-in-aid-to-wealthy-
    countries.html [accessed October 17 2012].

10 'How Aid Money is Being Spent in Barbados' (2012) *The Telegraph*, 23 September. At: http://www.telegraph.co.uk/news/worldnews/centralamericaan dthecaribbean/barbados/9560410/How-aid-money-is-being-spent-in-Barbados.html [accessed October 17 2012].

11 Alexander, H & Sawer, P., 'British Aid Used to Train Waiters at Billionaire's Playground' (2012) *The Telegraph*, 23 September. At: http://www.telegraph.co.uk/news/worldnews/centralamericaan dthecaribbean/barbados/9560292/British-aid-used-to-train-waiters-at-billionaires-playground.html [accessed October 17 2012].

12 Mendick, R., 'Revealed: £800,000 in Aid Given to Water Park in Morocco' (2012) *The Telegraph*, 29 September. At: http://www.telegraph.co.uk/travel/destinations/africaandindian ocean/morocco/9576154/Revealed-800000-in-aid-given-to-water-park-in-Morocco.html [accessed October 17 2012].

19. DfID and NGO Culture and Ideologies

1 Graham Hancock, *Lords of Poverty*, pp.32-33.

2 Peter Bauer, *Equality, the Third World and Economic Delusion*, p.100

3 See Guest Blogger, 'The Accidental NGO and USAID Transparency Test' (2010) Aid Watch, 18 August. At: http://aidwatchers.com/2010/08/the-accidental-ngo-and-usaid-transparency-test/ [accessed October 17 2012].

4 Bruckner's gruelling battle to get information from various major agencies became well known after William Easterly wrote about it in the *Wall Street Journal* in August 2010. Easterly, W., 'How Not to Win Hearts and Minds' (2010) *Wall Street Journal*, 16 August. At: http://online.wsj.com/article/SB10001424052748703999304575399 422302747074.html [accessed October 17 2012].

5 Guest Blogger, 'The Accidental NGO and USAID Transparency Test' (2010) Aid Watch, 18 August. At: http://aidwatchers.com/2010/08/the-accidental-ngo-and-usaid-transparency-test/ [accessed October 17 2012].

6 Human Accountability Partnership, 'Current Members' (2012) Human Accountability Partnership, August. At: http://www.hapinternational.org/members.aspx [accessed October 17 2012].

7 Grant, J., 'A "Third Way" for Aid?' (2011) *Think Africa Press*, 15 March. At: http://thinkafricapress.com/angola/third-way-aid [accessed October 17 2012].

20. DfID and Corruption

[1] PAC, 'MPs report on Department for International Development Financial Management' (2011) House of Commons Public Accounts Committee, 20 October. At: http://www.parliament.uk/business/committees/committees-a-z/commons-select/public-accounts-committee/news/dfid-financial-report/ [accessed October 17 2012].
[2] Wrong, M., *It's Our Turn to Eat*, p.208.
[3] Interview, Sir Edward Clay, 20 November 2011.
[4] Interviews, Michela Wrong, 5 November5 2011 & Sir Edward Clay, 20 November 2011.
[5] Interviews, Michela Wrong, 5 November 2011 & Sir Edward Clay, 20 November 2011

21. DfID and the Use of Aid as a Moral and Political Lever

[1] Their statement ran: 'While the intention may well be to protect the rights of LGBTI people on the continent, the decision to cut aid disregards the role of the LGBTI and broader social justice movement on the continent and creates the real risk of a serious backlash against LGBTI people... The imposition of donor sanctions may be one way of seeking to improve the human rights situation in a country but does not, in and of itself, result in the improved protection of the rights of LGBTI people. Donor sanctions are by their nature coercive and reinforce the disproportionate power dynamics between donor countries and recipients... In a context of general human rights violations, where women are almost as vulnerable as LGBTI people, or where health and food security are not guaranteed for anyone, singling out LGBTI issues emphasises the idea that LGBTI rights are special rights and hierarchically more important than other rights. It also supports the commonly held notion that homosexuality is 'unAfrican' and a western-sponsored 'idea' and that countries like the UK will only act when 'their interests' have been threatened.... Furthermore, aid cuts also affect LGBTI people. Aid received from donor countries is often used to fund education, health and broader development. LGBTI people are part of the social fabric, and thus part of the population that benefit from the funding. A cut in aid will have an impact on everyone, and more so on the populations that are already vulnerable and whose access to health and other services are already limited, such as LGBTI people.'

2   Walters, S., 'We'll Cut Your Aid if You Persecute Gays, Britain
     Warns African Nations' (2011) *The Daily Mail*, 8 October. At:
     http://www.dailymail.co.uk/news/article-2046965/Well-cut-aid-
     persecute-gays-Britain-warns-African-nations.html [accessed
     October 17 2012].
3   BBC World, 'UK and the Netherlands Withhold Rwanda Budget
     Aid' (2012) BBC News, 27 July. At: http://www.bbc.co.uk/news/
     world-africa-19010495 [accessed October 17 2012].
4   http://www.nytimes.com/2011/08/23/world/asia/
     23kashmir.html
5   As advocated by Michela Wrong and others.
6   This is yet another reason why DfID's new policy of giving more
     aid to conflict-ridden and very poor countries is probably
     misconceived.

PART 8: What Works and What Doesn't Work in Aid

23. *Aid Effectiveness*

1   Easterly, W., 'Measuring How and Why Aid Works–or Doesn't'
     (2011) *Wall Street Journal*, 30 April. At: http://online.wsj.com/
     article/SB10001424052748703956904576287262026843944.html?mo
     d=googlenews_wsj [accessed October 17 2012]
2   Easterly, W & Williamson, C.R., 'Rhetoric versus Reality: The Best
     and Worst of Aid Agency Practices' (2011) *World Development* , 39
     (11), pp. 1930-1949.
3   http://www.cfr.org/foreign-aid/effectiveness-foreign-aid/p12077
4   Interview, Clare Lockhart, 5 November 2011
5   Interview, Alex de Waal, 23 December 2011

24. *'Best Practice' in Development Aid*

1   Maren, M., *The Road to Hell: The Ravaging Effects of Foreign Aid and
     International Charity*, p.10
2   Easterly, W & Williamson, C.R., 'Rhetoric versus Reality: The Best
     and Worst of Aid Agency Practices' (2011) *World Development* , 39
     (11), pp. 1930-1949.
3   Banerjee, A.V & Duflo, E., *Poor Economics*, pp.257-258.
4   http://www.transparency.org/
5   Walsh, D., 'Rape Claims Against British Soldiers Are Fake' (2003)
     The Independent, 27 September. At:
     http://www.independent.co.uk/news/world/africa/rape-claims-
     against-british-soldiers-are-fake-581324.html [accessed October 17
     2012]

6   'Prostitutes 'told to fake rape claims'' (2003) *The Telegraph*, 2
     October. At: http://www.telegraph.co.uk/news/worldnews/
     africaandindianocean/kenya/1443083/Prostitutes-told-to-fake-
     rape-claims.html [accessed October 17 2012].

PART 9: Conclusions and Recommendations
25. *General Conclusions*

1   Gray, R., 'Foreign Aid Cash Spent Tackling Climate Change' (2012)
     The Telegraph, 18 February. At: http://www.telegraph.co.uk/
     earth/environment/climatechange/9090830/Foreign-aid-cash-
     spent-tackling-climate-change.html [accessed October 17 2012].

26. *Recommendations*

1   Alex de Waal believes that Guinea-Bisau is on its way to
     'becoming Africa's first narco-state and a base for Latin American
     cartels looking for a way into Europe' Interview
2   An injunction memorably urged on donors and international
     agencies by Collier, P and Dollar, D, 'Development Effectiveness:
     What Have We Learnt?' (2004) *The Economic Journal*, 114, pp.244-271.
3   'BBC World Service Cuts Outlined to Staff' (2011) BBC News, 26
     January. At: http://www.bbc.co.uk/news/entertainment-arts-
     12283356 [accessed October 17 2012].
4   Syal, R & Robinson, J., 'BBC World Service Broadcasts in Burma
     Face Axe' (2010) *The Guardian*, 7 September. At:
     http://www.guardian.co.uk/media/2010/sep/07/bbc-world-
     service-burma-axe
5   See e.g.. 'Senior Tory Accuses EU of Squandering Britain's Aid
     Budget' (2011) *Think Defence*, 17 July At:
     http://www.thinkdefence.co.uk/2011/07/mad-dogs-and-
     englishmen/ [accessed October 17 2012].

27. *Suggestions*

1   Wilson, D & Purushothaman, R., 'Dreaming with BRICs: Path to
     2050' (2003) Goldman Sachs, Global Economics Paper No. 99, 1
     October. At: p://www.goldmansachs.com/our-
     thinking/topics/brics/brics-reports-pdfs/brics-dream.pdf
2   Foroohar, R., 'Power Up' (2009) *The Daily Beast*, 20 March. At:
     http://www.thedailybeast.com/newsweek/2009/03/20/power-
     up.html [accessed October 17 2012].

3   See e.g.. Mendick, R & Gilligan, A., 'Senior Accuses EU of
    'Squandering' Britain's Aid Budget' (2012) *The Telegraph*, 29
    September. At: http://www.telegraph.co.uk/news/politics/
    9576399/Senior-Tory-accuses-EU-of-squandering-Britains-aid-
    budget.html [accessed October 17 2012].
4   See Easterly, W., 'How, and How Not to Stop Aids in Africa', a
    review of Helen Epstein's *The Invisible Cure*.
5   Porter, A., 'G8 summit: David Cameron Defends Foreign Aid
    Spending' (2011) *The Telegraph*, 27 May. At:
    http://www.telegraph.co.uk/news/worldnews/g8/8542475/G8-
    summit-David-Cameron-defends-foreign-aid-spending.html
    [accessed October 17 2012].
6   An ICM poll for *The Sunday Telegraph* found that 70% opposed
    raising foreign aid to 0.7% of GDP and 64% opposed ringfencing
    foreign aid at a time of cuts to other government departments.
    Sunday Telegraph, 24 September 2012.
7   McVeigh, T & Helm, T., 'Queen's Speech Omission Ignites
    Overseas Aid Row' (2012) *The Guardian*, 22 April. At:
    http://www.guardian.co.uk/global-development/2012/apr/22/
    international-aid-queens-speech-omission [accessed October 17
    2012].